EAST JERUSALEM

EAST JERUSALEM

THE FORMER GARDEN OF EDEN

Isiah Lawrence Nottage

Strategic Book Publishing and Rights Co.

Strategic Book Publishing & Rights Co., LLC
USA | Singapore
www.sbpra.net

For information about special discounts for bulk purchases, please contact Strategic Book Publishing and Rights Co. Special Sales, at bookorder@sbpra.net.

ISBN: 978-1-68235-470-4

EAST JERUSALEM: THE FORMER GARDEN OF EDEN

100% Irrefutable: iron-clad preponderance of compelling evidence and facts guaranteed to convince and to satisfy your inquiry. Beginning point of reference in the quest for the Garden of Eden is: The Temple Mount in Jerusalem – the center of the earth as far as God is concerned.

Scriptural quotations are taken from the King James Version and 'The youth bible, 21st century'.

(Bishop) Isiah Lawrence Nottage
Email: inottage533@gmail.com
Facebook: Isiah Nottage

vii

TABLE OF CONTENTS

PREFACE

Ladies and Gentlemen, I shall endeavor to prove to you without reasonable doubt, that the ancient land of Eden is the same land as "OLD JERUSALEM". Two: And that God had planted his Garden **'in the south eastern portion in east Jerusalem.**
I will also pinpoint the exact spot where God had planted it in Jerusalem. You will also be informed that the fountain of living water which watered the garden, emanated from the top of Mount Moriah or The Temple Mount in Jerusalem. As for the sources of my information, they are taken from 'The King James Version of the bible. And also from the 'Youth Bible, New Century Version'. And by extension, my sources of information are derived from the inspiration of the Holy Spirit. The names of my three witnesses are as follows: Jesus Christ. Two: the Israelites' legislator who was **'the god Moses', and** the prophet Ezekiel. You may wonder why I had referred to Moses as a god. Well, because it was God himself who had promoted him to the position of an earthly god.
Here is what Moses himself writes in Exodus 7: 1-2. "And the Lord said unto Moses, **"see, i have made thee a god to Pharaoh;** and Aaron thy brother shall be thy prophet". Verse 2," Thou shall speak all that i command thee: and Aaron thy brother shall speak unto Pharaoh, that he send the children of Israel out of his land."
So if God promoted Moses to the status of a god, then he was a dirt god.

INTRODUCTION

Ladies and gentlemen, I believe that you would love the pertinent information in this book, because you will see the logic and rational reasoning of its contents. This book presents iron-clad proof that the land of old Jerusalem is the same land as Eden which Moses records in Genesis 2:8.

Like everybody else, I didn't have the slightest clue as to where the Garden of Eden was located. This question as to where the Garden of Eden was located, is still a burning question in the minds of many people. It's my hope that this book will satisfy this burning question in your mind. But the truth is, many people, even today are walking up and down in the area where the Garden of Eden was planted without realizing it.

Let's have a dialogue on this subject. I will ask you lots of questions because they will put you in touch with the genius person in your mind. I'm asking you these questions, just to get you involved in our dialogue. But you will unravel the truth for yourself.

I'm also seeking to convince you that the most holy place was located on Mount Moriah, within a 875 feet square area. This was the spot or source where the spring of Living Water had proceeded from to water the Garden below it. And it was also the place where God's holy altar was built in the very beginning. I believe you will come to this conclusion by mere intellectual reasoning and logical deduction. But as for me, I have received this truth by divine revelation, inspiration, and searching the scriptures.

You will be given the size of the south side of 'East Jerusalem' where The Garden of the Lord, or Eden was planted. And also the dimension of the Garden itself. In addition: you will be enlightened as to what 'the tree of life' was **and what was 'the tree of the knowledge of good and evil.'**

You will love the following: the truth about the forbidden fruit which Adam and Eve ate. **And what was the fruit in the middle of the Garden of Eden.** You will also see that Adam and Eve lived in **The City Adam in the Jordan valley, by the Jordan River, near Zarethan,** after being expelled out of the Garden – and by the way, the City Adam is also mentioned in the scriptures.

Please know that whenever you visit Old Jerusalem, you will be in Eden. And whenever you visit **the south side of east Jerusalem, below the Temple Mount, you will be in the Garden of Eden.** All of this will be proven in this book.

All of this will be proof from the scriptures that the river which **was 'in Eden'** went and watered the Garden which was also **'in Eden'.** So it's obvious that the Garden was watered first. Now to be sure of this, let's revisit the second half of verse 10.

It says "And from thence (there) it was parted and became into four heads."

Question: what is this 'thence,' or there? Answer: it is the Garden of Eden.

So you see, the river indeed did water the Garden **first** before it went and split into four heads (yes?).

I sincerely ask you: do you see from scriptures that the river which was **in Eden,** went and watered the Garden 'first' which was **also in Eden?** And do you see that it was **'after'** the Garden was watered – **then the river of living water was parted into four heads?**

So you see that the countries where the four rivers flowed to, **could not have been the place, or country where the Garden was located.** So what this proves without contradiction is....that none of the four (4) heads of the river led to the Garden of Eden, but rather, **away from it.**

It's important to understand that all of what the angel told Ezekiel would have come into existence, after the Jews would have come out of captivity didn't materialize. The reason is, God had changed his mind because the Jews still didn't altogether please him after coming out of captivity, but continued to serve the gods of darkness.

Again the promises of God to mankind, or to nations are conditional, and predicated on us living righteously. See Jeremiah chapter 18:7'10. It shows where God changes his mind from keeping his promises to us if we refused to keep his righteousness. Now the burden of proof is on me to prove the above information.

CHAPTER 1

IN SEARCH OF THE GARDEN OF EDEN

My Beginning reference point is the Temple Mount in Jerusalem. Because this was the place from where the living water emanated or flowed eastward. Question, in which country would you say that the Garden of Eden was located? Well, by the time you would've finished reading this book to the end, you'll be convinced that it was in east Jerusalem.

Over the past many years, hundreds of people have been hard at work searching to find the Garden of Eden, but up to this point, no one has discovered it yet. The prevailing theories by some are that the Garden of Eden might have been located in Africa, because Moses says in Genesis 2-13: "And the name of the second river is **'Gihon'** the same is it that compasseth (surrounds) **the whole land of Ethiopia "(Cush)."** The truth and fact of the matter is that the Garden of Eden **was not in Ethiopia.** The fact is that one head of the river just ran to Ethiopia. I too thought that the Garden of Eden was somewhere in Africa, but only until I was made sensible by the Holy Spirit which is within me, and by further research, I've found the truth.

Some people even extrapolate that the Garden of Eden might have been located in Armenia, or Turkey, just because they read that Noah had landed on Mount Ararat in Anatolia in Turkey in the east. And some even guess that it must be around

Iraq, because the Euphrates river runs through it. Yet others say because Moses records that one of the river's heads flowed to the east of Assyria, that the Garden must have been in this area. Some even speculate that the Garden of Eden might have been somewhere under the waters in the Persian Gulf or in that region.

What one needs to consider is the fact that the four river-heads only flowed to these countries. Therefore, the Garden couldn't have been within any of these alleged countries because the living Water flowed, or emanated from somewhere else other than these countries to where it flowed.

It is of paramount importance that i quote two of Moses' statements from Genesis 2:8, and verse 10. These two verses will open up your understanding that both the river of living water, and the Garden were 'in Eden', or Jerusalem. **No other countries.**

Verse 8, "And the Lord God planted a Garden **Eastward...in Eden**, and there he put the man whom he had formed."

Verse 10, "And a river went **Out of Eden to water the Garden: and from thence (there)** it was parted and became into four heads." I want you to underscore the words 'in Eden'. Keep in mind that Moses says that God had planted a Garden ... 'in Eden'. So we know that the Garden **was in Eden**. Okay, let's see where we'll find the river of living water.

I also invite you to cast your eyes on these three words in verse 10: '**out of Eden**'. So let's put these two verses into context. One: the Garden was planted..'.**in Eden**'. Two: and the river went '**out of Eden**'. This therefore, should cause you to see that both the Garden of Eden, and the river of living water...**were in Eden/ Jerusalem.**

Now if you would carefully analyze Moses' narrative, you will discover that he is saying that the flow of the river of living water, watered the Garden of Eden 'first' – and from there, or from the Garden, then and only then, the river was parted, or divided into four heads...that is, it went or flowed into four directions. But the question is: Where was the spot where it was parted? Well, we'll see later.

Do you now see that indeed, the river of living water flowed **first** to the Garden, **in Eden, then it flowed...out of Eden – then divided into four heads?**

Again, I want you to see that both the Garden and the river were in Eden. The question must be asked...from where in Eden did the living water flow? Note: we know that water seeks its own level. So the water had to flow from the top of the mountain of Moriah/Zion. So when I say that one can't find the location of the Garden of Eden outside Eden, or outside Jerusalem, is a fact.

TAKEN FROM THE YOUTH BIBLE VERSION

Ladies and Gentlemen, I now turn my attention and discourse to the subject-matter at hand proving that the biblical Eden Moses writes about in Genesis, **is the same land as Old Jerusalem.** But first, I now present to you, Ezekiel, the prophet of God, who will tell you about his vision of how the Lord God brought him to Jerusalem in the land of Israel.

Ezekiel will give us the understanding that the altar of God was on Mount Moriah in Jerusalem. And the fountain of living water in the very beginning also emanated from Mount Moriah in Jerusalem. And that the water flowed downward to the Garden of the Lord at the lower level below Mount Moriah or the Temple Mount in Jerusalem, facing the east. I believe him.

Let's hear from the prophet about the whole matter as it relates to where the Garden of Eden was planted, or located.

3

He writes in Ezekiel 40:1: "It was the twenty-fifth year of our captivity, at the beginning of the year, on the tenth day of the month. It was the fourteenth year after Jerusalem was captured on the same day i felt the power of the Lord and he (the Lord) **brought me to Jerusalem.**"

Keep in mind, it wasn't Africa nor Armenia where Ezekiel was transported, or brought by the Lord. The reason why I say this, is because later, you'll see that the river of living water **flowed out of the Temple which was in Jerusalem** – no other country. And you'll also see **that 'the tree of life' which was in the Garden, was just outside the golden gate in Jerusalem.** And the living water went to the Garden **First ...** 'before', it went to any other countries.

Ezekiel goes on in verse 2: "In the vision of God He brought me 'to the land of Israel' and put me down on a very high mountain. On the south on the side of the mountain there were some buildings that looked like a city. I will show you, because that's why you have been brought here. **Tell the people of Israel all that you see**"

At the time of this vision, both Ezekiel and the Jews were in captivity in Babylon. So when he would have come out of his vision, his job was to explain all of what he had seen in it to all of the Jewish captives, especially the leaders. He was to let them know that not only they will eventually be set free, but the broken-down city of Jerusalem, and its Temple which Nebuchadnezzar had destroyed in bc.586 will be rebuilt.

This good news to them was to give them hope that God was indeed going to deliver them. And the truth of the matter is...As you know, that in the process of time, the city of Jerusalem and its Temple were rebuilt, and the Jews did return home to Jerusalem from Babylon in bc.516 – Just as the angel told Ezekiel, and just as Ezekiel told the Jewish captives.

The vision continues: Ezekiel is now being brought closer to the buildings. He now sees a man who was made out of copper which was an angel who would give him a tour as to how Jerusalem should look **after** it would be restored. And also the new Temple which Zerubbabel would have built, which was indeed, the second Jewish Temple. At this time Jerusalem was in desolation, and its former Temple, or Solomon's Temple / the first Jewish Temple was destroyed to its very foundation.

Here is a question for you before I go on: **Why is it the land of Israel where the prophet Ezekiel would see…The Garden of Eden located, or was planted…if it's not truly; that it was Jerusalem where it was located or planted? Think about it.**

FROM HERE ON – IMAGINE THIS SCENE

Ezekiel now continues on his tour with this copperish angel as he follows him measuring the Temple-area and the wall. He continues to say: Verse 5, "I saw a wall surrounding **the Temple-area. The measuring stick in the man's (angel) hand was ten and one half feet long So the man measured 'the wall' which was ten and one half feet thick; and ten and one half feet high."

This is the 875 feet square wall which had surrounded the Temple in Jerusalem. I'm sure Ezekiel couldn't have remembered all of what the angel was showing and telling him. So I feel certain that he was taking notes. The angel even gave him a pattern of the future rebuilt Temple in order to give to Governor Zerubbabel and the Jewish leaders.

It was this Jewish Governor Zerubbabel whom God had chosen to build this second Temple 'after' the Jews would have been freed out of Babylon. And indeed he did build the Temple 'after' they came out of captivity. God had chosen him because he was of the line or lineage of the Jewish kings. In fact, he was the holder of the key, or scepter of David, in captivity...because he received it from his father Salathel.

PUT ON YOUR THINKING CAP

Know this: Jerusalem was going to be **sanctified, and set a part as a holy land from the rest of the lands in Israel – just as it was separated or sanctified....AS EDEN in the beginning.** We now find the angel telling Ezekiel as to how the land of Israel should be divided **after** they would have returned home from captivity. The land of Israel is from Dan, formerly, Leshem in the north, **to Negev and Eilat in the south.**

It's interesting to observe how God was going to use Jerusalem as his Holy land 'again'-as **Eden was in the beginning, with his Garden being planted...'AT THE EAST, IN EDEN'.** Seriously, think about it.

Ezekiel is now being commanded in chapter 45: 1, by God to inform the Jewish people the following: "When you divide the land for the Israelites' tribe by throwing lots (choosing) **you must give a part of the land to belong to the Lord. It will be about seven miles long and about six miles wide (7x6) all of this land will be holy."**

Obviously, God still wanted Jerusalem to be his sanctified land, even years after the Jews would have come out of captivity. And it was to be seven miles long, by six miles wide. So the whole land of Jerusalem was to be holy after the Jews would have returned home out of captivity from Babylon. **But 'The Most Holy Place' was the Temple Mount which was situated in the middle of the seven miles long and three (3) miles wide.** This most Holy place was surrounded by a 875 feet square wall, which was on the **south side of Jerusalem.**

Verse 2, "From this land an area eight hundred seventy five feet square (875 ft) **Will be for the Temple. There will be an open space around the Temple that is eighty seven and one half feet wide (87 ½).**

Observe: a space of 875 ft. square was separated for the Temple in Jerusalem. That is, 875 ft. Square to the east, west, north, and south. So the Temple was to sit within this square, **or in the center of this 875 ft. square area-with a wall 10 ½ feet high, and 10 ½ feet thick.** So we have the Jewish Temple on the hill-top facing the east with the land sloping downward which entered the Garden of Eden below it.

Picture the former Jewish Temple on a hill-top with its land sloping downward, facing the east, or the sunrise – and with the Garden also facing the east, or sunrise. So what we have here is the former Jewish Temple **on the Temple Mount,** surrounded by a four square wall of 875 ft. Then

there was an open space nearest to the Temple which was 87 ½ feet-that is, **from the Temple porch's gate, to the outer court yard's gate, which was a distance of 87 ½ feet.**

Let's leave from this 2,440 feet high Mount Moriah, or hill-top for a moment, and let's go on and discuss Jerusalem and its division, or separation.

CHAPTER 2

THE DIVISION OF EDEN / JERUSALEM

Let's continue to verse 3, in order to pick up the angel's instructions to Ezekiel about Jerusalem's division. The angel goes on to say: "In the Holy area (Jerusalem) you will measure a part about seven miles long and three miles wide (7x3)...and it will be...the most holy place. This holy part of the land will be for the priests who serve him," Verse 4, This holy part (southern part) of the land will be for the priests who serve him in the Temple, who come near to the Lord to serve him. It will be a place for the priests' houses **and for the Temple"**

Take special notice of the following: Jerusalem is now being split in half straight down the middle. That is, from seven miles long by six miles wide ' to **7, miles long by 3, miles wide.** So now we have **TWO HALVES,** that is, 7x3, miles to the north and 7x3, miles to the south. Imagine Jerusalem in ancient times divided, or separated in **TWO HALVES.** This is how it should have been when the Jews would have come out of captivity from Babylon.

According to Ezekiel, the priests who would have served God in the Temple should have occupied the south side of Jerusalem, **or the southern 7x3 miles.** And the Levites should have occupied the **northern side of 7x3 miles.** Like Eden, Jerusalem faces **'east to west' with one half to the south, and the other half to the north.** But the 7x3 miles on the southern side was 'The Most Holy Place'. This was what the angel told Ezekiel as to how Jerusalem should have been divided after they would have returned to Jerusalem from captivity.

Again, the reason was, this half of Jerusalem to the south... was the place where Zerubbabel built the Temple. And it was the most Holy sanctified place, because God had his Holy altar up there. And that's the place where he himself said that he dwelt. This Temple Mount was the epic center because it 'was' the most holy spot on planet earth at that time.

For a short while, let's deal with the other half of Jerusalem, which was also seven miles long, by three miles wide (7x3) which was to the north. Verse 5, Ezekiel writes: "Another area about seven miles long and more than three miles wide, will be for the Levites, who serve in the Temple area. It will belong to them so they will have cities in which to live." So now the Levites get a portion of the city of Jerusalem to live in. Not the most Holy side to the south where the priests and the Temple were, but on the opposite side...to the north. Verse 6, "You must give the city (Jerusalem) an area that is about one and one half miles wide and about seven miles long, along the side of the Holy area. It will belong to the people of Israel.

In addition to the seven by three miles for the building of the Temple, and for the Priests, God ordered that an additional one and one half miles wide, by seven miles long – to be alongside of the Holy area. The reason God added this extra one and one half miles, by seven miles, alongside the most Holy area, was to make it easier for the Israelites to live and to attend services at the Temple.

However, this additional one and one half miles...was not a part of the most holy area, because it wasn't a part of the holy Jerusalem, which was seven miles long and three miles to the south.

EZEKIEL NOW EXITS THE TEMPLE

Ezekiel now leaves from that area of the Temple Mount and is being brought around to the front door of the Temple, by way of the northern gate. And based on what he says, you'll see that Jerusalem is being correlated with the land of Eden wherein God had planted his Garden.

Chapter 47: 1, Ezekiel writes: "The man led me back to the door of the Temple. **And i saw water coming out from under the doorway and flowing east,(the Temple faced east) the water flowed 'down'** from the south side wall of the Temple and then south of the altar."

Picture this scene as I go along: the angel brought Ezekiel back to the front door of the Temple. Bear in mind, that Ezekiel and the copper looking angel **are on the Temple Mount** standing outside by the front door of the temple. Now what he saw startled him. **He saw water flowing out from under the doorway, and flowing toward the east.**

Ezekiel is now being brought around to the east gate. He now sees the living water coming out on the south side of the gate. This gate is the eastern gate also called the goldengate.

WATER NOW FLOWS FROM THE TEMPLE'S DOOR TO THE GOLDEN EAST GATE

Keep in mind that you are all the way up there, at the top of Mount Moriah, some 2440 feet in elevation. Now picture Ezekiel standing by the golden gate which is a part of the 875 feet,square wall, that surrounded the Temple.

The fact that water was flowing **under the threshold of the Temple's door, which was some 2440 feet… 'above on Mount Moriah',** shows that the water was flowing…downward toward the eastern gate, or golden gate.

Remember, the water flowed from the Temple's door, then it dropped down on the floor of the Temple's porch – then flowed down the eight (8) steps, then finally to the golden gate.

EZEKIEL NOW TAKES A TOUR THROUGH THE WATER WITH AN ANGEL

Now Ezekiel and the copper angel are going to go toward 'The East', and to measure the distance from the golden gate to some four thirds miles, which is really...a mile and a third, which was some 9,333 feet, east to west.

I humbly submit to you that this was the total length of the Garden of Eden, or the Garden of the Lord. Ezekiel now follows this copperish man, or angel up to this point, because he couldn't walk in the water beyond this point. Verse 3, "The man went toward the east with a line in his hand and measured about **one third of a mile"(2,333 feet)** again and led me through water that came up **to my ankles."** Verse 4, The man measured about **one third of a mile (2,333 feet)** again and led me through water that came up **to my knees.** Then he measured about **one third of a mile (2,333 feet)** again and led me through water **up to my waist."** Verse 5, "The man measured about **one third of a mile 2,333 feet)** again, but it was now a river that I could not cross. The water has risen too high. It was deep enough for swimming: **it was a river that no one could cross."**

Verse 6, "The man asked me, human, do you see this? Then the man **led me back to the bank of the river."**

Do you see that the...bank of the river where the Garden of Eden was planted, was below the golden/eastern gate...IN JERUSALEM? Did you hear what Ezekiel say? He says that the man **led him back to the bank of the river.** Here is a question: so from where did he start when he began his tour through water with the angel? **Answer: He started from the golden gate where the bank of the river was located.** So Ezekiel was led back to the bank of the river which was below the Temple Mount in Jerusalem. **SO IF THE TREE OF LIFE...WAS ON BOTH SIDES OF THE BANKS OF THE RIVER**-where do you think the Garden of Eden should have been located? **WELL, BELOW THE GOLDEN GATE IN JERUSALEM.** So do you see that...no matter how we twist or turn, we always end up in Jerusalem as to where the Garden of Eden was planted or located?

ON THE WAY BACK TO THE TEMPLE'S GOLDEN GATE

Again this is where you need to read slowly in order to understand that the Garden of Eden was located below the Temple Mount at the south east in Jerusalem, or old Jerusalem...IN THE DAYS OF ADAM AND EVE.

Now Ezekiel couldn't cross the river because the water was too high for him to cross. So both he and the angel had to return to the Temple's golden gate. Or the eastern gate,

THE ANGEL NOW GIVES EZEKIEL THE DIRECTION THE RIVER WILL FLOW

Let's now read what Ezekiel saw on the way back as he returns to the golden gate of the 875 feet square wall where he and the angel started their tour.

Verse 7, "Ezekiel continue to say, "**AS I WENT BACK I SAW MANY TREES ON BOTH SIDES OF THE RIVER**" here is the question to ponder: **IS EZEKIEL 'IN JERUSALEM'** at this time where he saw those trees on both sides of the river.'

or is he outside of Jerusalem **by the marshes and swamps in the south in Israel?** Well, as you have just heard him say, **that he was in Jerusalem on the way back to the eastern /golden gate, where he started his walking tour with the copper angel.**

So we can safely deduce from this narrative that the Garden of Eden had to have been planted in Jerusalem, **facing the sunrise.** At this time Ezekiel and the angel...were not down by the marshes and swamps...which were outside Jerusalem –even though these swamps and marshes are in Israel's land.I say this to show you that the Garden of Eden and the tree of life.' **were not by the marshes and swamps in the south in Israel.**

Again after watering the Garden of Eden according to the angel's words, the river of living water would flow **to the east country which of course, 'IS JERICHO', which is in the Jordan valley...TO THE EAST OF JERUSALEM.**

After the living water would have left from Jericho, it would merge, or enter into the Jordan river which flowed and still flows from north to south, then both the living water and the Jordan river **flowed together into the dead sea.** However, even though The Jordan river empties itself into the dead sea and remains... **the living water would continue all the way down to the end of Israel's border to the south.**

INFORMATION ABOUT THE COUNTRY JERICHO

Before I continue with verse 8, let me digress to explain a little about Jericho. Again, the east country to which the angel told Ezekiel the river would flow to, after leaving the Garden of Eden, was none other than Jericho. So you see, it was no other country. Jericho is a tiny country in the Jordan valley in the west bank. it is15.9 miles from Jerusalem. The Jordan river is to the east of Jericho...and Jerusalem is to the west of Jericho. However, the Jordan valley is not only east of Jericho, but also east of Jerusalem. Therefore the country which the angel told Ezekiel about where the living water would flow...after leaving or watering the Garden of Eden was Jericho.

So there should be no doubt that if Ezekiel and the copper angel are in Jerusalem describing the route of the living water, 'after watering the Garden of the Lord – then he says that the water will flow...to the east country first – but we know that Jericho is the east country from Jerusalem. Shouldn't this indicate that the east country from **the land of Eden, or Jerusalem, should be the same land as Jericho?** So now we have both combined rivers in the remote past, continuing after they would have merged together. And they passed the various countries, such as Bethlehem, Hebron and En-gedi, etc. Again the living waterways flow all the way down to Eilat's gulf, at Israel's border. This is as far as the angel described it to Ezekiel.

However, Moses describes the route beyond the gulf of Eilat, or Aqaba, but he entered it and travelled the length of gulf Aqaba, or 99 miles. The gulf Aqaba and the living water then merged...AT THE JUNCTION OF THE RED SEA AND THE GULF SUEZ. it's right here the river of living water... divided itself into four (4) heads, or four rivers.

One head of the living water **turned left, that is to' the east' and went to the land of HAVILAH. But the second head turned right, that is to the west, then went and surrounded DJIBOUTI, ERITREA, and ETHIOPIA.** But in the beginning,Djibouti, and Eritrea, were a part of Ethiopia to the west in the horn of Africa **AS ONE LAND.**

Note: This route through the Gulf of Aqaba, then to the Red Sea, is the most ideal way by water to get to Ethiopia in the horn of Africa. This cannot be a coincidence! It was ideal for the river to travel from Jerusalem, then into the Jordan valley, then into the Jordan river-then into the dead sea – then to Israel's border – then to Gulf Aqaba – then to the Red sea, then to Ethiopia.

VERSE 8, FROM KING JAMES VERSION

Here is how it is recorded in Ezekiel 47: 8. "Then said he unto me, the waters issue out **toward...the east country (Jericho) and go down into the desert (plain/Jordan valley) and go into the sea: (dead sea) the waters shall be healed "(fresh)**

Again, the east country here in verse 8, by Ezekiel has to be Jericho, the country to the east of Jerusalem – that is, a country in the Jordan valley. You see, the living water had to have flowed to Jericho..'.first' after leaving the field, or the Garden below the Temple Mount, because it had to have flowed to it, **before** it entered the Jordan river.

If you would Google Israel's map, you'll see that Jericho...**is east of Jerusalem.** And you'll also see that the dead sea is next to the Jordan river. In fact, the river flows to it.

The above information were to occur, **AFTER THE LIVING WATER WOULD HAVE LEFT FROM THE GARDEN OF EDEN.** So as a twenty first (21st.) century person, I'm sure you can see that the Garden of the Lord had to have been planted **EASTWARD, IN JERUSALEM IN PALESTINE.** So do you see that the Garden was in Jerusalem? that is, according to the angel and Ezekiel's words?

BACK TO THE YOUTH BIBLE NEW CENTURY VERSION

The angel continues to tell Ezekiel in chapter 47: 9, "Everywhere the river goes, there will be many fishes. Where-ever the water goes, even 'the dead sea' will become fresh, and so. Where the river goes there will be many living things." Verse 10, "fishermen will stand by **the dead sea, from en-Gedi all the way to En-Eglaim (end of Israel's border)** there will be places to spread fishing nets. There will be many kind of fish 'In the dead sea',as many as in the Mediterranean Sea." Note: this part of the vision never came to pass, i will explain it later.

Verse 11, But it swamps and marshes will not become fresh; they will be left for salt Google Israel's map to see the swamps and marshes. Now read slowly, for here-in lies your first proof that Jerusalem was ancient Eden. **Verse 12, "All kinds of fruit trees will grow on both banks of the river, and their leaves will not dry and die. The trees will have fruits every month, because the waters from them come from the Temple. The fruits from the trees will be used for food, and their leaves for medicine".**

Power Point: Think about this reader: in this vision, where is Ezekiel and the angel? answer, '**IN JERUSALEM'.** that is, in Israel's land. So according to verse 10 – 12, isn't the angel describing the land of Israel **from En-gedi all the way down to En-eglaim/ Eilat?** So in verse 12, the Garden with its fruits and leaves **HAVE TO BE IN ISRAEL'S LAND. (do you see it)**

Do you see why the Garden of Eden couldn't have been planted in Iraq, Turkey, Armenia, Africa nor under the Persian Gulf? The prophet Ezekiel says it was in Israel's land where the Lord brought him where he saw the Garden of Eden.

Ponder this: If the water came **from the Temple to water the trees in the Garden of Eden as Ezekiel says, then where do you think the tree of life, or the Garden of the Lord must have been planted? The answer should be…**'in Jerusalem'. But why do i say…'**IN JERUSALEM'?** Well, because Moses says that God planted his Garden…'in Eden'. And we do know that both the living water and the Garden were in Jerusalem. Because Ezekiel says so.

Again, because the living water which watered the Garden and the tree of life were both in Jerusalem-as Ezekiel says, don't look for the Garden of Eden to be located, 'outside Jerusalem'.

EZEKIEL SEES FRUIT-TREES IN THE LIKE MANNER AS THE GARDEN OF EDEN

Question: To where did Ezekiel return after following the copper angel who was measuring the distance to the point of the river where he couldn't cross? Answer: to the place where he left from '**before**' he started to follow the angel. And where was this place? Answer: **by the eastern/golden gate which was a part of the Temple-wall of 875,feet square, which surrounded the Temple area in Jerusalem.**

Reflect on this: When Ezekiel returned, **HE SAW MANY TREES ON BOTH SIDES OF THE BANKS OF THE RIVER WHICH WERE NOT THERE WHEN HE LEFT TO FOLLOW THE COPPER ANGEL WHO MEASURED A MILE AND A THIRD, OR 9,333 FEET OF WATER UP TO HIS NECK.**

But the question must be asked: Was this place where he saw many trees on both sides of the bank of the river, below the eastern/golden gate, '**The Garden of Eden?** I put it to you dear people, that it was truly the Garden of Eden, or the Garden of the Lord, which was just below God's house on top of the Temple Mount. You see, this Mount sloped downward and levelled off at ground level into a field. This field in the days of Adam and Eve was a part of the Garden of Eden.

Be reminded at this time, Ezekiel and the angel **are not all the way down to, the south by the marshes and swamps where**

17

he sees these trees but he is on the way back to the eastern/ golden gate which was attached to the 875 feet square wall WHICH LEADS TO THE TEMPLE IN JERUSALEM. I'm stressing this because you just might think that the Garden of Eden was located by the swamped and marshes in the south.

Bear in mind the Garden of Eden couldn't have been that far south in Israel, because both Moses and Ezekiel state that **the Garden was in Eden/Jerusalem.** But the marshes and swamps were and still are...OUTSIDE JERUSALEM' And they are all the way down past En-gedi, Bethlehem, Hebron and the dead sea, or salt sea.

COMMENTS ON THE ANGEL'S DIRECTION OF THE RIVER

Again, the angel now gives Ezekiel the route the river should have taken after it would have exited the Temple; **and 'before' it parted into four (4) heads or directions.** First it flowed from under the Temple's threshold door. Two: Then it flows from there to the right, or southside of the altar of sacrifice. And three: it flows straight out of the golden gate eastward. Again, this gate was a part of the 875 feet square wall, which surrounded the Holy area of the Temple.

The angel then tells Ezekiel that the river will flow ... toward **the east country.** That is, the east area, or direction, and would go **down into the Jordan valley or desert /field.** Then the river will enter...the dead sea, and when it does, the dead sea will turn fresh. Again, we know that this east country, 'is Jericho', and not some other country in the east; because the river would go down Into 'THE JORDAN VALLEY, AND THE DEAD SEA'.

So do you see for yourself that the angel is making reference to Israel's land, as to where the Garden of Eden was located? But you see, in order for the living water to flow to the dead sea, it had to first enter the Jordan river which was flowing from north to south. When the living water which flowed eastward **from the Temple's door entered the Jordan river, it had to turn and flowed southward.** Do you see that this whole affair about the Garden of Eden, had to do with Israel's land, and Jerusalem? Think about it.

The copper angel goes on to explain to Ezekiel that wherever the river goes, there will be many fish and many living things. The reason everything would have been in abundance in life, is because its living water flowed **from the Sanctuary of God in the Temple, in Jerusalem. Not any other country, but rather from Jerusalem.** So do you see from where the river of living water emanated or flowed in the days of Adam? It flowed from Mount Moriah / the Temple Mount in Jerusalem.

Now even though the Jordan River would have ended in the dead sea, **the living water continued all the way down to Eilat / en-eglaim /Aqaba's Gulf.**

The angel also told Ezekiel that the fishermen would be catching and hauling fish from En-gedi with their nets-that is, even to the end of Israel's land to the south. So you see, we are indeed **at En-gedi, in the south** in Judah, or Israel's land. This Garden which the angel was describing to Ezekiel, was going to be..**a physical Garden God was going to replant in Jerusalem after the Jews would have come out of Babylon. But God changed his mind because of man's sin. This Garden was not that spiritual Garden which John the revelator describes in his book, which is in New Jerusalem above. BECAUSE THERE IS NO EN-GEDI OR BETHLEHEM UP THERE.**

In order to get a good understanding of the direction the river would have taken, you should Google Israel's map and follow the angel's trail, all the way past Beer-Sheba and Negev, then to Eilat from Jerusalem. You will discover that En-gedi is on the same trail. All of the above should prove to you, according to Ezekiel's words that the Garden of the Lord...had to have been planted in Jerusalem, in the land of Judah / Israel.

Now the Gulf of Aqaba/ Eilat is a large gulf at the northern tip of the Red Sea, east of the Sinai Peninsula, and west of the Arabian mainland. Its coastline is divided between four countries, namely: Egypt, Israel, Jordan, and Saudi Arabia.

MEDITATE ON THE FOLLOWING:

I want you to bear in mind that in the processing of explaining the water route, Ezekiel stopped at Eilat / Aqaba Gulf. He only takes us up to the point at the south end of Israel's border. This indicates that the Garden of Eden had to have been watered 'before' the living water reached to the end of Israel's border, or 'before' we arrived at Eilat / Aqaba's Gulf. SO THE GARDEN HAD TO HAVE BEEN IN ISRAEL'S LAND. If you agree then give feedback on Amazon.com

Again the river of living water would have continued through Aqaba's Gulf, then through the Red Sea, or the southern end of it in order to get to Ethiopia. Now if you have reached the point of Eilat in Judah /Israel, you would have passed 'THE GARDEN OF EDEN'. You would have to return, or back-track to find it.

Power point: Moses states that the Garden of Eden...was in the land of Eden. Note this: But Ezekiel and the angel state that the Garden of Eden was in Jerusalem. One can extrapolate from this that the land of Eden must have been the same as the land of Jerusalem. Again this proves that the land of Eden is the same land as Old Jerusalem.

If we are to believe the prophet Ezekiel's account as to where the living water began to flow from, and as to where the Garden of the Lord was located, we should at least comprehend that it was in Jerusalem.

Ponder this: in order for the living water, or river to flow from Israel's border to Ethiopia, and surrounded it in the horn of Africa, it would have flowed through the Gulf of Aqaba, or Eilat, all the way down **to the south of the Red Sea, to Djibouti, then into Ethiopia and surrounded it as Moses says.**

To the seekers who are looking for the Garden of Eden, you cannot find it by following the route, or direction of the four heads of the rivers. The fact is...because the living water of life flowed directly to the Garden of Eden 'First', **and watered it – then it branched off into four heads Just as Moses says. But it branched off at the junction of the Red Sea and the Gulf Suez, in the water.**

If you want to find the Garden of Eden, you have to trace the living water **from the Sanctuary in the Temple of God on the Temple Mount in Jerusalem, to the end of Israel's border.** You see God's physical Sanctuary wasn't in any other country... but it was in the city of Jerusalem. So this should prove to you that the living water had emanated from the Temple of God, from the Temple Mount in Jerusalem. So the Temple Mount is the point of reference to begin your search to find the spot where the Garden of Eden was planted or located. And you shouldn't go beyond Eilat, Israel's border in the south.

Again, Ezekiel says that when he returned from his walking tour with the copper-angel through the water up to his neck, and returned to where he first started at the golden gate...**IT WAS A WATER BANK...AND HE SAW ALL KINDS OF TREES ON BOTH SIDES OF THE BANKS OF THE RIVER.**

Bear in mind, in the physical Jerusalem during the time Ezekiel was having this vision...no Garden of Eden was in existence. This was only a vision he was having. However, God was going to **recreate his Garden as it was in the days of Adam and Eve, but he repented, or changed his mind because the Israelites refused to worship him wholly.** So you should know that the trees which Ezekiel saw on both sides of the banks of the river when he returned to the golden gate, **HAD TO HAVE HAD HANGING FRUITS ON THEM, INCLUDING THE FRUITS OF THE TREE OF LIFE.** But when we come to verse twelve (12) it will show that these fruits will be good for food, and their leaves for the healing of the nations, or for medicine. All of this should prove that indeed, the Garden of Eden had to have been in Old Jerusalem, below Mount Moriah, or below the Eastern golden gate.

Take special notice of the following: **Ezekiel saw the same kind of fruit trees below the Temple Mount which the apostle John saw in New Jerusalem above.** We know that John's description of New Jerusalem, contrasts with the Garden of Eden on earth. Also it's safe to say that Ezekiel was referring to the same river which Moses also referred to, as it relates to the Garden of Eden. Even though Ezekiel's vision of the Garden of Eden was in contrast with John's vision of New Jerusalem above, Ezekiel and Moses referred to the Garden on earth

If you would observe: the fruits for food and leaves for medicine...had to have been in the plain or area below the Temple Mount, in Jerusalem – this plain area, was indeed the area where the Garden of Eden was planted.

The fact that Ezekiel didn't see these trees of the Garden of Eden, in no other country in the world, but rather right there in Jerusalem, should convince you that the Garden had to have been planted in Jerusalem facing the east.

Now even after the waters of the flood of Noah had receded, the topography, or the physical features of the earth still remained in the same position as before the flood. However, the original land where Adam, and the first ten (10) generations lived, remained intact. That is, the land of Palestine with its Judean hills, including the Temple Mount / Zion, and acre remained.

Note: no other parts of the earth, were inhabited by human beings who were made in the image of God, or Adam's race **before the flood-except the area where Adam...and up to the tenth (10th) generation, or where Noah lived. This was the area from Dan in the north to Negev in the south.** Now despite what anyone may say, this area of Palestine,' **IS THE CRADLE OF HUMAN CIVILIZATION.**

When I talk about the cradle, or origin of civilization, I'm making reference from Adam, the first man who was created after the image and likeness of God himself. Not about the Neanderthals, or the prehistoric man. Now by the time God had created Adam those prehistoric creatures, or ape-like men, had already become extinct millions of years prior, including the dinosaurs.

Now even though some of the ape-like men were almost human-looking, they still were not humans or Homo sapiens. But it was Adam and Eve whom God had created to look just like himself, and his wife, '**MOTHER SHEKINAH WISDOM**' (Sophia) See my next book.

Don't allow yourself to be deceived that God had created the universe, or the earth in six literal days, because he did not. It was six (6) periods of time, with each period being called a day. But God had created Adam at the end of the six period, or last of a million years. **See my next book.**

Okay, now in the process of explaining the water route which flowed from the Temple of God in Jerusalem, and watering the trees on both sides of the river, Ezekiel also brings into this narrative,' **the tree of life which is used for food'. And even 'the** leaves of this tree for medicine just as the apostle John explains in Revelation chapter 22:1-2

POWER POINTS TO PONDER

If the apostle John and the prophet Ezekiel placed 'the tree of life'...in the midst or center of Jerusalem, then it should be obvious ...' that the tree of life which Moses writes about in Genesis chapter 2: 9, when he says: ' that the tree of life was planted in the middle of the land of Eden...had to have been ...'the land of Jerusalem. So Moses had to have been referring to the land of Jerusalem, As the land of Eden where the tree of life was planted... Meditate on it.

MORE QUESTIONS TO PONDER

Question: what does the tree of life have to do with Jerusalem, which bears twelve kinds of fruits? And yielding her fruits every month – and the leaves of the tree for medicine-or the healing of the nations – and with living water proceeding from the Temple of God-watering the Garden of the Lord...if Jerusalem wasn't the same land as Eden. Are you reasoning with me?

Another question: why is Eden and Jerusalem similar? or what relationship Eden has with Jerusalem...if they aren't one and the same land? Know this: Ezekiel was describing the future restored Temple, that is, the second Jewish Temple which God was going to have governor Zerubbabel to build after the Jewish people would have returned to Jerusalem from captivity, or out of Babylon, where they stayed for seventy years.

Power Point: Why would the angel link 'the living water', 'the Garden of Eden', and 'the tree of life' with Jerusalem...if

Jerusalem wasn't being portrayed as Eden, and the Garden' in Eden', or in Jerusalem? Think about it.

Two: if the Garden of Eden was in any other country, why didn't the Spirit of the Lord transport Ezekiel to that country where the Garden of Eden would have been, instead of transporting him. **TO THE LAND OF ISRAEL, AND SPECIFICALLY TO THE CITY OF...BROKEN-DOWN JERUSALEM?**.

Also if the Garden of Eden was in Iraq, Armenia, Africa, Ethiopia, or the Persian Gulf region, why didn't the angel mention it to Ezekiel? why did the angel tell Ezekiel to make sure to inform the people who were in captivity, of all of what he saw in the land of Israel/Jerusalem, including one: 'The living water', And two, 'The tree of Life' in the garden...if what he was showing him and explaining to him were not expected to come into realization in their lifetime and in Jerusalem?

The fact that the Jews were eventually freed out of captivity, and the Temple rebuilt, proves that this part of Ezekiel's vision came to pass, or came into being after they were freed. Now verse 12, is the clue which will open-up your eyes / minds to the fact that Jerusalem was Eden wherein God had planted his Garden below the Temple Mount.

Power point to ponder: fact, it was in Jerusalem below the Temple Mount where Ezekiel saw all kinds of trees growing on both sides of the banks of the river. And yes, the trees also had to have had fruits on them. Therefore, I humbly submit to you...that this area had to have been the location of the Garden of Eden. yes. Right here below the Temple Mount.

In addition: to prove that this was the Garden of Eden, the angel told Ezekiel **that the leaves of the trees would not get dry, nor die. And that the trees will have fruits every month, because the water which flowed to the Garden to water the fruit**

25

trees, will proceed from the Temple which was in Jerusalem...
do you see it? The angel goes on to inform Ezekiel. I quote him.
"The fruits from the trees will be used for food." Now, Doesn't
this sound like these trees were...in the Garden of Eden? Oh yes!
However, here is the kicker: **This narrative refers to Jerusalem
on earth because the angel talks about the river passing the
dead sea, and En-gedi.**

Could you comprehend from this statement by the angel
to Ezekiel, that this place which he was pointing out to
him...HAD TO HAVE BEEN THE LAND OF EDEN
ANALOGICALLY? This description could only be referring
to Eden, and the Garden.'

Again, because the water which flowed from the Temple's
door threshold, ended by Eilat as the angel explains – you may
be inclined to believe that the Garden of Eden must have been
located somewhere by the marshes and the swamps in the south
in Judah.

Consider the following to prove that the Garden of Eden
couldn't have been by the marshes and swamps, at the southern
portion of Israel's border. One: Eilat...it is not in Jerusalem. And
two: it is not east of Jerusalem, but rather at the southern end in
Israel's land.

Ponder this: according to the angel's narrative, after the
living water would flow eastward from the Temple's door, it
would flow to the Garden of Eden-then to Jericho, a country
in the east, which is in the Jordan valley. Then it would merge
with the Jordan river which was flowing from the north to the
south. Then it would continue all the way down to Eilat. Three:
neither Beer Sheba, Negev, nor Eilat are located in the holy area
below Mount Moriah / Zion. Only Jerusalem was Holy land.
Four: Moses says that God had planted a Garden, 'Eastward in
Eden'. NOT SOUTHWARD OUT OF EDEN. So the Garden

was planted...inside Jerusalem, not outside Jerusalem, nor to the south in Israel/Judah. Therefore, we have to rule-out all other countries or areas outside Jerusalem. So these two words-' IN EDEN 'are the key words which indicate that the Garden was in Jerusalem.

After going eastward, the living water would enter into the Jordan Valley, or desert, or Garden, then join into the Jordan River which was already flowing from the north, or from the foothills of Lebanon and Syria, as stated before. After joining into the Jordan River, which was flowing to the south, the living water continued going south...all the way past En-gedi, continuing all the way down to Eilat / Aqaba 's gulf, and flowed through it some ninety nine (99) mile **then entered at the junction of the Red Sea and Gulf Suez, where it split into four heads or directions.** I repeat the above information just so you may remember them.

We know that the Garden of the Lord, had to have been inside Jerusalem, because it's in the Garden of Eden, or the Garden of the Lord where it was originally planted – which area was eastward in Jerusalem below Mount Moriah / the Temple Mount.

Now compare this verse 12, in the Youth Bible version, with Genesis 2:8, from the king James version. "Verse 8, And Moses says, "The Lord planted a Garden eastward...'IN EDEN: "and there he put the man whom he had formed, that is the Garden faced the East, or the sunrise.

Observe this strange twist: The land of Jerusalem and its Temple were also positioned eastward: that is, facing the sunrise. Coincidence? oh no! Because Eden is the same land as Jerusalem. It was called Eden before the flood of Noah, but in the process of time...after the flood, its name came to be called Moriah, Jebus' land, Salem, and finally, Jerusalem.

Verse 9, "And out of the ground made the Lord God to grow every tree that is pleasant to the sight, and good for food. 'The

27

tree of life' also in the midst of the Garden, and the tree of knowledge of good and evil"

Consider this: the tree of life in the Garden was also in the midst of the physical Garden. So you should know that, 'the tree of life', had to have been in the midst of the many trees in Jerusalem which Ezekiel saw when he returned to the Temple Mount, from his walking journey through the water with a copper looking angel. But we know that where-ever these trees were positioned, they must have been 'in Eden' but we know that Ezekiel and the angel were ' in Jerusalem'. So you see, 'the Garden ' must had been below the Temple Mount in Jerusalem'

Moses continues in verse 10, "And a river went out of Eden to water the Garden and became into four heads." Note this: The river went out of Jerusalem. So observe: according to Ezekiel's vision, it's the same scenario as to how the water went out of the Temple to water the Garden below the Temple Mount in Jerusalem. So the river had to have emanated out of Jerusalem. Don't forget that the Lord planted a Garden ...'IN EDEN'... And also a river went 'out of Eden'. Therefore, both the Garden and the river,.were 'in Eden'. It was the same land ! This is in comparison as to how the river flowed out of Jerusalem, and flowed to the Garden eastward in Jerusalem.

Therefore, you see, there was a similarity between Eden, the Garden of the Lord by Moses, and Ezekiel's Garden of Eden in Jerusalem...the former city of God. As you can see for yourself that the Garden couldn't have been planted...in Armenia, Turkey, Iraq, nor Anatolia, just because it was in that region where Noah had landed with the ark on Mount Ararat.

Obverse this famous Christian song: "We are marching upward to Zion, that beautiful city of God" However, it was the ancient Israelites who would have marched upward to Mount Zion/Moriah the Temple Mount to worship God in their

Temple. But when the Christians would sing this song today, they are referring to...**the heavenly New Mount Zion in New Jerusalem**... But it all started here on earth in the original old Jerusalem.

Power point: if you can read between the lines, you'll discern that not only Mount Zion was here in the beginning, but it is still here on earth in Jerusalem. So the Garden of Eden also had to have been in '**Old Jerusalem**' in the beginning with Adam and Eve.

Power point: Since Jesus says that if you overcome the evils of this world, he will give you food to eat **from the paradise of God above...which is now in New Jerusalem above...then isn't it logical to believe that the paradise of God had to have been...**'IN OLD JERUSALEM BELOW ON EARTH'? So no matter how hard we try, we cannot shake-off Jerusalem as Eden. Are you beginning to believe that the land of Eden is the same land as Jerusalem in Palestine?

EZEKIEL'S VISION WAS NOT ANY TEMPLE IN THE MILLENNIUM REIGN

There is a misconception by some that the Temple which Ezekiel saw in his vision will be the future Temple in the so called, up-coming millennium reign. However, this view is far from being true. The reality is, it was Zerubbabel's Temple, which was the second Jewish Temple which the angel was explaining to Ezekiel which was to be rebuilt.

Why would the angel go to all of those explanations to Ezekiel about those events, especially about the rebuilding of the Temple...then turn around and told him to make sure and explain them to the Jewish captives in Babylon...if those events were intended to occur many thousands of years '**AFTER**' they would have been set free out of Babylon? And in addition to this, those events wouldn't even come into existence in their life-time, but rather in the **far future in the spiritual millennium reign?**

Now to prove that the Jerusalem which the angel was informing Ezekiel about was the Jerusalem in the middle east, and **not Jerusalem above…** is the fact that the Jerusalem above is 1,500 by 1,500 by 1,500 miles high, wide, and in length. But Jerusalem in Palestine, to which the angel was explaining to Ezekiel, was seven miles long and six miles wide. And he told Ezekiel to tell the Jews that this 7x6 miles must be holy to God.. So in the same way the rebuilding of the Temple was in reference to Jerusalem, after their captivity…**So was the Garden of Eden in reference also to Jerusalem on earth 'after' their captivity. Do you see this reality reader?**

Again: why would the angel tell Ezekiel to inform the Jews in captivity of events in Jerusalem in the millennium reign which would come into existence many thousands of years later? It just doesn't compute at all.

VERY IMPORTANT INFORMATION TO REMEMBER

Even though mankind had failed to satisfy the expectations of God's desires, he being so merciful, still planned to recreate Jerusalem for the enjoyment of his former people…then for these blessings to be spread into the wider world.

God wanted to give Jerusalem a make-over. It was his plan to recreate the Garden of Eden also, when the Jews would have come out of slavery from Babylon. God wanted to redo his Garden like in the beginning, but mankind had disappointed him again. **So he didn't bring into realization, 'all' of the events in Ezekiel's vision.** But some of the events were indeed realized such as, the liberation of the Jews out of captivity, and the building of the second Temple by Governor Zerubbabel on the Temple Mount in Jerusalem.

Even after God's former people had been freed out of captivity, they still committed grievous sins before him, by secretly calling upon demons and false gods. Therefore, in the process of time, God had allowed this same second Temple which the angel was informing Ezekiel about to be desecrated by King Antiochus Epiphanes 4, the Syrian king in bc.168

Even though the Temple was indeed rebuilt after the Jews returned to Jerusalem out of Babylon, **God didn't allow the living water to flow from the Temple's door from his holy house which was on top of his holy mountain, as in the very beginning with Adam and Eve. God didn't even replace the ark of the covenant in the second temple.**

This recreating, or restoring of the Garden of Eden in Jerusalem, after the Jews would have come out of captivity...was to have been the greatest wonder of the world. It was to have brought people from all over the world as Tourists, but alas ! it never came to fruition. However, the powers that be in Palestine today should still **recreate or...replicate the Garden below East Jerusalem. Or below The Temple Mount.**

So again, God didn't allow all of what the angel was showing and telling Ezekiel to come into existence in the earth; including the Garden of Eden. Therefore, God had decided to replant his Garden and river of life...**In The New Jerusalem above instead.** So the Dead Sea in Israel remains salt even today.

Know this truth: all of the good plans God had intended for the earth and the original Eden/Jerusalem, after the Jews came out of captivity he had decided to **make all things new above instead.** So all of what was to have been done, in the earth, **are now in the Spiritual New Earth Above, and in New Jerusalem above.**

Now what the angel was showing Ezekiel in his vision was to be a Garden which God was planning to recreate in Jerusalem on earth **after the Jews' captivity.** So the direction which the river would have taken after leaving Jerusalem, or Eden **was the original route which the river took in the very beginning.** However, this route or direction never came into existence after the Jews exited their captivity out of Babylon. Again, because they didn't please God.

Therefore, in order to see and to enjoy all of God's new creation, we have to go through the spiritual door, or tunnel into **The New Earth's atmosphere, then to the center of the New Earth where New Jerusalem had descended and rested** – which Jerusalem is 1,500 miles long – 1,500 miles wide, and 1,500 miles high. That is, like a cube or square. This is the capital city for the New Earth – **'this is the metropolis.**

Observe: just like the earthly Jerusalem is in the center of the earth, as far as God is concerned; so is the spiritual New Jerusalem in the center of the Spiritual New Earth above. Think about it.

ENCOURAGEMENT

I believe you will appreciate the following information which the churches don't know.

Now, when we die, we'll be living in **the New Spiritual Earth above, which surrounds New Jerusalem.** But we will visit this new Jerusalem where the 144,000 ancient pure Israelites live, that is, 12,000 from each of the twelve tribes of Israel.

When we who would be living in the Spiritual New Earth above visit New Jerusalem, we'll not only eat from the tree of life, but will bring back leaves as medicine to the New Earth in order for us to live forever. Now this glorious new creation which the prophet Isaiah predicted in chapter 65:17-25, **was the same environment which the prophet Ezekiel predicted about which was to be experienced...' after the Jews would have come out of Babylon.** However, all of what was predicted by these two prophets didn't come to pass...but some did. The reason why all didn't come to pass was because of the lack of faith in God.

Before you continue to read, please, please, read Jerimiah chapter 18:5-10 where you'll see that God changes his mind at times, **even if he made a promise to you.** So all of what God promised to bring into realization as it relates to the new creation, didn't come to pass after the Jews came out of Babylon. Some assume that both Ezekiel and the prophet Isaiah, 65:17-25, refers to the same vision as the apostle John in revelation chapter 22:1-2. This isn't the case. Isaiah chapter 65, **speaks about a New Earth which is below,** because obviously, he couldn't have been referring to the New Spiritual Earth above, nor the New Jerusalem above, because in the New Earth above **NO ONE WOULD DIE AS AN INFANT,** But in the New Earth of Isaiah 65, he says: **"For the child shall die an hundred years old...but the sinner being an hundred years old shall be accursed."**

If you would notice, in Isaiah chapter 65, his narrative **speaks of death in the New Earth, and in New Jerusalem.** He also speaks about...SINNERS BEING IN IT, LIVING AT LEASE A HUNDRED YEARS OLD. But in the apostle John's vision New Jerusalem, and the New earth: **THERE IS NO DEATH IN THEM.** So we shouldn't confuse Isaiah chapter 65:17-25, with John's vision in revelation chapter 22:1-2. **and there is no need for the sun because the Lamb or Jesus and God are the light of them. So there is no sunrise, nor sunset in New Jerusalem and the New Earth above because there is** no twenty four (24) hours a day-because...it's a brand New Earth...not this old one below.

This proves that Isaiah's vision of the New Earth which was prophesied about to come into being, didn't come into fruition in all of its fulfillment – just like all of the events in Ezekiel's vision about the Garden of Eden didn't come to pass in the earth after the Jews came out of captivity from Babylon, because **God had repented, or changed his mind because man still was too wicked, and he would have ruined it all over again. I repeat, read Jerimiah chapter 18:5-10 again.**

So God recreated all things new ...' **in the spiritual heavens above. Not parallel to this earth below...but VERTICAL TO THIS EARTH BELOW.** So if you are pleasing the Almighty God and his son Jesus Christ Eliakim, don't be afraid to die. Because after death, he will assign you to the Spiritual New Earth above.

LOOKING FOR THE SECOND RIVER GIHON, WHICH FLOWED AROUND ETHIOPIA IN THE BEGINNING

Forgive my digression. You see, one mystery leads to another okay, let's continue.where we left off. Okay, these rivers which the researchers are looking for in the earth, are the ones which Moses writes about which stemmed from the Temple,on Mount Moriah-then flowed to the Garden of Eden. But in reality, the four rivers were divided out of the one living water.

Picture in your mind: We are now at the southern end of Israel's border again. This is at Eilat /Aqaba's gulf. This gulf of Aqaba is the same gulf as the gulf of Eilat. It's a large gulf at the northern tip of THE RED SEA, EAST OF THE SINAI PENINSULA, AND WEST OF THE ARABIAN MAINLAND. The max.

Width of Aqaba's gulf is 24km, (15,miles) Max. depth is 1850 m. (6,070 feet) and Max. length is 160 km. (99 miles).

The living water which flowed from the Temple's door which was built on the Temple Mount in Jerusalem, according to Ezekiel's vision, flowed all the way down to the gulf of Aqaba in the south where he stopped. However, in order for Moses to take us to Ethiopia, or Havilah, his narrative would've continued to flow through it some 99, miles to the end of it, **where it connected to the Red sea, and the gulf of Suez.** Now, as a result of the Gulf of Aqaba and the Red Sea coming together with force, they clashed and caused the river of living water...**to split into four directions.** Note this:: this is how the river flowed in the very beginning of creation. And this is how God was planning to recreate it after the Jews came out of captivity from Babylon; but he changed his mind. Because of their ill behavior.

Now it's at this northern end of the Red Sea where the living water split, or divided into four (4) heads. The first head of the river, **Pison, then turned and connected into the Gulf of Suez** along the midline of the Suez Gulf. It is bounded between Africa and Asia. The Gulf of Suez is shallow approximately 180-210 feet deep, and it is boarded by a broad coastal plain.

However, as the river of living water or the fresh water flowed through the Suez's Gulf, **it found a way into the Adal region located in East Africa. Its port city Zaila, is believed to take its name from 'HAVILAH' CUSH'S SON.**

In the past, the living water, or river surrounded this area of Havilah...even though there is no visible river surrounding this region today. However, the mere fact that Moses says that...'**The River Pison**' surrounded this region of Havilah where there was gold, and the gold was good...proves that there was indeed such a river there surrounding it. Therefore, the fact is...the river stopped flowing to Havilah in the process of time...'AFTER MOSES MADE THIS CLAIM'. This is therefore evident.

In reference to the second river in Genesis 2:13, Moses says, "And the name of the second river IS 'GIHON' THE SAME IS IT THAT COMPASSETH (surrounds) THE WHOLE LAND OF ETHIOPIA "(Cush)

At the time Moses wrote this, or made this claim… "like Havilah' **the whole land of Ethiopia, including Djibouti and the land of Eritrea, which connect to Ethiopia, the second river head was still flowing to them.** However, neither of the two rivers, nor the living water are in existence today.

Here is what Moses writes about the sons of Ham in Genesis chapter 10: 6-7 "And the sons of Ham, **CUSH, AND MIZRAIM, AND PHUT, AND CANAAN.**" Verse 7, "And the sons of Cush: Seba **and HAVILAH,** and Sabtah, and Raamah, and Sab-te-chan; the sons of Raamah Sheba and Dedan." **Therefore, CUSH was/is the Ethiopian people. MIZRAIM, was/is the Egyptian people. PHUT, was/is THE LIBIAN / NUBIAN PEOPLE, AND CANAAN, was /is the Canaanite people /Palestinian people. So Havilah and his land was/ is, of the son of Cush/ the Ethiopian.**

First, the mere fact that Moses uses the words "**IS IT**"-not "**WAS**" which compasseth the whole land of Ethiopia, **proves that it was in existence during the time he wrote about it. Moses even uses the word 'COMPASSETH' not COMPASSED. NOT SURROUNDED but SURROUNDS.** This was in the present tense at the time he was portraying the narrative in the wilderness. So even in his days in the wilderness, **Ethiopia, was still surrounded by...The river Gihon-the second head of the four rivers.** But of course, it's now withdrawn.

Ponder this: seeing that Ethiopia **is land-locked today, and isn't surrounded by a river; proves that it had already dried-up in the process of time...after Moses made the claim. And it also proves that DJIBOUTI AND ERITREA WERE ALL A PART OF ETHIOPIA AS ONE LAND IN THE PAST.** This means that the river Gihon, also surrounded Eritrea and Djibouti which means Ethiopia was really surrounded by the river Gihon in the remote past. If you Google them and observe the map, you'll see the reality of it.

BACK TO THE POINT OF THE RED SEA WHERE THE RIVER SPLIT INTO FOUR HEADS

Moses says the second head of the river was named 'Gihon'. Here is the route to Ethiopia.

When the river flowed 99 miles through the gulf of Eilat/Aqaba, it then flowed to the northern end of the Red Sea and the Gulf Suez. It was right here it split into four (4) heads, but instead of turning into the Gulf of Suez, **like Pison,** where it went and surrounded Havilah. Gihon continued to flow straight down to the southern end of **the Red sea, at the junction of BABEL MANDEB STRAIT / STRAITS OF TIRAN,** and into the Djibouti then into Ethiopia which is the land-lock northern horn of Africa.

Today, Djibouti and Ethiopia share borders with Eritrea, And the three of them are in the horn of Africa. In the past all of these three lands were named...Ethiopia. This is why Moses says that the river surrounded' **The whole land of Ethiopia.** This could not have occurred unless it surrounded Djibouti and Eritrea, At that time there were no Djibouti nor Eritrea.

Again, there is no more riverview surrounding Ethiopia today as Moses claims, This could only mean one thing-that is,

37

the river Gihon, had to have already dried up, or stopped flowing, sometimes 'after Moses had written about it. Be reminded of this.

Again, in ancient times, these two lands of Eritrea and Djibouti, were all classified as Ethiopia. But the river Gihon did run through the Red Sea from the northern tip to the southern end – then to Ethiopia and surrounded it, just as Moses recorded. So since then it has dried up. That is. by receding, or backing-up **into the Red Sea-then eventually, into the Babel strait/strait of Tiran.** But instead of backing-up into the Gulf of Aqaba/Eilat, **it flowed into the Gulf of Eden and into the Indian Ocean.**

However, it's a fact that the Red Sea, even today, connect to both Djibouti and Eritrea, which connect to Ethiopia. As you can see, that the river was still in existence After the flood of Noah. And to prove it again, is the fact that Moses says that it was flowing during the time he wrote about it.

Here now is a quote from the prophet Isaiah chapter 18: 1 "Woe to the land shadowing with wings (Babylon) **which is beyond the rivers of Ethiopia."** Obviously, it appears that even in the days of the prophet Isaiah, that there were still many rivers in the land of Ethiopia. So Ethiopia was indeed known as a land of rivers, and was famous in the days of the prophet for its many rivers, However, the river which completely surrounded Ethiopia, had vanished. But today there are not as many rivers in it as in ancient times. Because with the passing of time, many were dried up or stopped flowing.

So Pison and Gihon which were in Africa had disappeared out of view. But the other two rivers, Hiddekel/Tigris, and Euphrates on the Asian side are still visible, even though it is believed that Euphrates is gradually diminishing. So in the future Euphrates will be no more.

BACK AT THE TOP OF MOUNT MORIAH

Now from this holy land of Jerusalem which was set aside for the Lord, 875 feet square, was for the Temple area. This 875 feet square wall here, 'was not' the city wall, or the wall which surrounded Jerusalem, but rather the wall which was to be built around the Temple – which contained the gate called, ' THE EASTERN GATE/ GOLDEN GATE',

In addition, another open space of 871/2 feet square was to be measured within this 875 feet square area. This 871/2 feet square area was to be measured from the Temple porch's gate, extending 871/2 feet up to the outer court's gate. This 871/2 feet square was to be an opened space.

So ancient Jerusalem was seven miles long by six miles wide. But notice how God was going to have this seven miles long, and six miles wide, divided, or split smack down in the middle, from East to West. This is seven miles by three in half miles to the south. And seven by three miles to the north.

Picture this scene as you read. Now within this 875 feet square, or the most holy place, the Temple was constructed. Verse 4, "This holy part of the land will be for the priests who serve in the Temple, who came near to the Lord to serve him. It will be a place for the priests' house and the Temple."

At this time, I want you to imagine this scene of Jerusalem being divided in half. But bear in mind, that it is the half toward the south, which was seven miles long and three miles wide that I will be dealing with for now, not the other half of 7x3, miles to the north, which was given to the Levites. So now picture a land 7, miles long and 3,miles wide at the south in Jerusalem.

Verse 5 "Another area about seven miles long and more than three miles wide will be for the Levites, who serve in the

Temple area. It will belong to them so they will have cities in which to live."

This other area about 7 miles long and some three miles wide, **is the other half of the 7, miles long by 6 miles wide which was for the dwelling of the Levites.** This 7x3 miles was to the north in Jerusalem.

Let me quote another portion of the scriptures so that you may understand **THAT THE TEMPLE, ON THE TEMPLE-MOUNT, WAS REALLY IN THE MIDDLE OF THE 875 FEET SQUARE.**

In chapter 48:9, the angel goes on to tell Ezekiel to tell the Israelites the following: "The share which you will give to the Lord, **will be about seven miles long and three miles wide** "(7x3)

Verse 10, "The holy area will be divided among these people. The priests will have land about seven miles on the north and south sides, and three miles wide on the west and east sides. **THE TEMPLE OF THE LORD WILL BE IN THE MIDDLE OF IT."**

This is the rectangular shape of the portion of land to the south which is paralleled to the 7x3, miles to the north. So you see, the Temple was going to be constructed' **IN THE MIDDLE OF THIS 7 MILES LONG AND THREE MILES WIDE RECTANGULAR AREA WHICH WAS TO THE SOUTH.**

Whenever you go to East Jerusalem, or Old Jerusalem, and would visit the Temple Mount, then rest assured, that you would be standing in the former most holy spot on earth. This is because this is where **the fountain of living water proceeded to water the trees in the Garden of the Lord, including ' THE TREE OF LIFE.**

This was where the altar and throne of God were situated in the beginning on earth. And this is also why God had his holy

Temple built up there in the process of time by Melchizedek, the Priest of the most high God, even 'before' the days of Abraham. But in the days of Adam, there was no physical Temple built up there. Nonetheless, this was the mountain and spot where Adam and Eve went to workshop God...not where they lived below the Mount...that is before they were expelled out from there.

Do you see why Jerusalem is what it is even today, especially, 'East Jerusalem'? The struggle is in part, **for the former real estate, or property of God, as to where his throne and altar were originally set-up.** Now he who controls the Temple-Mount, possesses the former most holy spot on earth, making it the most expensive piece of real estate on planet earth.

CHAPTER 3

THE DIMENSION OF THE GARDEN OF EDEN

ANCIENT BIBLICAL MEASUREMENT OF A MILE

In biblical ancient times, the Israelites' measurement of distance was quite different from today. **Example: One mile was a measurement of 7,000 feet, instead of 5,280 feet as being used today. And the month was calculated as 30 days in a month-and 360 days in a year.**

I am equating 7,000 feet as one mile in this chapter as ancient Israel did. So my measurement of the dimension of Jerusalem, and the Garden of Eden, is 7,000 feet, to equate one mile...not 5,280 feet as today. So please remember this 7,000 feet to one mile. And now, on with my narrative which you will enjoy.

One: The holy area of ancient Jerusalem constituted seven (7) miles long and three (3) miles wide. This of course, was in ancient times. But since then, the size of Jerusalem, and the boundary of the building of the walls around it had changed a few times.

This size or dimension of Jerusalem, is not in relation to the overall dimension of it which was 7, miles long by 6, miles wide.

But this is in reference to the half of the southern portion of Jerusalem… 'The Holy area'.

Two: the 875 feet square, which surrounded the Temple, constituted '**The Most Holy area**'. But the question is, what was the size or dimension of the Garden of Eden according to the prophet Ezekiel?

Follow me closely: **This holy area was on the south side of Jerusalem, and it was 7, miles long by 3, miles wide. Now one mile equals 7,000 feet. So seven (7) miles equals 49,000 feet. Let's now minus the 875 feet, from the 49,000 feet. This leaves a balance of 48,125 feet. So this balance of 48,125 feet is the number we have to deal with.**

Next, we have to divide this 48,125 feet in order to have…HALF TO THE EAST OF THE TEMPLE-WALL WHERE THE 875 FEET ENDS AND THE OTHER HALF…TO THE WEST OF THE TEMPLE-WALL, WHERE THE 875 FEET ENDS. And as you know already, the Temple sat in the center of this 875feet square area. That is, between the eastern portion of this 875 feet wall.

After dividing this 48,125 feet, **in two halves,** we have a quantified number of **24,062, and one half feet 'GOING EAST'** from where the 875 feet ends – that is, at the end of the **EASTERN WALL WITH ITS GOLDEN GATE. And we have the other 24,062, and one half feet 'AT THE WEST'** from where the 875 feet ends-to where the 24,062, and one half feet, ends ' IN THE WEST'.

IMPORTANT POINTS TO PONDER

Ladies and gentlemen, boys and girls, I submit and declare to you – **that the dimension, or size of the Garden of Eden, or the Garden of the Lord…WAS A MILE AND A THIRD LONG**

(9,333 ft.) BY THREE MILES (21,000 ft.) WIDE. This is three (3) miles from north to south, AND A MILE AND A THIRD, (9,333 ft). 'FROM EAST TO WEST'.

In fact, just as you step out of the area where the golden gate was erected, which was a part of the 875ft. Wall at the east, you would automatically be stepping down the slope into the Garden of the Lord. This is, at ground level in a plain where the Garden of the Lord / Eden was planted. **And also where ' the olive tree of life was planted...IN THE CENTER OF THE 9,333 FT, OR MIDDLE OF A MILE AND A THIRD, WHICH IS...4,666 FEET ON BOTH SIDES OF THE RIVER.** This is where the river was flowing in the very beginning in the days of Adam and Eve.

If you would follow Ezekiel, or the copper angel's instructions, you would be going straight ahead **toward the east, from the golden gate into the Garden. Then straight ahead eastward, into the Jordan valley through Jericho, and would then enter the Jordan river which was flowing south from the north. Then you being merged into the Jordan river which was flowing south, would automatically be going SOUTHWARD. Then down by En-gedi, then pass Beer Sheba, and Negev. Then you would end up, all the way down to Eilat, at the end of Israel's border.**

FOLLOW ME CAREFULLY

Follow this narrative carefully: From the golden gate, which was a part of the 875 ft. square wall, which surrounded the Temple To the very end of the former holy land of Jerusalem, **was 3.417, miles long (3,point 417 miles) or 24,062 feet.**

Two: The distance from the golden gate where the beginning of the Garden of Eden began, **to where it ended...was a mile and a third, which is equivalent to 9,333 feet.**

This mile and a third, or 9,333 feet, is based upon the fact that it was at this golden gate or eastern gate where Ezekiel and the angel began their walking journey through the water. **And it's a fact that they walked up to 'a mile and a third'** – because Ezekiel couldn't walk any further as a result of the water being too high for him to cross. He was neck deep and tipping on his toes in the water.

Now because the angel and Ezekiel stopped walking at a mile and a third, or 9,333 feet eastward, I feel inspired to end the Garden Eastward at this point. Because the water rose so high, they didn't complete their journey to the end of Jerusalem, eastward **which was some 3.417 miles, or 24,062 feet FROM THE EASTERN OR GOLDEN GATE.** So now we leave with approximately **14,729 feet from where the angel and Ezekiel stopped walking to the entrance of the city itself which was eastward. This is to the entrance of Jerusalem itself.**

When Adam and Eve were expelled out of the Garden, God placed cherub angels with flaming swords at **the entrance of this 14,729 feet area eastward.** The reason was to make sure that no one including Adam and Eve wouldn't return to have access to the Garden and the tree of life. This 14,729 feet **was a kind of a buffer zone from the eastern entrance of Jerusalem to the Garden. That is from where Ezekiel and the angel stopped walking, to Jerusalem's entrance at the east.**

CONSIDER THIS ALSO

Seeing that the Garden of Eden began just outside the Eastern / Golden gate – and sloping downward, going 9,333 feet eastward – and the tree of life being in the middle or center of the Garden, indicates ' **THAT THE TREE OF LIFE WAS PLANTED SOME 4,666 FEET FROM THE GOLDEN GATE.** this must be the case, because **the length of the Garden was,9,333 feet-and some three miles, or 21,000 feet wide from north to south.**

We must remember that the angel told Ezekiel to tell the Israelites that they must give a portion of the land of Israel to the lord, when they would have come out of captivity and return to Israel. This portion was Jerusalem, and it was to be holy to him. Then he commanded that Jerusalem to be **DIVIDED STRAIGHT DOWN IN THE MIDDLE FROM EAST TO WEST.**

But this Jerusalem was to be seven miles (49,000 feet) long by six miles (42,000 feet) wide: that is, 7x6 or 49,000 feet x 42,000 feet. Now as a result of splitting Jerusalem in half, we now have **one half to the north, which was seven miles long from east to west, by three miles wide from north to south.** Now this southern side of Jerusalem, was also 7x3 miles or, seven miles long from east to west by three miles wide from north to south.

So what I'm going to deal with is that portion of Jerusalem **to the south which was seven miles long by three miles wide.** Therefore, the Garden of the Lord in Eden, or Jerusalem **was three miles wide – that is, from north to south, and it was a mile and a third long – that is, from east to west.**

Ezekiel and the angel stopped one and a third miles after leaving the eastern gate because the river had risen too high for him to cross.However in Adam's days the 14,729 feet eastward, from the Garden's entrance, was an open space. But in Ezekiel's vision a river passed through it. This river which was too high for Ezekiel to cross, continued into the east country of Jericho, which was /is in the Jordan valley.

Again, after this the river flowed to the Gulf of Eilat/Aqaba- then it flowed to the junction of the Red Sea, and the Gulf of

Suez, where it split into four (4) heads, or four directions. One direction flowed into **the Gulf of Suez, then to Havilah. And the other head flowed to Ethiopia in the horn of Africa and surrounded it.**

EZEKIEL NOW DESCRIBES THE GARDEN OF EDEN

When Ezekiel returned to where he started his tour he was surprised. Observe this: **it is now turned into a garden with many trees on both sides of the banks of the river. And the leaves of the trees were for medicine.** This is the same narrative the apostle John describes in Revelation chapter 22:1-2. However, John's vision was the New Jerusalem above. But Ezekiel's vision was to be the one God was going to replicate on earth from the original Garden of Eden. This was to be replicated **after the Jews would have returned to Jerusalem after coming out of captivity from Babylon.** And the vision of the Garden was to be in **the same position it was in during the days of Adam and Eve, in the beginning.**

Now Jesus Christ speaks to John's vision in which John speaks about the paradise of God. In fact, it was Jesus who said that if you were to overcome this evil world-system, he would then give you **food to eat from the tree of life which is in the midst of the Paradise of God** This is the spiritual Garden of Eden in Revelation 2:7.

Do you see that Ezekiel was describing the paradise of God, which was the Garden of Eden in the beginning, **AND NOT THE ONE IN HEAVEN?**

Even though the paradise of God, or the Garden of the Lord which was on earth below, **is somewhat similar to the Paradise of God, or the Garden, or paradise of God in New Jerusalem**

above, they are still different in their nature, even though they look alike. Put another way. Are you able to observe **the similar scenario between the paradise of God above wherein the tree of life is planted, and the Garden in Eden /Jerusalem, below Mount Moriah/Zion, in the days of Adam?**

Even after God was disappointed with his people, he still wanted to replicate Eden, or Jerusalem again on the earth. And to replant his Garden **'again'** in it as in the beginning, And this is the Garden of Eden which the angel was showing Ezekiel...But it never came into being because of the peoples' disobedience.

God's intention was to give the Jewish captives another chance to live in his potential Paradise especially the ones who were born in captivity in Babylon...after they would have come out of captivity. But sadly, they still didn't please him to the point to cause him to make it happen. Again read the book of Jerimiah chapter 18:7-10, so that you may see that God would change his mind from doing what he promises...if one does not keep his integrity.

So from that point forward, God had decided to replant his Garden or Paradise in Jerusalem, which he calls 'NEW JERUSALEM' which is in the spiritual realm above. Note this: the reason God calls it,'NEW JERUSALEM', was because the people in the Old Jerusalem had disappointed him again. This has nothing to do with the Jews today. **They are good modern days people.**

TAKE NOTE OF THE UP-COMING POINTS

In his Temple, the living water is currently flowing to his Garden, or Paradise, and watering all of the trees including the tree of life. And There is also a river like a street which leads **from his throne to his Garden,** just like the river which formerly flowed from Mount Zion / Moriah / Temple Mount in the earthly Jerusalem to the Garden. (re-read)

Power point: So if the above narrative is in the Paradise of God in New Jerusalem above, then Ezekiel's vision had to have been the Paradise of God also on earth in Jerusalem in the beginning with Adam and Eve. Therefore, Jerusalem on earth...had to have been...the Paradise of the Lord, and the same land as ancient Eden. Now like in New Jerusalem above, so was it in 'OLD JERUSALEM, IN PALESTINE BELOW ON EARTH'.

Look at this: by the time of St. Paul, and St. John's ministries in the first century, New Jerusalem had already been completed above **'with the tree of life' and the river of living water within it.** See Galatians chapter 4:25-26 And Revelation 22:1-2'

In Ezekiel's vision the Temple also had living water **flowing outward from the Temple's threshold door, and flowing toward the east. And It also watered the trees in the Garden. Consider this: and the trees were also on both sides of the banks of the river which were below the Temple-Mount, just like the living water flowing.OUT OF GOD'S TEMPLE IN NEW JERUSALEM ABOVE.**

Powerpoint question: isn't it rather strange that Ezekiel saw these fruit trees, and river, **in Jerusalem rather than any other country? This could only mean that the Garden of Eden had to have been in the land of Jerusalem. (yes?) Also: these trees bear fruits every month. And the leaves on the trees were for medicine. That is, for the healing of the nations-just like John's vision in the book of Revelation 22:2.** This my friend was indeed the Garden of Eden which Ezekiel was describing...but look where it was? yes, **IN JERUSALEM ON EARTH!** I put it to you that **the area below the Temple Mount in Jerusalem is the same spot as the Garden of Eden.**

MEDITATE ON THIS ALSO

Power points: if the Garden of Eden was in any other country on earth, **why would Ezekiel describe it as being...at the east in Old Jerusalem, below Mount Moriah/ the Temple Mount... and the living water flowing from the Temple's threshold-door from Mount Moriah...downward, to water the Garden? Think about it!**

Two: and why would John the Revelator describe,' **The Garden of the Lord, or the Paradise of God, being within 'New Jerusalem also'...if it weren't within ancient Old Jerusalem on earth in the beginning with Adam and Eve? Why Palestine?**

Know this truth: Moses' narrative about the creation of mankind, and the first ten (10) generations of 1656 years, from Adam to the flood of Noah, was in reference to the Middle East in Palestine – beginning with Eden, or Jerusalem. God didn't start the creation of mankind **from a corner on the earth, but rather in the middle of it.**

Think about this: If you have a pond in your yard filled with water, and you want to create ripple-waves within it – would you drop your pebble-stone at the corner in your pond, or would you drop it or throw it to the center of the pond of water? If you say, at the center...likewise, when God had started his creation of human beings...'not the Neandertals,' he started from the center, or middle of the earth near a great sea, called, ' **The Mediterranean Sea as their western border in Palestine. This Sea means, 'Middle of the earth' Strange isn't it?**

CHAPTER 4

SIMILARITY BETWEEN EDEN AND JERUSALEM

Here are a few convincing pieces of evidence for you to deliberate upon as you read, so that you may be convinced that Eden was indeed Jerusalem. And the Garden of the Lord, was located within it-which location was in a plain below Mount Zion / Mount Moriah/ the Temple Mount.

What reasonable evidence can be provided that the river of living water which watered ' the tree of life' in the Garden of Eden...was indeed in Jerusalem, in the middle east? The answer is: **Because we find it in New Jerusalem above watering the tree of life in the Paradise, or Garden of God also.**

John writes in Revelation 21:1, ' And he shewed me a pure river of water of life clear as crystal, **proceeding out of the throne of God and the Lamb. "(Jesus)** So there should be no reasonable question that the river which was in the Garden on earth, which watered 'the tree of life' **proceeding from Mount Moriah or the Temple Mount was indeed in Jerusalem.**

Why would I say this? Well, because we find a similarity **of the same river of water proceeding out of the throne of God and the Lamb from MOUNT ZION/ in New Jerusalem above.** Please give this some serious thoughts.

51

At a point in time past, God said the ancient Israelites had forsaken him **who is the fountain of living water.** This is why we see the clear crystal water proceeding or flowing out of the throne of God in New Jerusalem.

Moses writes in Genesis 2:10, "**And a river went out of Eden to water the Garden:** and from thence (there) it was parted, and became four heads."

Do you see that the spot or place in Eden, from where the water originated, or sprang, **had to have been Mount Moriah, or the Temple-Mount, God's former holy mountain where he dwelt in time past when he would have visited the earth?**

Power Point: Let me try to put this statement as simply as I can. Watch the parallel: In the same way the river went out of Eden to water the Garden in Genesis 2:10, **is the same way in New Jerusalem above, it went and watered 'the tree of life' in the paradise of God.**

Even Ezekiel says that the living water flowed...**out of Jerusalem.** So who is right? Moses says the river **flowed out of the land of Eden, and went and watered... 'the tree of life'** which was, (Note this) 'IN EDEN'.

Again, Ezekiel says that the living Water flowed.. OUT OF THE TEMPLE, THROUGH ITS DOORS 'THRESHOLD...WENT AND WATERED THE TREE OF LIFE, IN JERUSALEM ON EARTH. Now could you deduce from both Moses and Ezekiel, that they were referring **to the same Garden, and the same 'tree of life in Jerusalem'?**

Both Moses, Ezekiel and John the Revelator are right, because both Moses and Ezekiel's Garden of Eden, **was the same physical Garden or Paradise of God on earth.** However, in John's vision...his Paradise or Garden, **was a spiritual one in**

New Jerusalem above, with Eden, and its Garden as a symbol of the Garden of Eden in Jerusalem in the beginning. This therefore, should open-up our minds' eyes, **that the earthly Garden of Eden had to have been in Jerusalem, that is....South East Jerusalem.** So both the living water and the Garden must have been in Eden / Jerusalem.

MORE POWER POINTS

Contemplate on these power points. **One: The earthly river flowed out of Eden. Two: The heavenly river currently flows out of Jerusalem above, even today: And three: In Ezekiel's vision, the river flowed out of the Temple of God and...out of Old Jerusalem, in the past. Strange isn't it?** So both Moses and Ezekiel and the apostle John, had experienced visions of the Garden of Eden' facing the east.

Now ponder this: how could you satisfy yourself that the Garden of Eden and Eden itself which both Moses and Ezekiel wrote about...**were the same Garden, and that Jerusalem was Eden?** Well, because Moses says that God planted a Garden **eastward in Eden. And Ezekiel also says that the Temple...faced east, or the sunrise. And that Jerusalem and the Garden...faced the east.**

Here is a rational and reasoning question for you to consider, so that you may believe that God's throne and Altar must have been...on Mount Moriah in Jerusalem in the very beginning.

So where-ever the living water proceeded from on earth, in the beginning to water the physical Garden, and the tree of life, just as it is doing in New Jerusalem today (Revelation 22:1) **must have proceeded from the throne of God...**which should mean that the throne of God, had to have been in Eden / Jerusalem on Mount Moriah in the beginning.

More Power Points

Again, how would you know that the tree of life which was in the Garden of Eden, **was in South East Jerusalem in the Middle East, or Palestine? Well, because it is found in New Jerusalem above. So it must have been here on earth...in Old Jerusalem below the Temple Mount.** Do you see the connection between the Garden of Eden and Jerusalem? Here is what the apostle John writes in Revelation 22:2. In the midst of the street of it, and on either sides of the river, **there was the tree of life which bear twelve (12) manner (sorts) of fruits, and the leaves of the tree are for the healing of the nations "(nations of the new earth above...not this physical earth down here)**

So if Adam and Eve had eaten of the tree of life first, then they would have lived forever as righteous people, bringing forth righteous children, thus making God pleased. They also could have used the leaves of the Spiritual Female Olive Trees **as medicine to prevent sickness.** But they blew their opportunity to live forever on earth. Therefore, only those persons who believe **ON THE SECOND ADAM.**who is of the Spirit of God will live forever above, after this life on earth.

This second Adam is also the Son of God just as the first Adam was the Son of God. See Luke chapter 3: 38. This son of God is Jesus Christ, the Messiah...and anyone who believes in him, can take advantage of the tree of life, and live forever, when they would leave this earth and enter 'the spiritual New Earth above, which God had prepared for righteous people after physical death.

STILL COMPARING EDEN AND ITS GARDEN BELOW...WITH JERUSALEM AND ITS PARADISE / GARDEN ABOVE
Taken from the King James version

Here is what Moses says God did to Adam and Eve, after they sinned in the Garden of Eden, or in his Garden. Genesis 3:23-24." Therefore, the Lord God sent him forth from the Garden of Eden, to till the ground from whence (where) he was taken. "Verse 24, "So he drove out the man; and he placed at the east of the Garden of Eden, Cherubims, and a flaming sword which turned every way, to keep the way of the tree of life."

So we see that 'the way to the tree of life...WAS BLOCKED OR CLOSED, so that neither Adam nor Eve could have returned, and to eat of the tree of life and to live forever. Again, the earthly Garden was closed. That is, the Cherubs or angels with four faces, who were 'The watchers'...WERE LIKE A CLOSED GATE, to prevent Adam or anyone from entering it. However, you'll see a parallel, or a comparison between 'this block way' or 'closed gate' of entering the Garden in Palestine... to the spiritual Garden or Paradise above with ' the opened gates' to the city in New Jerusalem. This should also prove to you that both the earthly Eden, and its Garden are symbolically the same as the spiritual New Jerusalem and its Paradise or Garden above. Because the New Jerusalem above, was prepared 'AFTER' the earthly Jerusalem below. So if you would remember, Jesus told his apostles that he was going to prepare...a place for them...which means that at that time, it wasn't prepared yet.

Now after many years, St. Paul stated that there was at that time a Jerusalem above, which was a spiritual one. The apostle John confirmed it, and gave us a description of that spiritual or New Jerusalem above.

THE OPENED GATE IN NEW JERUSALEM

Remember now, that the 'pathway' or the gate in Eden to the Garden ' was closed ' as a result of the angels blocking the entrance from anyone entering into it. Now watch how the twelve (12) gates of the city of New Jerusalem were going to be opened, 'to all' who are found worthy to enter in, and to eat of the tree of life, and to continue to live forever.

John writes in Revelation 21:21-25, concerning the gates of the new city of Jerusalem. ..." And the twelve (12) gates were twelve pearls, every several gate was of one pearl: and the street of the city was pure gold, as it were transparent glass."

Verse 22, "And I saw no Temple therein: for the Lord God Almighty and the Lamb are the Temple of it."

Verse 23, "And the city had no need for the sun, neither of the moon, to shine in it: for the glory of God did lighten it, and the Lamb is the light thereof."

Verse 24, "And the nations of them which are saved shall walk in the light of it: and the kings of the earth do bring their glory and honour into it."

Verse 25, "**And the gates of it shall not be shut at all by day: for there shall be no night there.**"

Ponder this: In Eden, the way to the tree of life 'WAS BLOCKED' but in New Jerusalem above, the way, or gateway to the tree of life...'IS UNBLOCKED and the gates' ARE WIDE OPENED'.

Here is what John writes concerning the gates and the city.

Revelation 22: 4, "Blessed are they that do his commandment, that they may **have right to the tree of life, and may enter in through the gates into the city.**"

Think about this: with this Jerusalem above, **you do have a right to the tree of life.** And you will be able to enter in through the gates into the city. But with the Garden in Eden on earth, Adam, and Eve, had no more rights to the tree of life, because they had become sinful. **So they were barred from re-entering it through the passage-way into the Garden, or into the Paradise of God.**

John writes in Revelation 21: 5, "He (God) that sat upon the throne said, **Behold, (look) I make all things new."** Question: what were the...**all things which God had made new?** Well, all of those things which he had previously made in his first creation. You should ponder my next statement in order to understand that God did make all things new.

Note: God's second creation was a spiritual and new one. Now with this new creation, if one would accept the Lord Jesus Christ Eliakim, as the Lord of their life, then he or she would live forever, in this new spiritual world – that is – **in the New Spiritual Earth above.**

After Adam had failed God in his Garden, and caused the whole human race to become sinful, God eventually destroyed all of his creation leaving only eight (8) persons alive. That is, he destroyed everything during the tenth generation from Adam to Noah. But God being so merciful, he **started all over again with a new people.** But they too became sinful, but this time, he didn't kill them all, but he scattered them from Babel, and caused them to travel throughout the earth and to establish new colonies and to inhabit them.

Now because of God's long patience, he started all over again after the great confusion and departure from Shina/ Babel. However, because ten (10) is his number of completion, he waited **for another ten (10) generations, that is from Noah to Abraham, to start over again.**

It was Abraham who was the tenth generation from Noah. It was Abraham whom God had blessed, then his son Isaac, who was the father of Jacob. And it was from this Jacob who was the father of the twelve (12) tribes of Israel. And it was these special people who God had called to be an example to the world by living righteously. Some of them had tried but they couldn't hold out.

Here is what God did for his former special chosen people. He took away a portion of Canaan land and gave it to them for their possession. This land to them was called, '**the promise land**', because he had promised his friend Abraham that he will possess the land of Canaan, and it will be for his seed or descendants. However, God had struggled with them for many years trying to lead them in his way of righteousness, but they still failed him also in the end.

However, today I can testify that many of them are pleasing God, **by accepting his son, 'The Lord Jesus Christ Eliakim', and living as Christians. And if this former original branch of the natural olive tree would continue to be watered by the living words of Jesus Christ Eliakim, then they will bounce back and be the next leading Christian nation 'AFTER' THE NATION OF THE BAHAMAS, WHICH IS THE PRINCIPLE CHRISTIAN NATION ON EARTH.**

WHAT MUST GOD DO NOW?

Should God have given-up on the human race at that time? Here is what he did. He sent his beloved son Jesus to teach his chosen people, and by extension, to choose apostles and disciples to go throughout the then world, and to teach them of his way of righteousness.

However, the gravitational pull of the powers of darkness in one's mind, is so strong, that it's very difficult to break free and to gravitate to the light. Know this: the way of darkness is death. And the way of light is, 'LIFE '.But you know, that deeds being done in the darkness...appear to be sweeter than in the light, But we have the choice to choose.

God being the God of light would not allow the evil powers of the gods of this world to cause him to abandon his earth (foot stool).

But God had another plan which was plan "B". Now plan 'B' was the following: God had made a spiritual New creation. That is, a Brand New Spiritual Earth Above, with a Brand New Spiritual Jerusalem above – and a Brand New Spiritual Paradise in Eden above.

In this second, or new creation of God, he sent the second Adam who is of the Spirit, to salvage the souls of mankind in order to inhabit...**This New Jerusalem and New Spiritual Earth Above.** And all who accept God's beloved son Jesus, will become a citizen of this spiritual New Earth.

As for the Spiritual New Jerusalem, no other persons are added into it, apart from the 144,000 ancient Israelites, that is, 12,000 from each of the twelve (12) tribes of Israel who are already there. **But the Spiritual New Earth above, is the place where all of us go when we die provided we please God and his son Jesus Christ Eliakim.**

Know this: Jesus would have been disappointed if he wasn't crucified. So the former Jews are vindicated. But why do I say this? Well, it was Jesus who said, **"As Moses lifted up the serpent in the wilderness, so shall the son of man be lifted up".** So he knew that he was going to be lifted up upon a pole, or was to be crucified. In Fact, he came to this earth to initiate or to form a spiritual kingdom for himself, and to bring a new way to God. But his kingdom would be within you. That is, in your mind. And this new Spirit within you would cause you to demonstrate Love, Joy, Peace, Long suffering, Meekness, Gentleness, Goodness, and Faith.

Jesus made another statement by saying: **"if I be lifted up from the earth, I will draw all men unto me."** So if he had missed being crucified in the **year 30 ad.** He would have had to wait for the following year or 31ad, to try again. However, all went well according to his plan as was prophesied. By Jesus being crucified was the only way for him to become the second

Adam in God's new creation. The first Adam of the flesh, failed, But the second Adam who came after the Spirit of God was successful. If the first Adam would have taken off the Spirit of the Olive Tree of Life 'first', he would have been successful as was the second Adam. But Adam took off the wrong tree ' first', which was the tree of the knowledge of good and evil,

Simon, the Jewish Priest, prophesied to Mary the mother of Jesus, at the time he was christened, that he would have suffered a terrible death. Even Jesus told his apostles that he was going to Jerusalem where they (the Romans) would crucify him, but on the third day, he would arise. So it was destined for him to be crucified. **So please stop blaming the Jews for the death of Jesus. They are now vindicated again.**

So with this new creation of God, the new arrangement was that only those persons who believe in Jesus Christ Eliakim, God's son, will have a chance, including all **races to have the right to enter the Spiritual Garden of Eden above, or Paradise and to enjoy the best he has to offer. However, the earthly Eden was the ancient Jerusalem in Palestine.** Now this physical earth is like a school building, and we are in our various classes. At the end of our school term, or when we die, it will be decided if we will pass our examination. If we do, then we will graduate **to The Spiritual New Earth Above where we will live forever and enjoy the best the Almighty God had created for us. We'll be with our families and friends.**

GOD HAD CREATED A VERTICAL NEW EARTH ABOVE AND A VERTICAL NEW JERUSALEM ABOVE

First, it's important to understand that the New Jerusalem and the New earth **are 'not' parallel, or suspended vertically to one** another. But the New Jerusalem came down...out of Heaven... and rested in the center of the Spiritual New earth which is also above. So the Saints in the Spiritual New Earth can go to the Spiritual New Jerusalem and present their crowns before the throne of God.

Know this: This physical earth is vertical to the spiritual New Earth above. It's not horizontal, nor parallel like the planets which are at a great distance from one another. However, The Spiritual New Earth and the Spiritual New Jerusalem are indeed both vertical to the original heaven above them.

Bear in mind that the apostle John says that he saw 'A NEW HEAVEN AND A NEW EARTH. This New earth he saw...was not this physical earth where we now live down here. It's indeed a Spiritual New Earth which is located Above,...and away from this one here. Again, not away in a parallel position-but in a vertical Position. John didn't say he saw 'A RENOVATED EARTH, BUT RATHER, A BRAND NEW EARTH. Even though it may look somewhat like this one, it is more polished and without any Seas or Oceans.

Now unlike the earthly Jerusalem which is some seven miles long and six miles wide, according to Ezekiel, this New Jerusalem above, is 1,500, by 1,500 by 1,500, square miles It is square like the Holy of Holies in the former Temple in Jerusalem.

MORE IMPORTANT INFORMATION

At the time John wrote his book of the Revelation of Jesus Christ in 62-63 ad, The New Earth Above and the New Jerusalem Above, had already been created by God.

Here is the truth: when John saw the New Jerusalem descending from God out of Heaven – IT RESTED, OR

DESCENDED UPON THE SPIRITUAL NEW EARTH WHICH WAS ALREADY CREATED. It's not in the future that New Jerusalem will come down and rest on this earth in Palestine. God has New Jerusalem positioned **in the center of the spiritual New Earth Above.**

THE POSITION OF THE NEW EARTH AND THE NEW JERUSALEM

Here we are on this physical earth, where the physical Jerusalem is located on this same earth in the Middle East. Now when you look up, even though you will not see **the Spiritual New Earth, it is located far beyond the blue. Above this old Earth**

Now within the Spiritual New Earth above us, the Spiritual New Jerusalem is located **directly in the center of it;** and the light of God and the Lamb, or Jesus, shines all over the whole Spiritual New Jerusalem, and the New Earth. So there is no night, nor darkness up there.

Directly above New Jerusalem, far, far, 'vertically,' is the **area where Heaven is located.** In this Heaven, or location, is the place where all of the angels of God do inhabit. This is God's most Holy place, even though he has another throne in New Jerusalem, and in the New Earth.

Again, God had created this New Earth for all righteous people who would die to live in. But New Jerusalem was / is for the 144,000 ancient Israelites – who are already there. New Jerusalem is somewhat set-up as it is on the earth, that is, with the nations of the New earth situated around her. This is why you would have heard the apostle John say, **"The kings of the earth do bring their glory into it. That is, the kings from the Spiritual New Earth do bring their glory into the Spiritual New Jerusalem where Jesus and God's throne are set-up.**

Know this: If you please Jesus to his expectation, then some of you will be given a crown, not only of everlasting life, **but a crown of a Spiritual King, Queen or Priest.** Do you want to be a King, Queen or Priest in the Spiritual New Earth? well, just please God and Jesus.

This lofty position as King, Queen, or Priest, would be given to you based on your righteousness. And predicated upon you working for God and Jesus Christ Eliakim...on this Earth down here. However, these positions are not given to you just because you accept him as Lord...the reward for accepting him as Lord and saviour, is that you will enter into the Spiritual New Earth which some call heaven. But these lofty positions as Kings, Queens, and Priests, are based upon your suffering on Earth for him and the kingdom of God.

In the New Earth, there will also be **teachers to teach the people.** I don't mean to teach the saints about accepting Jesus Christ as Lord, but teachers who God will give special knowledge about the various planets and beings who inhabit them etc. Yes, there are hundreds of billions of Spiritual beings and other worlds up there. So because God is a God of order, there will also be order up there also...just like a country has orders.

You may wonder why I'm saying..Spiritual New Earth? Well, because all of the people are spiritual beings. They died, then they ascended to the New Earth. Bear This in mind:**you'll not be a citizen of 'New Jerusalem.** The reason is because you are not an ancient ethnic Jew. Even the present-day ethnic Jews who do not believe in Jesus Christ, will not live in New Jerusalem, but rather, **in the Spiritual New Earth.**

Let me inform you: New Jerusalem is not created for you nor me to live in. But rather for the ancient 144,000, ancient Israelites **'ONLY'.** This is also why the spiritual New city of

Jerusalem contains twelve (12) gates which symbolize the twelve (12) tribes of ancient Israel.

Here is a question: which of the twelve (12) tribes of ancient national Israel are you from? Did you say none? **well then, New Jerusalem was not created for you to live in when you die. It's only for you to visit and to partake of a part of ' the tree of life', then to return home to ' The New Earth', to the specific city where you and your family would live in.** There are hundreds of thousands of cities **within the Spiritual New Earth..** So much so, that John the Revelator couldn't count the huge numbers of the saints in the New Earth. See Revelation chapter 7: 9, for proof.

The New Jerusalem above symbolizes the 875 feet square area in the earthly Jerusalem in which the former Holy Temple of God sat. But of course, it is magnified from the earthly 875 feet square, to 1,500 miles in length,1,500 miles wide, and 1,500 miles high. Again, it is also square like the 875 feet square, **on the former Temple-Mount in Old Jerusalem'.**

Think about: the very same objects which God had planted ' in Eden', and in the Garden on earth – he put the same objects in the Paradise, or Garden in the Spiritual Eden, or in New Jerusalem above. However, there are no Seas or Oceans in New Jerusalem, nor in the New Earth above. Therefore, the space in the New Earth is expanded, or enlarged for us to live in.

MORE PENETRATING QUESTIONS.

Some of my fellow Christian families may doubt my statement that there lies a Spiritual New Earth Above where we go when we leave this earth; so allow me to ask you a question that you may be convinced. Ponder this: **If you can believe that there is** a Spiritual New Jerusalem above...why can't you believe that God had also created a New Earth Above...for New Jerusalem to be a part of? and seeing that the scriptures and the prophets prophesied about...A NEW EARTH WHEREIN DWELLS RIGHTEOUSNESS?

Some persons believe that it's this same earth down here which God will eventually make new. But the truth is, in the book of Revelation he says, "**Behold (look) I made (past tense) ALL THINGS NEW:**

If you would notice, that at the time the apostle John made this statement about all things being made new, all things had already been made new by God. So the New Jerusalem and the New Earth had already been made New since the **first century.** So if New Jerusalem was already in existence in the first century, **then it should have already descended on the New Earth above since in the first century.**

But as you can see, New Jerusalem was not descended on this physical Earth in the first century because it was never intended to descend on this physical Earth...but rather it was in the spiritual New Earth above, which was already created by the time the first century came along.

Even St. Paul further stated that in his own days, **that New Jerusalem had already been made New above.** He speaks of Jerusalem above which is free, compared to Jerusalem below which was in bondage. Think about it !

POWER POINTS TO REMEMBER

Here is what the Lord did. He created a brand New Jerusalem above. But look at this:Within this New Jerusalem, **he created a brand New Mount Moriah which is called Mount Zion...** **He planted a brand New River of Water, and he even created** brand New Opened Gates up there to enter the city of Spiritual Jerusalem.

In New Jerusalem above, God even placed or put 'the second Adam' in it who is Jesus Christ Eliakim, who is of the Spirit of God, and who is. Unlike the first Adam in Old Jerusalem, who was of the flesh. This Brand New Adam is also 'The Bridegroom of the 144,000 former Israelites who is his symbolic bride, and who symbolizes THE SPIRITUAL NEW EVE.

Think about this.: if the second Adam, or Jesus, was placed or put in New Jerusalem above where there is the tree of life... where do you think the first Adam of the flesh or dust must have lived? Observely,...in 'Old Jerusalem below on Earth. Does this compute to you?

Let's read between the lines and consider this: The objects which were in the Garden of Eden, in Palestine, were made up of earth. But the objects which God had placed in New Jerusalem, 'were not' the physical earthly elements, but they resemble, or look like them...but they are made of spiritual essence. That is, heavenly elements.

Power Points:

Seriously think about this: God had duplicated what was in Eden, or Jerusalem below, and recreated them in Jerusalem above. Shouldn't this therefore, indicate that indeed the land of Jerusalem was Eden? So the Garden of Eden in the beginning must have been in Old Jerusalem / East Jerusalem below according to Ezekiel. But why? Well, not only because Ezekiel indicates this, but because we find that all of those objects which God had originally put in the Garden on earth, he placed them... in New Jerusalem above.

Contemplate on this

When St. Paul was in Old Jerusalem in Palestine, didn't he say at that time that there was a Jerusalem above? (see Galatians 4:26) Two: was that Jerusalem above **separated and apart from this Earth?** well then, should it be so difficult for one to believe **that the New Earth is also above...and separated, and apart from this one down here?**

It could be that no one never told you that the New earth was already completed during the first century when Paul said That New Jerusalem was already above. However, the Lord Jesus wants me to be the one to up-date you about these matters.

Power Point: This is what I'm saying: since one can believe that there is **a vertical Jerusalem or two Jerusalems – that is, one here on earth, and one above...then one should believe that there is also a vertical Earth, or two earths,** that is...like Jerusalem, one here, or physical, and one spiritual up there.. And if the physical Jerusalem in Palestine **is a part of this Earth...then one should be able to believe that Jerusalem above, IS ALSO APART OF THE SPIRITUAL NEW EARTH.**

The problem is, we were never informed by preachers that there is a spiritual New Earth already in existence above, **and this is the place where we go when we die after touring New Jerusalem with Jesus.**

We see in Revelation 21:1, where the apostle John speaks about this New Earth which God had already created by the time he was writing about it.He says he saw A NEW HEAVEN AND A NEW EARTH. But what I want you to see, is that the New Earth...IS NOT – AND WILL NOT BE THE ONE WHERE WE ARE TODAY but it is above, just as New Jerusalem is above. Now that you may believe that the New earth is Above, I can continue to explain the New Earth Above.

BACK TO THE NEW EARTH

Please read slowly in order to be up-dated about spiritual truths, as to where you'll go after you die. The spiritual New Earth is indeed the place where you or your spirit-man will go when you die provided of course, you make the passing grade and p[lease God. Believe me, the spiritual New Earth today, contains so many trillions of souls, or spirit-people, that the apostle John the Revelator says, that he couldn't even count them: they are numberless.

These new spirits – people who live in the New earth today are people who once lived on this earth, but still retain the appearance of their physical bodies, But God has given them, and will give you too, **a make-over.** But you will still look like you. Your new spiritual body **will be a vibrant and polished New you, just like Jesus' New body looked like his old body...but only more divinely polished.** This was why some of his apostles doubted that it was him at the beginning when he appeared to them on Easter Sunday (Jesusday) evening.

Here is the divine truth: all good people who die; first go through a tunnel and are then escorted by two of God's angels to Jesus Christ. This tunnel is the passage-way **between the realm of this earth, and the realm of the spiritual New Earth above.** I know this is true because I too have gone through this tunnel a few times in my dream This tunnel is not parallel, but is vertical. That is, it is positioned as a passage-way from the physical earth, going straight up to the New Earth above. Again, far, far upward beyond the blue.

After exiting this tunnel which is vertical in its position from this earth, you'll find yourself in the atmosphere, or realm of the New Earth. Now, for the lack of the proper name of this realm people call it heaven. But the truth is, even heaven itself is not only in space, **but space itself.**

After entering the New Earth's atmosphere, two angels will escort you **to New Jerusalem** to have an audience with Jesus Christ Eliakim.But before he would transport you to your eternal home where your families are, and where you will live forever, he will first give you a tour through New Jerusalem where you'll visit **the city of God, or city of Gold as a guest.** He will also introduce you to his father, the prophets, his apostles, and Adam and Eve, and even Moses.

After taking up residence in the New Earth above, after leaving New Jerusalem, you'll always have the opportunity to return, or to re-visit New Jerusalem, **and to partake off, and to eat from, ' THE TREE OF LIFE', and to take back home, some of the spiritual leaves from the female Spiritual Olive Tree of life' for medicine – in order to avoid sickness.** This is why there is no sickness up there.

I'm not just writing this because this is what i think. But rather, **because Jesus Christ himself gave me...that is, put books in my hands and told me "to carry them there when I go.** This was at a time I had visited him in my dream. So these writings are inspirational from the spirit of God. You'll also be sealed in your forehead with the name of **ELIAKIM, and the lord God Almighty-and the city... 'NEW EARTH'** This is your passport when travelling to other regions.

I have proven without reasonable argument. **that the new name of Jesus Christ – in my book, 'A QUEST FOR DIVINE KNOWLEDGE'.**.And you'll also read about my several encounters with both Jesus Christ, and God Almighty. In the book I **stake my precious soul on this truth that Jesus Christ had put books in my hand and told me to carry them to the earth. And I also stake my soul on the truth that I have seen both Jesus and God face to face many times in my dreams and they spoke to me. This information is also in my**

69

book, ' A quest for Divine Knowledge ' (see Amazon.com and get your copy. I promise that you will be blessed when you read it /them.

MORE PERTINENT INFORMATION

Again, New Jerusalem is only home for the 144,000 ancient pure virgins Israelites. That is, 12,000 from each of the twelve tribes of Israel whom God had salvaged out of millions. Bear in mind again, no new spirit-persons are being added to this group of 144,000 Israelites which are already there since in the first century. All other persons who die these days, do go to...and live in the various cities in the spiritual New Earth above.

These 144,000 ancient Israelites do have a seal on their foreheads, and on this seal, the city where they live, which is, 'New Jerusalem '. **and also the New name of Jesus Christ – which is 'Eliakim,' is written on their foreheads.** Unlike the seal of the Saints who live in the New Earth with the name-'**NEW EARTH ' on their foreheads, the Saints in New Jerusalem have the name. ' NEW JERUSALEM' instead.**

MORE POWER POINTS PARAGRAPHS

Consider this: After the apostle John saw the 144,000 ancient Israelites' Saints, or virgins, he says that he saw **a crowd of people that he couldn't even number.** So the fact is: if New Jerusalem was prepared for the 144,000 Israelites, **where do these unlimited or numberless people of all tribes and languages live?** Obviously...Not in New Jerusalem, because New Jerusalem has twelve (12) gates, and each gate has the name of each of the twelve tribes of Israel.

Question: Which of the twelve tribes of Israel are you from? Don't panic ! You are not left out of God's plan of an eternal home. Here is the truth: This crowd of people or Saints from all races, **are the ones who live in the spiritual New Earth above. I mean they are there right now.** You should know that New Jerusalem is 12,000 furlong, which is 1,500 miles in length. 1,500 miles in width, and 1,500 miles high cannot contain **all of those numberless people John saw.**

John says when he looked on Mount Zion / Mount Moriah, he saw the 144,000 former Israelites' Saints up there along with the Lamb, or Jesus...and where-ever the Lamb or Jesus went, the 144,000 saints went with him.

If you would notice, it was only the 144,000 ancient Israelites **who were Jesus ' Bride, and were with him on Mount Zion.** Because in the earthly Jerusalem, it was the ancient Israelites who worshipped God on Mount Zion.

Consider this also: **One: it wasn't the crowd of people of all nations and tribes who were without numbers who were able to stand on the sea of glass mingled with fire. Two: It was the 144,000 ancient Israelites. They were the only ones who had the harps of God. And three: they were the only ones...who were able to sing the song of Moses and the Lamb (Jesus).** It's time for Christians to know the truth. The reason the 144,000 **former Jewish Saints were – 'The Bride of Christ' and not the numberless Christians Saints,** is because the former Israelites were the first ones who God had chosen from Abraham's loins. They were indeed the first people who were promised to inherit the kingdom of God, and New Jerusalem, because they were God's former chosen people in Old Jerusalem on earth. Note: Jesus told the Samaritan woman that salvation was of the Jews.

The ancient Jews symbolized **The Original Olive Tree. And the other people symbolized, 'the wild olive branches'.**

But God allowed the wild olive branches to **be grafted into the original olive tree.** However, the promise was only to the ancient Israelites, God's former people.

Now as for the citizens of the New Earth, who are the numberless crowd of people, who John says he saw **with palms in their hands, are not jealous of the bride. They were quite happy to be called, and to be invited to the wedding of the (144,000) Bride and the Lamb, or Jesus – and as a part of the bridal party, and to be chosen as 'THE BRIDE'S MAID'-because in the earth they weren't ethnic Jews.**

Remember this: The Bride symbolizes,' **the natural olive tree, or the original 144,000 ancient Jews, but the other nations of Christians were GRAFTED INTO THE NATURAL TREE OF LIFE.** However, all of us, natural olive branches, or wild olive branches have one source of spiritual life and this is the Spirit of God. However, the Bride lives in New Jerusalem above. And the Bride's Maid lives in the spiritual New earth, But know this: **The New Jerusalem is a part of the New earth, and is situated in the middle of it.**

Observe this: The numberless Christians which John saw, who live in the New Earth, **do wear white clothes with palms in their hands indicating victory. Note this: they couldn't learn the song of Moses and the Lamb...because they weren't Israelites' Saints when they were alive in the earth. again, they weren't ethnic Jews.**

Two: They weren't in the wilderness along with the Israelites, Moses and Jesus, **who was the angel who accompanied them to the promised land.** That is. the angel who appeared to Moses in the burning bush...so the non-Israelites' Saints in the New Earth, were not jealous of her being ' The Bride of Christ '.

THE BILLION DOLLAR QUESTION

Power Point: Here is the question for you to ponder before you go on.One: why did God replicate what was in the Garden of Eden, and re-created them in Jerusalem above...if the earthly Jerusalem wasn't Eden and the Garden wasn't within East Jerusalem?

Two: Why did God recreate Jerusalem above as his Paradise with ' the tree of life, and a river running to his Garden...IF THE PARADISE BELOW, OR THE EDEN BELOW WASN'T THE JERUSALEM BELOW? If you would think you would see that it's the same set-up as in Old Jerusalem in Palestine.

Three: If Africa, Turkey, Armenia, Ethiopia or Iraq were Eden, with the Garden of the Lord, why didn't God re-create one of them as his Paradise above? Again. Why duplicate Jerusalem instead of the mentioned countries above?Do you see it?

Four: if the river of living water proceeded from Mount Zion in New Jerusalem, to water the Garden, or Paradise above, and the tree of life today...where do you think it must have proceeded from in Eden in the days of Adam? well, the truth is, from Mount Zion / the Temple Mount in Jerusalem.

Five: So since Mount Zion on earth was God's former holy Mountain in Jerusalem, would you agree or disagree, that the river must have flowed from Mount Zion / Moriah, or the Temple Mount in Jerusalem as Ezekiel states?

FINAL POINTS TO PONDER

Six: in Revelation 2:7, we hear Jesus say, he will give you food from the tree of life which is in the midst, **OR MIDDLE OF**

THE PARADISE OF GOD ABOVE. Check this out: So shouldn't this indicate that the Tree of Life which was in the Garden of Eden, had to have been in the midst of Jerusalem below, or in Paradise on earth?

So the question is: where is the Paradise of God today? The answer is: **IN NEW JERUSALEM ABOVE. But if you would notice that the Paradise of God...is in New Jerusalem above.** So again, Therefore, it stands to reason that the tree of life must have been '**in the Paradise of God...in Old Jerusalem on Earth.**

CHAPTER 5

ADAM AND EVE LIVED IN THE CITY ADAM-IN THE JORDAN VALLEY

After Adam and Eve had sinned in the Lord's Garden, or in Jerusalem, he expelled them, or drove them out from below the Temple Mount in East Jerusalem. God was indeed heart – broken when his earthly son Adam, whom he had created in his own image and likeness, or who looked exactly like himself had sinned. As a result, he had no righteous choice but to exile him and made him pay by sentencing him to hard labor – that is, by working hard by the sweat of his face for his food. If God didn't take this drastic action against Adam, then all of his angels would have expected to sin against him with impunity, or exemption from punishment.

Now Lucifer, or the Devil was watching God like a hawk to see how he will deal with Adam – knowing quite well that it was he himself who had instigated the trouble. **If God had forgiven Adam for his sin, then he had to either apologize to Lucifer, or to forgive him and his co-conspirators for trying to usurp his kingdom, or to seize and hold power illegally, and by force. And God would have to have restored them to their position in Heaven.**

In verse 23. Moses writes: "Therefore the Lord God sent him (Adam) forth from the Garden of Eden to till the ground – from where he was taken". I put it to you that where-ever we find Adam tilling the ground, we can logically conclude that it was **the place, or ground from where he was taken, or was created. Obviously, he wasn't taken from the ground of the Garden of Eden, because he was expelled from the Garden of Eden. And to prove that it wasn't the ground of Eden, or the Garden where he was taken … is the fact that when he died he wasn't buried in the Garden of Eden, or in Eden. So the ground from where he was taken must have been another place.**

After Adam was expelled out of the Garden of the Lord, he returned to the same area from where he was taken or created. That is, before God put him in his Garden. This place where he returned to till the ground was the same place where he was taken from which is – **THE AREA OR LAND NEAR, 'BETH-SHEAN' IN THE JORDAN VALLEY BY THE RIVER JORDAN, SOME 65, MILES AWAY FROM EDEN – THAT IS, FROM JERUSALEM AND THE GARDEN. THIS PLACE OR AREA IS ALSO BY ZARETHAN BELOW JEZ-REEL.**

Again, this proves that the ground of the Garden of Eden wasn't the ground where Adam was taken-because if it was that ground, then Adam would have tilled the ground right there in the Garden, 'In Eden' or in Jerusalem.

Don't forget, Adam wasn't created in the Garden of Eden but was PUT THERE, after he was created. Also, Eve wasn't created in the Garden neither but elsewhere – then was brought to the Garden to join Adam. So where was she created? Well, like Adam, she was created in the same place where Adam was created, which was in the Jordan valley by the Jordan river on the Israelites' side, to the west of the Jordan River.

DESCRIPTION OF THE JORDAN VALLEY

The lower Jordan valley is between the Sea of Galilee, and the Dead Sea. The term 'Jordan valley', often applies just to the lower course of the Jordan River, from the spot where it exits the sea of Galilee, in the north, to the end of its course where it flows into the Dead Sea in the south and empties itself.

In a wider sense, the term Jordan valley also covers the Dead Sea basin and the wadi Arabah, or Arau valley which is the Rift Valley segment, beyond the Dead Sea, ending at Eilat/Aqaba Gulf, 96 miles further south.

The valley is a long and narrow trough, it is 105 km. (65 miles) long with a width averaging, 10,km. (6.2 miles) over most of the course before widening out to a (12, miles) Delta when reaching the Dead Sea.

Due to meandering, the length of the valley itself is 140,miles that is the deepest valley in the world beginning at an elevation of (696 ft..) below sea-level.

CHAPTER 6

THE CITY ADAM MENTIONED IN SCRIPTURES

In the ancient days during the time of the crossing of the Israelites over the Jordan River – Joshua, the general of Moses, tells us that there was a city near the Jordan River in the Jordan Valley called, 'THE CITY-ADAM', and it was next to a city called, 'Zarethan'.

I'm trying to make the case that this City – Adam, was the place where Adam and Eve travelled to, after being banished from the Garden of Eden, which was in Jerusalem / Eden, some 65, miles away. If this is believed, which it is, then it proves that this City – Adam, Eden, or Jerusalem must have been the cradle of civilization where mankind first lived.

Some researchers postulate that this City-Adam was on the east side of the Jordan River. Some even believe that this City-Adam was situated on the west side of the Jordan River, near Zarethan. But they believe that it was in the Jordan Valley in the land of Israel.

The truth is: **this City-Adam was located…on the west side of the Jordan River, in the Jordan Valley near a city called, ' ZARETHAN.** This I will prove as I go along, and from a scriptural perspective without reasonable question.

This City – Adam and Zarethan are some twelve (12) miles in distance from one another. Remember it was Joshua who is going to tell us that the City-Adam was beside Zarethan, even though one may not be able to locate the exact spot of Zarethan on today's map. However, we can position the location where it was.

My point of reference in finding the area of both, the City-Adam and the City-Zarethan, **is to locate, 'BETH-SHEAN/ BEIT-SHEAN, AND LOWER JEZ-REEL ON THE MAP OF ISRAEL.** Once you can locate **Beth-shean on the map... well, the scripture will tell you that Zarethan...was next to it.** And once you can find Zarethan, then the City-Adam was beside it, as the scripture itself says.

Now once you can locate **'JEZ-REEL'** on the map, then the scripture says **'Beth-shean and Zarethan are beneath, or below it.** This lower Jez-reel is approximately 86.9 miles from Jerusalem / Eden. So when Adam and Eve were expelled out of the Lord's Garden, **they walked some 65 miles north to the area of the City-Adam.**

All of what I've said so far, shows that the City-Adam had to have been located **on the west side of the Jordan River in the Jordan Valley. How?** Well, because the City-Adam... was by Zarethan, and Zarethan...was by Beth-shean... and Beth-shean was beneath Jez-reel. Note this reader: AND ALL OF THESE TERRITORIES ARE IN THE LAND OF ISRAEL. So yes, The City-Adam was in Israel's territories.

Remember there were no Israelites living on this side of the Jordan River yet. But despite this, **we find a whole city called, 'The City Adam' on this side of Canaan land.** It's obvious to the Canaanites and the people of Palestine in ancient times, **that it was the place where Adam and Eve lived after they were expelled out of the Garden of Eden...which was Jerusalem.**

It wasn't the Israelites who named this area 'The City-Adam' when they crossed over the Jordan River and entered the promised land. **They met the City-Adam already populated with Canaanites.** So obviously, the Canaanites knew about 'The City-Adam' many years before the Israelites arrived.

In fact, they were the ones who named it, 'The City-Adam'. Isn't it strange that we do not find the City-Adam in Babylon, or Mesopotamia, where the Canaanites migrated from, but rather in Palestine where they migrated to? All of this indicates that Palestine had to have been the land where human life, or civilization began. When God parted the Jordan River which flows from the foot-hills of Syria and Lebanon, and going south, it stopped flowing and it backed-up ' **as a dam, a good distance from the City-Adam.** This is what Joshua says in his book, chapter 3:16.

Think about this: So if the city Zarethan was some 65 miles from Jerusalem, **and the City-Adam was next to Zarethan, then the City-Adam, had to have been some 65 miles or thereabout, from Jerusalem. So Adam and Eve had to have walked some 65, miles north, from the Garden of Eden to the place later named, 'The City-Adam'.**

SCRIPTURAL FACTS BY JOSHUA

Joshua chapter 3: 14-17 states: "And it came to pass when the people (the Israelites) removed from their tents, to pass over Jordan, and the Priest bearing the Ark of the Covenant before the people, "Verse 15, "And as they bear the Ark came into Jordan, and the feet of the Priests that bear the ark were dipped in the brim of the water, for Jordan over flowed all his banks all the time of harvest.'

Verse 16, is very important to consider. Joshua continues: "That the water which came down from above stood (stopped) and rose up upon a heap ' **very far from...THE CITY – ADAM**

THAT IS BESIDE ZARETHAN: and those (water) that came down toward the Sea of the plain (Valley) even the salt sea (dead sea) failed (stopped) and were cut-off: and the people (Israelites) passed over right against Jericho"

So as you have just read Joshua's statement, **that the City-Adam was indeed beside Zarethan.** So there is no question that Joshua himself confessed that there was a City-Adam, when he and the Israelites crossed over into the promised land – later to be called, ' **the land of Israel'.** And that the City-Adam was beside Zarethan.

Ponder this Question: but why would Joshua mention ' The City-Adam, if the City-Adam wasn't an important and significant one? And if it were the City-Adam, then it had to have been...**The cradle of civilization** – seeing that he was the first man, or father of the human beings (Homo sapiens) and, land where he lived after being expelled from Eden.

As you can see, Joshua had knowledge of **the place where Adam was created and where he lived after he was expelled from the Garden of Eden or from Jerusalem, below the Temple-Mount.**

It's important also to remember that the City-Adam was already in existence from the beginning of creation of Adam who was the father of it. All of this should convince you that the City-Adam, **was in the Jordan Valley, and it was there where Adam, Eve, Cain, and Abel lived until he Cain was expelled, or banished from the Jordan Valley...and went...TO THE EAST OF EDEN...WHICH WAS EAST OF JERUSALEM...TO THE LAND OF ARABIA, OR NOD.**

In ancient times, the various lands were always named after the fathers or leaders of them. So stop and think: **if the land on the west side of the Jordan River, in the Jordan Valley, or Plain...near Zarethan was named; ' The City-Adam",** doesn't this indicate that Adam must have been the first, or the most notable man to live there and the father of that land? Think about it.

So when I say that Adam and Eve were created in the Jordan Valley...in the City Adam, near Zarethan, and out of clay of that area – then was put, or placed approximately 65, miles in Eden / Jerusalem, is true.

It's interesting that it was none other than Joshua himself who gives us the understanding that Adam must have lived in the Jordan Valley near the River Jordan, in Palestine. Apart from Joshua chapter 3: 16, there are no other parts of the bible where the City-Adam is mentioned. But the reality is, it existed in the Jordan Valley, by **Zarethan, Beth-shean and Jez-reel.** So we know that the City-Adam wasn't located in Africa, Ethiopia, Armenia, Turkey nor Iraq.

PINPOINTING THE AREA OF THE CITY-ADAM

Now that you have seen that the City-Adam was beside Zarethan, let's look for the country next to Zarethan. This would pinpoint the area in the Jordan Valley where the City-Adam was located, or where Adam, Eve, Cain and Abel lived, I humbly submit to you that after Adam and Eve were banished out of the Lord's Garden, or from Jerusalem, **they walked northward some sixty five (65) miles to an area, later called...'The City-Adam'. This area was next to Zarethan...and this Zarethan was next to Beth-shean-and both, the City-Adam, Zarethan, and Beth-shean were beneath, or below Jez-reel in the Jordan Valley on the west side of the Jordan River.**

So if the City-Adam is by Zarethan as Joshua says, **and we find that Zarethan...is beside BETH-SHEAN-then the City-Adam has to be in the area of the Jordan Valley, by Zarethan and Beth-shean....**

THE SCRIPTURE: 1 KINGS 4: 12

Where-ever you find Adam living, you can safely say that the land was the cradle of human civilization – because he was the first man to be created.

1 Kings 4: 1-19, gives the names of the princes and great men in King Solomon's Government, when he became King. And it states the lands which they ruled over. Here is one of the men who Solomon gave territories to rule over

Verse 12, "Baa-na the son of Ahilud; to him pertained Taa-nach and Megiddo...AND ALL BETH-SHEAN..WHICH IS BY ZAR-TA-NAH (Zarethan) BENEATH JEZ-REEL, FROM BETH-SHEAN TO ABEL-MEHOLAH even unto the place that is beyond Jok-ne-am: "

The mere fact that king Solomon gave Baa-na, Taa-nach and Migiddo, **and all Beth-shean, which is by Zar-ta-nah (Zarethan) which are located...beneath Jez-reel, in Israel to rule over, proves that Jez-reel, Beth-shean, Zarethan and the 'City-Adam are also in Israel's land.** This shows that Adam did live in the Jordan Valley, in the land of Adam, in Palestine.

Now this verse states that Solomon gave Baa-na, many territories, namely: **Taa-nach, Megiddo...And all BETH-SHEA...(which is by Zar-ta-nah, which is the same name as Zarethan) WHICH IS BENEATH, OR LOWER JEZ-REEL.**

Again, versc 12, is straightforward **that Beth-shean,... is indeed by Zar-ta-nah** which is the same as Zarethan. And this Zarethan **is beneath Jez-reel. That is, below Jez-reel. This Beth-shean is 62.63 miles away from Jerusalem, or from Eden.**

POWER-POINT STATEMENT

Therefore if Jez-reel and Beth-shean are in the Jordan Valley 'IN ISRAEL on the west side of the Jordan River, then it

stands to reason that 'THE CITY-ADAM' had to have been also in the Jordan Valley…'in Israel' on the west side of the Jordan River. So if you can pin-point Jez-reel on the map, then you should know 'that Zarethan is just below it'. This Jez-reel is 86.9 miles from Jerusalem, or away from Eden.

Again, if Zarethan is Just Beneath, or below Jez-reel…and the City-Adam is by Zarethan…THEN THE CITY-ADAM IS BY BOTH ZARETHAN AND BETH-SHEAN. Therefore, both the City-Adam, Zarethan…and Beth-shean are located – just beneath Jez-reel in the Jordan Valley by the River Jordan. Do you see why the City-Adam, and Adam, and Abel, had to have been living in the Jordan Valley? **Sorry to have repeated it.**

YOUR HOME WORK

Here is an exercise for you to do. Now the City Beth-shean, And Jez-reel are all still, not only on the map, but still in existence today.so in order to see the location where Adam and Eve lived… in the City-Adam, you only have to Google, ' **Distant from Jerusalem to Jez-reel**'. You should get some 86 miles. And from **Beth-shean to Jerusalem, you should get some 62.63 miles.**

If you do this research, then you would be able to see the area to where Adam and Eve walked and settled down, after being expelled out of God's Garden: **which was approximately 65 miles.**

FINALLY JUROR

As you can see, the City-Adam was not discovered in Africa, Ethiopia, Iraq, Turkey, nor Armenia…but rather right there in Palestine, on the west side of the Jordan River, in the plain, or valley beside..the City Zarethan, and Beth-shean, which is below or beneath Jez-reel, which is also Israel's land.

What this also mean is at that time the Israelites crossed over into the Promised land, **The City-Adam was already populated with many of Ham's children who were the Canaanites. It was so well populated, that Joshua says it was' A CITY'... not just a town, or village, 'BUT A METROPOLIS'**

All of this should prove that the Garden of the Lord was also in the land of Israel...but in the area which was called, **'JEBUS', which the Jebusites inhabited, which was later called Salem, then Jerusalem.** So what better land do you think God would have planted his Garden? Well, it would have been in his own holy land which land ended-up being called Jerusalem.

So this chapter should really prove to you **that the land of Israel was the cradle of civilization where mankind lived in the beginning before the flood of Noah.** I'm aware that many people believe the cradle of human civilization began in Africa. I too formerly believed this, but from a scriptural and logical perspective, **one should now see that civilization really began in Palestine in the Middle East in the land of Israel.**

Now why would the people in ancient times named this area beside Zarethan ' The City-Adam if Adam wasn't from this area? Just the mere fact that we find The City-Adam in the promised land, should tell us that Adam must have lived in that land. So if Adam lived in this vicinity in the Jordan Valley beneath Jez-reel, then it follows that this area was indeed the country where the cradle of human civilization began and where he lived.

I'm hoping the above paragraph opens-up your mind's eyes that the Jordan Valley was the cradle of human civilization in the Middle East.

I do hereby declare that the land of Israel, is that land where Adam and Eve lived, after being banished from the Garden of Eden – and where human beings first existed.I also submit to you **that Adam was created out of a hundred and seventy (170) pounds of clay…and Eve was created out of a hundred and thirty (130) pounds of clay, coupled with Adam's rib. This gives a total of 300 pounds of clay which God scraped-up beside Zarethan, and from across the Jordan River to the area called Succoth.**

1 KINGS CHAPTER 7: 40 AND 46

When the Temple of the Lord was completed being built, King Solomon of Israel, hired king Hiram, to make accessories for it. Some of these items were the pots, pans, shovels, lavers, and many more accessories.

Verse 40, of 1 Kings chapter 7, says, "And Hiram made lavers, and the shovels, and the basons. So Hiram made an end of doing all the work that he made king Solomon for the house of the Lord "

Verse 46, says, "**IN THE PLAIN OF JORDAN DID THE KING (Hiram) CAST THEM – IN THE CLAY GROUND BETWEEN SUCCOTH AND ZARETHAN "**.

I quoted this verse so that you may see that it was **in the Plain, or Valley of Jordan in the clay ground between Succoth and Zarethan where king Hiram had made these items or accessories for the Temple of Jerusalem.** King Hiram got some of the clay from across the Jordan River from Succoth. This is the succoth where Jacob built his house, after he and his brother Esau had settled their differences. Also King Hiram got the rest of the clay **from the ground of Zarethan. And he cast or made these items – in the Plain or Valley of Jordan. Note: It was this** clay ground from Zarethan and The City-Adam which God used to create Adam and Eve.

JOSHUA CONFIRMS THAT THE CITY ADAM EXISTED

Here is Joshua's record from the scripture that the City-Adam was beside Zarethan, during the parting of the Jordan River. So allow me to repeat it so it may stay in your spirit.

Joshua chapter 3:16, "That the waters which came down from above stood and rose up upon an heap **VERY FAR FROM THE CITY-ADAM, THAT IS BESIDE ZARETHAN:** and those (waters) that came down toward the Sea of the Plain, and were cut off: and the people passed over right against Jericho"

So Joshua tells us that the City-Adam did exist in his days. And we see that this City-Adam was by Zarethan, as Joshua says – and we see that Zarethan was by Beth-shean – and we see that Beth-shean, Zarethan, and the City-Adam, **were beneath or below Jez-reel, in Israel. So wouldn't you position the City-Adam… in the Jordan Valley also, and on the west side of the River Jordan? ()**

Again, the scripture says that Zarethan was by Beth-shean. And the City-Adam was by Zarethan, Therefore it's obvious that the City-Adam was in Israel's land ' **to the north ', in the Jordan Valley.**

CHAPTER 7

THE GREAT STONE AND ALTAR OF ABEL REMAINED UP TO THE DAYS OF THE PROPHET SAMUEL

Allow me to relate a brief narrative about how the Philistines captured the ark of the Lord from the Israelites, and the consequences they received for their actions. This narrative is indeed germane, or relevant to the subject – matter, and it connects to '**The Great Stone of Abel'**

In 1 Samuel 4:1-22, he tells the story of how the Philistines defeated the Israelites by slaughtering some thirty thousand (30,000) men. In chapter 5, the prophet says that the Philistines captured the Ark of God from Ebenezer and brought it to their city of Ashdod, and put it into the house or shrine of their god Dagon.

He records in verse 6, "But the hand of the Lord was heavy upon them, of Ashdod, and he destroyed them and smote them with Emerods (piles) even Ashdod and the coast thereof. "

After God smote the Philistines with **Emerods/ Hemorrhoids in their rectum/anus,** they realized that they had made a serious mistake by stealing the power of Israel's God. So they gathered all of the lords of the Philistines together and asked them what they should do with the Ark of God So they decided to carry the Ark of God to the city Gath.

Samuel records in verse 9, "And it was so, that after they had carried it about the hand of the Lord was against the city (of Gath) with a very great destruction.and he smote the men of the city both small and great, **and they had Emerods in their secrets parts" (rectum)**

The Philistines then took the Ark of God to the city Akron. But the people complained about the Ark being brought to their city. So they gathered all of the lords of the philistines in Akron, and told them to send the ark of God out of their city. However, there was still a deadly destruction throughout the city of the Akronites.

Here is what the Prophet Samuel says in verse 12, "And the men that died not, **were smitten with the Emerods (piles)** and the cry of the city went up to heaven". Now the Philistines called on the priests and diviners to advise them as to what they should do with the ark of God. Both the priests and the diviners told them that if they sent it away, make sure to send it with gifts and a trespass offering. The Philistines then asked the priests and the diviners as to what kind of trespass offering should they send?

Here is the advice which the priests and the diviners gave them. They were advised to send five golden Emerods, and five golden mice, according to the number of the lords of the Philistines. The lords were struck with Emerods and the land was infested with mice. So they made golden images of the Emerods, or piles, with which they were struck, and images of golden mice which marred, or infested the land.

Here is the recommendation which the priests and diviners gave to the Philistines:

Samuel writes in chapter 6:5, in his book, the following: "wherefore ye shall make images of your Emerods (piles) and images of your mice that mar the land: and ye shall give glory unto the God of Israel:peradventure (hopefully) he will lighten his hand from off you, and from off your gods, and from off your land".

They continue to give the Philistines advice as to what to do. They told them to get two (2) Cows and tie them to a new cart, then put the Ark of the Lord upon it. And send the Lord God some money, that is, some jewels of gold in a jewel box. The cow will be for the trespass offering, and the jewel of gold as a gift. Then send the two Cows and the ark of the Lord on its way, and see which route it would take.

The priests and diviners continue to give their advice to the lords of the Philistines. **Now if it takes the route to the city-Beth-shemesh in Judah,** then we would know for sure that it was God who had put these plagues on us. But if the Cows were to take another route, then we will know that it was just a coincidence.

THE ARK WAS ACCEPTED AND SETTLED IN BETH-SHE-MESH, IN THE LAND OF JUDAH

In this narrative we're going to see that the Cows and the Ark would end up **'in Judah' the land where Abel built his Altar and sacrifice to God.** Now the five lords of the Philistines were following the Cows and the Ark of the Lord to see which direction it would take. The Prophet Samuel writes in verse 12, **"And the Kine/Cows took the straight way…to the way of 'BETH-SHE-MESH',** and went along the highway, lowering as they went, and turned not aside to the right hand or to the left: and the lords of the Philistines went after them unto **the border of Beth-she-mesh."**

Verse 14, "And the cart came into the field of Joshua, a Beth-she-mite and stood there, where there was a great stone: and they clave (cut) the wood of the cart, and offered the Kine (Cows) a burnt offering unto the Lord"

Samuel goes on in verse 15, "And the Levites took down the Ark of the Lord, and the coffer (jewel box) that was with it, wherein the jewels of gold, were, and put them ' ON THE GREAT STONE': and the men of Beth-shemesh offered burnt offerings and sacrificed sacrifices the same day unto the lord."

Ponder this: the great stone was an Altar whereon the men of Beth-shemesh, offered-up their burnt sacrifices to the God of heaven. But the question is: who built the great stone for sacrifice? well, whoever is named in honor of it, rest assured it was the person who would have built it. You'll soon know who he was.

Observe: the five lords of the Philistines who followed the new cart with the two Cows, and the ark, to the...'LAND OF JUDAH were observing the whole thing. Samuel goes on in verse 16, "And when the five lords of the philistines had seen it, they returned to Ekron the same day"

Verse 17, "And these are the golden Emerods (piles) which the Philistines returned for a trespass offering unto the Lord: For Ashdod one, for Gaza one, for Ashkelon one, for Gath one, for Ekron one".

Verse 18, "And the golden mice according to the number of all the cities of the Philistines belonging to the five lords, both of fenced (fortified) cities, and of country, villages...EVEN UNTO THE GREAT STONE OF ABEL, WHEREON THEY (the Levites priests) set down the Ark of the Lord: WHICH STONE REMAINETH UNTO THIS DAY IN THE FIELD OF JOSHUA THE BETH-SHE-MESH."

This great stone of Abel had to have been so sacred that the ark of the Lord was set down upon it. But why would Samuel say that the great stone of Abel remaineth even until his day...if this great stone of Abel wasn't in existence in the days of Abel? And we know that Abel was indeed the son of Adam.

If you would notice, that this great stone for sacrificing was named, or called,' after a man who lived before the flood. Not even righteous Noah, even though he had built altars of sacrifices. This stone wasn't even named after Abraham who lived 'after' the flood. He was the most righteous man who lived after the flood, and he was God's friend.

Even though Melchizedek was greater than Abraham, and as king of Salem, and Priest of the most high God, he was beamed-down from heaven to be Priest of the Jebusites, Ham's descendants in Salem, or Jerusalem. However, he wasn't fully human. So I will not enumerate his name in this list.

Note, Abraham built several Altars to sacrifice to God, even the altar on Mount Moriah. However, it wasn't any of the stones he set-up as an altar to sacrifice to God which was so famous, but rather, **it was this great stone of Abel. But why Abel, if it wasn't Abel's stone?**

If you could only read between the lines, you would readily discern that Samuel had great reverence and a special respect for this great stone of Abel.

If you would think out of the box, you would come to the conclusion that ' **this great stone of Abel,** was one that was in existence from the days of Abel. This is why Samuel had so much respect for this great stone of Abel. You too may discern that it wasn't the great stone of abel, because someone else had built it, and named it...but rather Abel himself.

If you concluded that it was Abel who built the great stone, or altar for sacrifices, then you should conclude, **that this same land of Beth-she-mesh, in Judah which is some 25, miles from Jerusalem, had to have been the cradle of human civilization, and by extension, the whole land of Israel, or Palestine, and even...to Arabia/Nod, east of Eden, or Jerusalem.**

Again, it's obvious that Samuel had great respect for this great stone of Abel which existed, **even until his own days,** because he realized that it was built by none other than Adam's righteous son Abel.

So we can see that this great stone of Abel, survived the great flood of Noah, **but it's interesting that we find it in Palestine in the Middle East afterward, and owned by the Israelites in a field of one Joshua a Beth-she-mite, in the land of Beth-shemesh...in Judah.** But why wasn't this altar found in Africa, or Europe? Now if you desire to see this great stone of Abel, just google 'the Great Stone of Abel'.

FINAL THOUGHTS TO PONDER

Samuel records that the great stone of Abel **"remained'** even up to his own days. But why would the prophet Samuel make such a curious and amazing statement about the great stone of Abel, **remaining even up to his own days – if this great stone of Abel wasn't in existence since in the beginning of Abel's days – that is, from the foundation of the world?**

I submit to you that it was truly Abel's Altar of Stone which remained even up to Samuel's days. It's quite obvious that this great stone of Abel was used as an Altar by the people of Beth-shemesh, **'in Judah',** after they possessed the Promised land. **This is the very same Altar of Stone where Abel sacrificed his Lamb to God.**

Note: it had to have been the Canaanites who told the Israelites about this special stone of Abel. You see, It was the Canaanites who were living in the Promised land for hundreds and hundreds of years, **before the Israelites crossed over the Jordan River and possessed it.**

How is this true? Well, if you would notice...God had promised Abraham that after 430 years, that he God would raise up a nation of people from his loins (Abraham's) and they would become a great nation. And if you would remember that the Israelites had inhabited **Goshon, in Egypt, for exactly 430, years. Then they spent forty (40) years in the wilderness, which gives a total of 470, years, BEFORE THEY ENTERED THE PROMISED LAND. in fact, the Canaanites were living in it...Even before Abraham departed out of Haran/Turkey and entered Canaan land.**

As you can see, this stone of Abel was already set-up when the Canaanites entered the promised land after leaving Babel, during the days of the division, or confusion. So the Canaanites knew about this stone, or Altar of Abel...and yet didn't destroy it when they possessed Canaan land. But why didn't they destroy it? Well, even though they worshipped and sacrificed to their gods, they still didn't destroy Abel's Stone of Altar. **The reason is, they knew that it was the stone of Abel, Adam's son.**

Now it was because of the longevity of this great stone of Abel which remained up to Samuel's days which caused him to make this curious statement about it. It seems logical that the great stone of Abel was the one in which he had built to offer-up his sacrificial Lamb to God. But why did Samuel give so much honor of the naming of this stone after Abel, **if it wasn't Able who built it?** Samuel couldn't use Moses' name, because Moses never went to the Promised land. He only saw it from a distance.

Deuteronomy chapter 34:1, states: "And Moses went up from the plain of Moab unto the mountain of Nebo to the top of Pisgah, that is over against Jericho. And the Lord shew him all the land of Gilead unto Dan."

So Moses viewed the Promised land from Mount Nebo, at the top of Pisgah, but he never set his feet in the Promise land. Samuel couldn't use Joshua's name either, because it was **after Joshua came into the Promised that he had discovered...'The City Adam', and later, the Great Stone of Abel.** So we ought to see that it was truly in Canaan land, or the Promised land where Adam, Abel and Seth lived.

Remember, the Prophet Samuel was no ordinary man. This prophet was very close to God, and God respected him. However, God himself says that even if Samuel, Job, Daniel or Noah were to ask a request of him, on behalf of the ancient Israelites, at that time, that he would refuse even their request.

The great reverence Samuel had for this stone of Abel, was not in respect of its size, but respect of its longevity. So the great stone of Abel in the eyes of Samuel, must have had some great importance, and significance in the past ages.

ANOTHER IMPORTANT QUESTION

Why is this Great Stone of Abel found in Beth-she-mesh, in the land of Judah rather than in any other country...if the land of Judah wasn't the land where Abel set-up his stone of worship? This should indicate that the land of Judah...is indeed a part of the cradle of human civilization. And not only Judah in the south, but the whole land of Israel from Dan in the north to Negev, and Eilat in the south, by its coastline.

Shouldn't this question prick your spirit to the reality that the people **before the flood,** must have lived in the land, now called. Israel, or the former Promised land? Indeed, all of Canaan land from north to south, **and the great Mediterranean Sea on the west was the cradle of civilization.**

Again, this is also why you would find 'The City-Adam' next to Zarethan in Israel...because it was in the City of Zarethan where God had scraped-up a hundred and seventy (170lbs) pounds of clay and created Adam.

This area was known for its plentiful rich clay. Truly, it was this refined mud, or sifted dirt, which God had used to create the physical body, and red blood cells of Adam and Eve. He got it from this area called, ' The City-Adam, next to Zarethan and also from Succoth.

So the fact that Adam's City was found in the land of Israel, **on the west bank of the Jordan River, and in the Jordan Valley,** should prove also...like Abel-that the land of Israel is indeed, the cradle of human civilization. This is the place where the human race first began, and by extension, **the land of Arabia/Nod ' east of Eden/Jerusalem' where the first sets of giants walked the earth.**

Could we rationally conclude that, the fact we find **The Great Stone of Abel'...in Beth-shemesh, some twenty five (25) miles from Jerusalem...and the City-Adam approximately sixty five (65) miles north from Jerusalem, that the area must be the place where the cradle of civilization really began? Ponder it.**

This land of Israel is the country where the first ten generations from Adam to Noah lived...which was some 1656, years...that is, **from Adam to Noah. Then after the flood, Noah and his family landed on Mount Ararat in Anatolia, in the east by Turkey and Armenia.** Then from there they travelled to the valley or plain in Shinar, or Babylon where they lived until the disbursement into all parts of the earth. **As a result, some of Ham's tribe went, or returned to the former land where the people lived from Adam to Noah. But most of Ham's tribe travelled to Africa, Egypt. Australia, India, and elsewhere.**

Read the following two verses of Genesis chapter 9:18-19, to see that the earth was just overspread by Noah's three sons ' after the flood'. Verse 18, **"And the sons of Noah, that went forth of the ark, were, Shem, and Ham, and Japheth: and Ham is the father of Canaan." Verse 19, "These are the three sons of Noah: AND OF THEM WAS THE WHOLE EARTH OVER-SPREAD'**

Again, this proves that the whole earth...truly was not over-spread by humans...'BEFORE THE FLOOD', other than the area where Noah and his family came from...which was ' THIS SAME LAND OF CANAAN IN PALESTINE. In the process of time after the flood of Noah, some of Ham's tribe returned right back **to the land where Noah and the first ten (10) generations lived.** Again, this land is Canaan land.

So apart from the land Shinah/Babylon where Noah and his family left from, no other parts of the earth were populated by human beings. Know this, Africa, China, Europe, and all of the nations of the world, or the earth-**were virgin lands and were just populated...' After the flood for the first time...and were indeed populated by the three sons of Noah, Namely: Shem, Ham, and Japheth.** And it was Moses who says...' **by these three sons of Noah that the whole earth was over-spread."**

What all of this also proves is that all of the humans on earth are derived from the three (3) sons of Noah. That is, the sperms of these three sons of Noah came from his loins/ Scrotum. And Noah's sperms came from his father Lamech. And Lamech's sperms goes all the way to Seth's sperms, and to Adam's sperms and Eve's Eggs.

You should also know that it was God who had placed three (3) nations in the womb of Noah's wife, in the same way he placed two (2) nations of people in the womb of Isaac's wife. Yes, Noah's wife had triplets when he was 500 years old, Not 501 years, 502 years, nor 503 years. This is proven in my book ' **BLACK BIBLICAL HISTORY'** on amazon.com.

CHAPTER 8

WHO DID CAIN MARRY – AND WHICH COUNTRY TODAY IS THE LAND OF NOD?

It is true that in the beginning of human history, God had created Adam and Eve in the image and likeness of the Gods. **He had created Adam in his own image.** That is, in the image like that of a man, not any other creatures. God also created Adam in **the likeness of himself. That is, Adam looked exactly as to how God himself looks... That is in his spitting likeness. Yes, Adam looked exactly like God. He had created Adam like himself because he wanted his own Godlike image in the flesh to be the head of the earth. But his earthly son Adam failed in the end. So he sent the second Adam, Jesus Christ, who also looks like himself to the earth, but he was successful.**

Eve was created in the image of **God's wife whose name is (MOTHER) SHEKINAH WISDOM. Yes, God's Wisdom looks exactly like a woman. Eve was also created in...the likeness of God's wife. She looks exactly like the Wisdom of God, who is the Divine Queen of heaven, and Goddess of the earth. (Mother Nature /Sophia) see my book on Amazon 'THE WIFE OF GOD'.**

Now, in the process of time, Cain murdered his brother Abel because of jealousy. That was due to the fact that God had accepted Abel's sacrifice and rejected his own. After Cain murdered Abel, God put a curse on him, and banished him from the face of the earth. Know this: the **face of the earth ' was the area of the Jordan Valley-west of the Jordan River.** This River was the dividing line to the east. between the face of the earth, and the outer world. Again, it was separating the Jordan Valley from the lands **on the east side of the River Jordan.** That side was counted as, **'THE FACE OF THE WHOLE EARTH' in the beginning before the flood.**

Moses writes in Genesis 4:16-17, "And Cain went out from the presence of the Lord, **and dwelt in the land of Nod, on the East of Eden."**

It was in Jerusalem, on the Temple-Mount, where the presence of God dwelt. And where his living water flowed from to water his Garden below it. But Cain never went up there because he was born **'after'** Adam and Eve were expelled out of it...and where God had stationed Cherubims' angels to guard the Garden, so neither Adam nor his descendance to have access to it.

However, before Cain was expelled, he was living in the Jordan Valley, so he was still under God's protection. In fact, in the beginning in Adam's days, all of the lands which became Canaan land, after the flood was considered, **' The face, or presence of the Lord...**this was from the area of Dan, (Leshem) in the north, to the current border of Israel today, by the Gulf Eilat.

After being cursed, just like his step-father Adam, Cain picked-up his Georgie-bundle, **' with his wife'** and crossed over the Jordan River-which was/is to the east of the Jordan Valley **and went to the land of Nod to the east of Eden/Jerusalem-which Nod, is present-day Arabia. Note: Cain travelled some 1,163 mile to Arabia, away from the presence of the Lord.**

Before he left home he was living in The City Adam, with all of his half sisters and brothers, which was next to Beit-shean. And Beit-Shean was next to Zarethan. Beit-shean is a city in the northern district of Israel. Geographically, Beit-shean is located ' AT THE JUNCTION OF THE JORDAN RIVER VALLEY AND THE JEZREEL VALLEY.'

However, Adam didn't cross the Jordan River when he was banished from Eden/Jerusalem, **but he and his wife Eve, journeyed some sixty five (65) miles North from Eden, or Jerusalem...to an area which was later to be called...'The City-Adam', which was next to Zarethan, and Beth-she-an, below Jez-reel.**

Moses writes in Genesis chapter 4: verse 17:: "And Cain knew (had sex with) his wife and she conceived and bare Enoch: and he builded a city, and called the name of the city, after the name of his son Enoch."

Now this is where it gets somewhat enigmatic for many people. That is, ' a thing that baffles the understanding of the mind. One wonders as to where would Cain find a woman to marry-seeing that it should only have left Adam and Eve?

Secondly, researchers are still trying to figure-out where is the land of Nod, where Cain married his wife...had a son... and even built a city? But they are walking in it every day without realizing it.

Moses writes in Genesis chapter 4:25; "And Adam knew (had sex with) his wife again, and she bare a son, and called his name '**SETH**'; for God, said she, hath appointed me another seed instead of Abel whom Cain slew."

Observe: **Seth was born 'after' Abel.** So when Moses says that Adam knew, or had sex with his wife again, He means that it was **after Abel-who was really his own flesh and blood. God made sure that Adam knew that this son, this time, is his own,...SO**

GOD MADE SETH IN THE SPITTING LIKENESS AS ADAM.

What this verse proves is the fact that in the beginning of human history, it was indeed **only Adam, Eve, Cain, and Abel.** Because here in verse 25, Eve says that God had given her another son or seed, whom Cain slew. This obviously means that **Eve didn't have any other sons after the death of Abel, to the birth of Seth.**

Moses writes in genesis 5:3-4: "And Adam lived an hundred and thirty years (130 yrs.) and begat a son in his own likeness, after his image: and called his name Seth." This statement here by Moses is a very strange one. Why would Moses record that when Adam was 130 years he had a son **in his own likeness, and after his image?** First of all. Moses is saying that Seth looked exactly like his father Adam. This means that Eve's first son Cain, was not in Adam's likeness neither image. So Cain didn't look like Adam. But the question is, why did Moses say that Adam's son Seth was **after his image?**

Image means that Seth was a normal man like his father Adam. That is, his image was not that of a bird, monkey, lion, or any other creature. But isn't it normal for Seth to be in the image of a human like Adam? The answer is yes. Then why would Moses have to say **that Seth was after the image of Adam? The answer is because: One, CAIN WAS NOT IN HIS LIKENESS, THAT IS, CAIN DIDN'T LOOK LIKE ADAM. Two: Because the image of Cain wasn't exactly like Adam's image,** Yes, Cain had two hands, feet, and body like a human, **BUT HE WAS A HYBRID HUMAN BEING – VERY HUGE, OR THAT OF A GIANT WHICH MEANS THAT CAIN WAS NOT ADAM'S SON, BUT OF THE EGGS OF EVE AND THE SPERM OF THE SERPENT. Now I don't mean like a snake which one sees today. This serpent was walking** on its feet. However, Seth looked exactly like Adam, and of a normal size just like his father Adam.

Moses goes on in verse 4, "And the days of Adam after he had begotten Seth were eight hundred years (800yrs. AND HE BEGAT SONS AND DAUGHTERS." So we see when Adam was 130 years old, he begat a son he named Seth who looked exactly like himself. You should also remember that the scripture says THAT AFTER ADAM BEGAT SETH, HE HAD MANY MORE SONS AND DAUGHTERS. That is, a whole group of children.

Here is what Moses records in Genesis 4:26: "And to Seth; to him also there was born a son; and he called his name ENOS: THEN BEGAN MEN TO CALL UPON THE NAME OF THE LORD." Here Moses tells us that all of those sons and daughters which Adam begat 'after Seth was born, did not call upon the name of the Lord, WOW! So those sons and daughters of Adam, up to 105 years, or up to Seth's 105 years-... DID NOT RECOGNIZE GOD'S NAME.

How ungrateful ! So whose name they called upon? Well, they called upon the names of fallen angels, Lucifer, and the gods of the original forces of darkness. Therefore, they too were wicked children of Adam. I want you to remember this. I want you to remember this group of Adam's children who didn't call upon the name of God.'

When Seth was 105, years old, he had a son named 'ENOS'. These sons and daughters whom Adam had begotten just after Seth was born – which was up to the birth of Enos, were in the age-range of some 100,years old, down to the age of say, one, (1) year old.

Why do I say Adam's sons and daughters were ranging from about 100 years and under? Well, if Seth was 105 years old when he begat his son Enos, and at this same time Adam had sons and daughters after Seth was born, then Seth's brothers and sisters...had to have been some 100 years, or just younger than he was, provided of course, Adam and Eve took a four (4) years break from having children.

Some women give a space of four (4) to ten (10) years before they have another baby. But if Eve took a four years break, **then her older child...'after Seth' would have been about 101 years old.** The objective is: that Adam and Eve had many sons and daughters, **after Seth was born.** But when Seth reached 105, years, at the time he begot his son Enos, **Adam and Eve had many children, and grandchildren. This means that Seth had many brothers and sisters ranging from about, one year old to at least, 101 years old.**

Know this: these sons and daughters of Adam and Eve...were Cain's own half brothers and sisters. This is so, because Cain was Eve's son, but not Adam's son. Remember this: THESE WERE THE PEOPLE WHO CAIN WAS AFRAID OF WHO WOULD COME SEEKING HIS LIFE. because they knew that he had murdered their blood-brother Abel-and may want to revenge his death.

Again, from the time of Seth's birth, up to the birth of his son Enos, was 105 years. Here is what you should also ponder: DURING THOSE 105 YEARS...ADAM AND EVE WERE STILL HAVING CHILDREN. Because you should remember that it was 105 years from Seth's birth to his son Enos' birth.

HERE IS YOUR ANSWER AS TO WHO CAIN HAD MARRIED

Observe this: IT WAS ONE OF ADAM'S DAUGHTERS, WHICH WAS CAIN'S OWN HALF SISTER, WHO HE HAD MARRIED THEN TOOK HER TO THE LAND

OF NOD-WHICH IS MODERN DAY ARABIA-EAST OF EDEN / EAST OF JERUSALEM: that is beyond the Jordan River eastward.

After God had cursed Cain for murdering his brother Abel, Cain replied to the Lord in his defence in Genesis 4:13: "And Cain said unto the Lord, my punishment is greater than I can bear." Cain continues his defence in verse 14: "Behold, thou hast driven me out this day 'from the face of the earth', and from thy face shall I be hid; and I shall be a fugitive and a vagabond in the earth: And it shall come to pass, THAT EVERYONE THAT FINDETH ME SHALL SLAY ME."

Verse 15, "And the Lord said unto him, therefore whosoever slayeth Cain vengeance shall be taken on him seven fold, and the Lord set a mark upon Cain least any finding him shall kill him."

Think about this: IF THERE WERE NO OTHER PEOPLE LIVING DURING THIS TIME...WHY WOULD CAIN COMPLAIN TO THE LORD ABOUT HIS SAFETY? WHY WOULD HE BE AFRAID IF THERE WERE NO OTHER PEOPLE AROUND TO KILL HIM? However, you should know that this conversation between Cain and the Lord took place...many years 'After' he had murdered his brother Abel. This conversation took place when there were other people living. Yes, it was in the process of time when this conversation took place.

Two: Cain said to the Lord: "I am driven out from the face of the earth, (Jordan Valley) and hidden from your face – I will be a fugitive and a vagabond in the earth". This earth Cain mentions here is The outer earth beyond the Jordan Valley on the east side of the Jordan River. So if there were no people around... who were there to kill him? Cain believed that his half-brothers and half-sisters may have hunted him down to kill him. What all of this proves is that at the time Cain killed Abel in the beginning, it really was only Adam, Eve, himself, and Abel. So this conversation with the Lord **had to have taken place years after he murdered Abel BUT AT A TIME WHEN PEOPLE WERE LIVING WHO WERE ADAM'S CHILDREN.** Doesn't this statement by the Lord himself infers that there had to have been people around at that time? Why would God use the words, **'WHOSOEVER' and the word 'HIM'?** Wouldn't you agree that the word **'WHOSOEVER'** was in reference to people? Think about this also: if God meant a 'beast,' he wouldn't have said,' **WHO SO EVER'.** and even if it was a beast, why would the Lord say, **"and vengeance shall be taken ...'ON HIM' rather than, 'ON IT'?** So why would God use the pronoun, **'HIM' if 'THE HIM' wasn't in reference to a person?** So you see, people were really around at that time.

Even though Moses' narrative may not lend itself to clarity, one thing is certain-**that human beings were in the earth during the time God cursed and banished Cain.** Know this: Cain said to the Lord that he was being driven **'from the face of the earth' and that he will be hidden from his face.** But Cain turns around and says to the Lord...**that he will be a fugitive and a vagabond...'IN THE EARTH'** But Cain wasn't crazy nor was he smoking crack. He knew exactly what he was saying to the Lord about him being driven from the face of the earth.

Know this again: 'the face of the earth in the beginning, WAS A SPECIAL GEOGRAPHICAL AREA...AND THIS AREA WAS IN THE JORDAN VALLEY BY THE JORDAN RIVER. This face of the earth was positioned from Dan in the North to the Gulf of Eilat in the south, and by the Mediterranean sea in the west. This area was the face of the earth where Adam, Eve, Cain, Abel, Noah and all of the people were living during the first ten (10) generations for **1656, years.**

Cain realized that he was being driven out of the land where the presence (face) of the Lord was. He realized once driven out of this area, where-ever he would have gone, the presence of God wouldn't have been there. Because he would have been a vagabond, '**IN THE EARTH...not the face of the earth...BUT THE LANDS 'OUTSIDE' THE FACE OF THE EARTH BEYOND THE JORDAN RIVER ON THE EAST SIDE. THAT IS, IN THE LAND OF ARABIA AND BEYOND.** This indicates that these people Cain was complaining about **were living during the time he was complaining to God.** This should open-up your eyes that among these people who Cain was afraid of...women had to have been among them. Two: and if females were among them, then it should prove that it was one of them,**whom Cain took to the land of Nod, or to the east of Eden, or the east of Jerusalem...married, built a city... and named it after his son.**

The land of Arabia was first named **Enoch by Cain.** The name Enoch means, **teacher. Cain means, 'to get'.** He was a go getter, when he was banished he didn't give-up on life. He didn't just build a house, or a hotel,' **but a whole city'. He was an entrepreneur. Think about this: if he was cursed and did all of this, how much more should a blessed person do?** After Cain was banished from the Jordan Valley where he grew-up with Adam and Eve, Moses writes in Genesis 4:16, "And Cain went out **from the presence of the Lord and dwelt in the land of Nod, ON THE EAST OF EDEN."**

When Cain was expelled from the Jordan Valley, he went and took up residence in the land **which is to the east of Eden, that is, the land east of Jerusalem...which land is Arabia, to the east of Jerusalem.** In the process of time, he built a city and called it after the name of his son Enoch, which means,

teacher. **Remember this: the first teacher on earth was Cain's son Enoch, He was a man the people looked up to.**
In verse 17, Moses writes: "And Cain knew his wife; and she conceived and bore Enoch and he builded a city and called the name of the city, after the name of his son Enoch". It is common intelligence that Cain had to have gotten married 'before' he left home, or the Jordan Valley, then carried his wife with him to the land of **Nod/Arabia, which is east of Jerusalem.** However, these lands had different names before the flood. The fact that Cain got married before he was banished and left home, proves that there had to have been people left in the Jordan Valley, but these people were his own half brothers and sisters, and Seth's children. Now what we are going to have is the land where Cain first lived which is **in the City-Adam, on the west side of the Jordan River...in the Jordan Valley, by Zarethan and Beth-shean, below Jez-reel.**
Even though some scholars put the City-Adam on the east side of the Jordan River, others put it on the west side of the Jordan River. What we now have is the land where Cain settled-down, which was in the land of Nod/Arabia. So we are going to have the children of Adam, and the children of Seth continuing to live in the Jordan Valley. And two: the children of Cain **living in the City Enoch, in the land of Nod across the Jordan River, on the east of Eden/Jerusalem**
Verse 17, also shows that Cain was an industrious person because he even built a City on the east of Eden, which was/is Ancient Arabia. Of course, he was inspired by his spiritual father, the serpent.
This is also what the serpent wanted Adam and Eve to do in the beginning; that is...**to use their own creative minds to achieve their desires instead of depending or waiting for God. The serpent also achieved his objectives through Cain and the children of both Cain, Seth, and Adam's children.**

Now that Cain is in the land of Nod, he is now going to multiply by having many personal family-members, **who were genius' and giants who never worshipped God.** Even Adam's children didn't call upon God's name until in the days of Enos which were some 235 years after Adam was created.

In Genesis 4:18 we see that Enoch's son was **Irad,** and his son was **Mehujael,** and his son was **Methusael,** then his son **Lamech.** He was Cain's great, great, great grandson. In verse 19, Lamech got married to two wives, the first was **Adah,** and the second was **Zillah.**

Now this is the beginning of men having **two (2) wives.** So remember Lamech was the first man to have two wives. So we see that right from the very beginning **in the City of Enoch** the serpent began to do just the opposite of what God did. God's intention in the beginning **was for one man to have one wife.** But Lucifer's intention was for man to have at least two (2) wives, or as many as they could take care of.

However, in the process of time, after the flood, some men began to have many wives. Not only wives, but many women as concubines or sweethearts-just like Abraham, and the people of his days had many concubines. I wouldn't even mention king David and king Solomon – they were the worst of the lots.

CAIN'S CHILDREN WERE THE FIRST INVENTORS, SCIENTISTS AND ENTREPRENEURS

Cain's children were exceptionally intellectual people who possessed the abilities of creative powers. They were the movers and shakers of the then world. They possessed a strong inclination of natural talents. They possessed a distinctive prevailing spirit to strive for excellence, just like Cain who was a work-a-holic. **They were the special-interest celebrities-the money people** and also the corruptors of men and women to sin against God. They were the smartie-pants people.

Cain's children were superior to Adam's children, that is, his half-brothers and half-sisters, as it relates to outward knowledge and wealth. They were even wiser and more skillful than Seth's children. But of course, they were more wicked and worldly.

In the process of time both Adam and Seth's children joined Cain's children in worshipping the forces of darkness. So God brought a destruction on all of mankind leaving only eight (8) persons alive.

I don't know if you thought I'm giving Cain's children too much credit.If so, then please read what Moses says about them in Genesis chapter 4:20-21. Here is the proof of what I've said.

Verse 20 "And Adah bare JABAL: he was THE FATHER (first) of such as dwelt in tents and of such as have cattle."

Now Jabal was tired living in caves, so being industrious, and a hard worker like Cain, he became **the first person to live in tents. And he was the first,or father...TO RAISE CATTLE. 'He was a cattle-rancher' and the first to have COWBOYS TO DRIVE CATTLE FOR HIM. So the City Enoch in the land of Nod, or ancient Arabia was the first to have tents as homes to live in.** So every time you see, or enter a tent, or see cattle, **remember Jabal.**

Here is what Moses writes about Cain's children in verse 21, "And his brother's name WAS JUBAL: he was the father (first) of all such as handle...THE HARPS AND ORGANS."

So who was the first organist? well, it was Jubal Cain's posterity. **Observe: JUBAL WAS THE INVENTOR OF MUSICAL INSTRUMENTS, SUCH AS HARPS AND ORGANS.**

Isn't it rather strange that it was the children of Cain who first invented the harps and organs, and the first ones to play them in their gathering, instead of Adam and Seth's children?

Yes, they were being played in their clubs and bar-rooms before they were played in the churches of shrines.

So Jubal's sounds were not of God, but of Cain's children. THEY WERE THE INVENTORS OF MUSIC. So Jubal sounds were and still are the sounds of the world, and even up to today. If you don't believe me then advertise about a singing concert to sing, or to praise God, then look to see how many people will show up. Then call a concert to sing Jubal's secular song, then see how many people will show up...there wouldn't even be standing room.

Verse 22, Moses goes on: **"And Zillah, she also bare... TUBAL-CAIN, AN INSTRUCTOR...'OF EVERY' ARTIFICER IN BRASS AND IRON: and the sister of Tubal-Cain was Naamah."**

EVEN TUBAL-CAIN WAS THE FATHER, OR FIRST...IN EVERY ARTIFICER IN BRASS AND IRON. He was an instructor or teacher as to how to make any, and everything in brass and iron; including musical instruments and statues of brass-gods. He was an inventor. **HE WAS THE FIRST BLACKSMITH, AND THE FIRST TO COMBINE METAL PARTS BY APPLYING HEAT AND PRESSURE. In other words, he was a genius.**

So it was Cain's children who made the City Enoch in the land of Nod, or the land which is now called, "ARABIA", in the beginning of the then modern world. They were the ones who were running things in the then modern world. It was their natural raw talents, coupled with a desire to excel which made them so great and professional. THEY WERE THE FIRST SETS OF SCIENTISTS AND INVENTORS ALSO IN RAISING CATTLE FOR SALE.

Take note: The land of Nod which is the ancient land of Arabia,...**HAS NOTHING TO DO WITH THE ARABIA,**

THE HAPPY, AND THE BEAUTIFUL TODAY. It was just that land where Cain went and created a City within it. In fact, all the people of that ancient land perished during the flood of Noah. However, the topography or exact physical land remains, after the flood, and will always remain. **So this is not casting any aspersion on Arabia.**

So yes, it was Cain's posterity who was indeed in charge of the world for the first 235, years after Adam's creation. Even Adam's sons and daughters whom he had after Seth was born, **didn't call upon the name of The creator God.** So the seed of the woman or Eve's children didn't bruise the head of the serpent. The truth is, they didn't even try to bruise his head, but instead, they joined-up with them causing God to destroy the whole world of people and his creation.

Men just began to call upon the name of the Lord from the days of Enos, or Seth's son. But it didn't last too long, **because they eventually crossed over the Jordan River and joined Cain's out-going erotic and sinful children, causing as stated before, God to drown all of his creation leaving only eight (8) person alive.**

Even though the City-Adam and the City Jericho were the oldest Cities in the beginning, the land of Arabia to the east of Jerusalem, **was the first modern country and City on earth before the flood.** Those ancient people had everything going for them, except the presence of the Lord God. Cain's first City, Enoch, which he built and named after his son-which City was called, Enoch. Was changed to Arabia in the process of time many years 'after' the flood. **The City Enoch was like the New York of today.** Anything they wanted they could have found in it.

Again, this City was so entertaining and modern, that both Adam, and Seth's children crossed over the Jordan River...went to the east country and joined them. This further exacerbated God's anger, so he killed them all.

The New Arabia of today comprises of Middle-Eastern people including Abraham's six sons **from KETURAH, THE EGYPTIAN WOMAN. It was this Arabia today where Abraham sent his six sons TO THE EAST COUNTRY WHICH IS ARABIA THE HAPPY.** And it was Moses who said that they were sent to the east country. (Genesis 25:6) And he also says Cain went out from the presence of the Lord, **and dwelt in the land of 'Nod', on the east of Eden (Jerusalem).**

CHAPTER 9

RE-POPULATING JERUSALEM AND THE JORDAN VALLEY: AS IN THE BEGINNING

After the flood of Noah ended, God had only preserved Noah with his wife, and his three sons, namely: Shem, Ham, and Japheth, and their wives for the purpose of re-populating the earth.

God used the original land of Eden symbolically as his new city called, Jerusalem. Of course this was in the process of time, after he had promised his friend Abraham, the land of Canaan, for a possession for his posterity, or future children.

After many hundreds of years living in Shinar/Babylon, the people became wicked just as the people before the flood. But this time God didn't kill them, but rather, scattered them all over the earth. **And this was going to be the first time that the earth was going to be overspread with human beings.**

Ham's fourth son Canaan, went and possessed the land afterward called, '**Canaan Land**', which included, the Amorites, Perizzites, Hittites, Canaanites, Girgashites, Hevites, and the Jebusites-which Jebusites' land eventually became Jerusalem.

Canaan's third son '**Jebus**' was the father of the land of Jebus: and his tribe was called,; **The Jebusites'.** They were the possessors or owners of the land of Jebus after the scattering, or disbursement of the population from Babel.

All through the ages after the flood, God still had his eyes on his original and special land which was Eden, in which he planted his Garden **in front of his earthly house, which house was his Holy Mount-and which Garden was planted below this Temple-Mount facing eastward, or the sunrise.** God knew that this Eden was eventually going to be called, **'Jerusalem'** **which he would eventually call, HIS HOLY CITY AND HIS HOLY MOUNT ZION / MORIAH.**

MELCHIZEDEK: THE FIRST ONE TO BUILD JERUSALEM, AND THE FIRST TEMPLE OF GOD ON THE TEMPLE-MOUNT AFTER THE FLOOD

Here now we have on the world stage after the scattering of the people from Babel/ Shinar, a mysterious personage whose name in the Hebrew language is **Melchizedek. He was the first priest and king of Jerusalem whom God had beamed-down from heaven to be a teacher/ priest, and a righteous king...for the Jebusite in Palestine. And he was the first person to build the Temple of God, even before Abraham met God.**

JOSEPHUS' NARRATIVE OF MELCHIZEDEK

After giving an account of the six times the City of Jerusalem, and its Temple were destroyed, Josephus, the Jewish historian/ priest, and general in the Jewish war in Galilee, and Jotapata, in 67ad, records, I quote: "But he who first built it (Jerusalem) was a potent (powerful) man **among the Canaanites,** and in our (Jewish) tongue called **Melchizedek the righteous king; for such he really was, on which account he was 'THE FIRST PRIEST OF GOD, AND FIRST TO BUILD A TEMPLE, THERE AND CALLED THE CITY SALEM**

WHICH WAS LATER CALLED, JERUSALEM. However, David the king of the Jews ejected the Canaanites and settled his own people therein" (un-quote)

So now we know that Melchizedek was the first righteous king who built the City of Salem, after the scattering of the people at Babel/shinar/ Iraq. Two: we are also informed by Josephus that Melchizedek was a powerful man among the Canaanites. **This means that he looked like a Palestinian.** Three: He states that Melchizedek **was the first priest of God, and also the first priest who built a Temple in Salem.** However, by the time king David fought against the Canaanites about 1,000 years later, and took Salem, or Jebus' land, King Melchizedek was long returned to heaven.

Now you can see why Abram respected Melchizedek. well, because he was a priest of the most high God, and the king of Salem, or Jerusalem. One may wonder why it was the Canaanites, or the cursed people by Noah..'. Not God', but by Noah that God sent his first righteous king to teach them the way of righteousness rather than the other tribes who were not cursed. Well, you see, after the scattering,or disbursement from Babel, the children of Canaan went and inhabited the whole land of Palestine,. But Jebus went and possessed ' **the very mountain where God had first planted the Fountain of Living Water and where he lived in the very beginning when he would have visited the earth.**

MELCHIZEDEK AND ABRAM'S FIRST ENCOUNTER

While living in Sodom, Abram's nephew Lot, was taken captive by king Chedorlaomer. Abram went and rescued Lot, and defeated the kings who took Lot as a prisoner. On the way back home, Abram met king Melchizedek, the priest of the most high God and paid him tithes of the goods he won in battle.

Now at this time Melchizedek and Abram met, Melchizedek was already living and reigning in Salem. Even though this was Abram's first encounter with Melchizedek I'm sure both Melchizedek and Abram had heard of each other before. And both of them worshipped the most high God.

Moses writes in Genesis 14: 17, "And the king of Sodom went out to meet him (Abram) after his return from the slaughter of Che-dor-la-o-mer, and the kings that were with him, at the Valley of Sha-veh, which is the kings dale." Verse 18, "And Melchizedek king of Salem brought forth bread and wine: **and he was the priest of the most high God**" Verse 19, "And he (Melchizedek) blessed him (Abram) and said, blessed be Abram of the most high God, possessor of heaven and earth:" Verse 20, "And blessed be the most high God, which hath delivered thine enemies into thy hand. And he gave him tithes of all."

So you see, Melchizedek did know about Abram before this encounter at this time. Because he said "**Blessed be Abram of the most high God** "At least he knew that Abram worshipped, "the most high God.

We see that Melchizedek was truly the first king and priest of Salem, later called Jerusalem. And we also see that Melchizedek was greater than Abraham-who was the tenth (10th) generation from Noah.

This strange priest Melchizedek who was greater than Abram, **was both a teacher for the Jebusites, and the guardian of Mount Moriah/Zion after the flood.** The reason God had Melchizedek to guard the Temple-Mount, was because this spot was holy to him. And it was his intention to have this Mount protected until he would have his Temple re-build up there.

St. Paul states in Hebrews 7: 7 that Melchizedek was greater than Abraham, because he being greater blessed the lessor one, who had the promise. Melchizedek was indeed greater than Abraham because he **was made like the son of God who truly was Jesus Christ in those ancient days.** Observe: just how the sons of God came down from heaven in the beginning and married to the daughters of men. **So this priest Melchizedek who was made like the son of God, was beamed-down from heaven to be God's king and priest for the Jebusites in Salem-Ham's descendants.** If priest Melchizedek was God's priest in Salem, he had to have had members/ parishioners/Students. And his members of his Temple which he built on the Temple-Mount, **had to have been the Jebusites. Because at this time, there were no Israelites yet.**

STUNNING INFORMATION

Note: the Jebusites were the first worshippers in the first Temple of God on the Temple Mount, hundreds of years before the Hebrews. And priest Melchizedek was their pastor...And he was Jesus Christ. This Melchizedek Was God's priest in Salem, **even while Abram was in 'UR' of the Chaldees, practising his craft of sorceries just like his father Terah, and by extension...all of the people in UR.**

However, if truth be told, this craft of sorcery was the normal practise among; not only the people in UR of the Chaldees, but among all of the nations of the world at that time. But God saw something good in Abram, so he appeared to him and promised to make him great. So God pulled him out of his country and blessed him and made a covenant with him.. God's plan was to make great nations out of his loins, and to make a special nation of people, who he would later call,' his people.

117

This special or chosen people was to return to the original land of Eden/Jerusalem, and be an example to the world in righteousness. Not only Jerusalem, or Eden, but the whole land of Palestine, which was populated in the beginning, from Adam to Noah, where they all lived for ten(10) generations, or 1656 years.

God's intention also was **TO RE-POPULATE THIS SAME LAND OF EDEN/JERUSALEM IN WHICH HE PLANTED HIS OWN GARDEN.** And he was hoping that this special people, this time, would please him, because the first ten (10) generations failed him. The land beginning from Le-shem, later changed to Dan, in the north, to Negev in the south, and even as far as the coast of Israel's land by Eilat. But for whatever reason, his expectation was not realized.

Know this truth: Man will disappoint you. So as a result of man' inability to please God-**he had decided to create a new spiritual Jerusalem above, and a new spiritual Earth above, wherein righteousness abides forever. So you have to die in order to live forever up there in the new earth.**

The reason man always fails God is because God gave him a mind of his own. or a tree of the knowledge of good and evil... that is to make his own choice. So because the ancient Israelites had choices to do as they wanted to do, most of them didn't choose God's ways of righteousness when they crossed over into the promised land, in Gilgal near Jericho.

CHAPTER 10

NEW JERUSALEM: WITHIN THE CENTER OF THE NEW EARTH ABOVE

Before I ask you a serious question, I want to remind you that the hill, or mount where the Jewish Temple was built, is Mount Moriah / The Temple Mount / Zion. 2,Chronicles 3:1, states: "Then Solomon began to build the house of the Lord 'at Jerusalem' in Mount Moriah where the Lord appeared unto David his father, in the threshing floor of Ornan / Arunah the Jebusite."

Why would king Solomon have his son Solomon **build the sacred Temple of the Lord, on the same spot where the Lord appeared to him on Mount Moriah?** So we see that the Temple of the Lord was built on Mount Moriah, not only because it was the spot where the Lord appeared to David, **but because it was the spot where the fountain of living water and the altar of God were first placed in the beginning.**

PUT ON YOUR THINKING CAP

Let's have a short but pragmatic conversation. If we discover in the book of Revelation chapter 22:1, **That the River of life... in New Jerusalem, flows from the throne of God, which is in Mount Zion/ Moriah, to water the tree of life, in the New**

Jerusalem above-then what country would you reason that the water of life, must have flowed from to water the Tree of Life,in the Garden in Eden, on earth, in the past or in the beginning? Is your answer – from the throne or dwelling place in the earthly Jerusalem, and specifically from Mount Zion / Mount Moriah? Well, if you did, it's also my conclusion. Now if you believe this, so where would you reason that the Garden of Eden should have been planted by God? Is your answer in East Jerusalem, or Old Jerusalem, below the Temple-Mount? If so, then you are right.

It was in Jerusalem, in the Middle-East where we found Mount Moriah /Mount Zion which was God's favourite holy Mount. Of course, his next holy Mount was, **Mount Horeb, the Mountain of God. then Mount Sinai in Arabia.**

Meditate on the up-coming paragraph. **Since Mount Zion/Mount Moriah...IN THE NEW JERUSALEM ABOVE, IS THE PLACE WHERE THE RIVER OF LIFE CURRENTLY FROWS FROM TO WATER THE TREE OF LIFE...it stands to reason logically, that it was truly, MOUNT MORIAH / MOUNT ZION IN JERUSALEM ON EARTH, FROM WHERE THE LIVING WATER FLOWED IN THE BEGINNING, TO WATER THE EARTHLY GARDEN OF EDEN, OR THE PARADISE OF THE LORD.** And it also proves that Jerusalem **was Eden, on Earth...And that Jerusalem above is also spiritual Eden.** Do you see the correlation between the two J esusalems?

Does this sound reasonable to believe? Know this: Mount Moriah in Jerusalem, in Palestine, was the fountain-head from where the water of life flowed to water the Tree of Life in the Garden of Even. Likewise, Mount Zion/Moriah in New

Jerusalem above-is the fountain-head of the throne of God from where the living water flows to water the tree of life even today.

Here is another serious question for you to mediate upon. **Why did God create a New Jerusalem above with a New Mount Zion/Moriah in it..and a tree of Life in it...and a River running from his throne, to the tree of life, just as in Eden...if the tree of life...Mount Moriah...and the river of living water were not in Jerusalem on earth, which of course, was Eden? Another question: WHY IS NEW JERUSALEM, CALLED ... 'NEW JERUSALEM'...IF THERE WASN'T AN 'OLD JERUSALEM'? This is why whatever you find in the 'New Jerusalem' above...you also find in the Old Jerusalem on earth in the beginning.** Do you see the correlation between the two Jerusalems?

PROOF: THERE IS A JERUSALEM ABOVE

During the ministry of St. Paul, he struggled with the Galatian Christians, Because even though they believed in The Lord Jesus Christ, some of them were still devoted to the law of Moses. So he writes to them in Galatian 4:21-25 Verse 21, "Tell me, ye that desire to be **'under the law',** do ye not hear the law?

Verse 22, "For it is written, that Abraham had two sons, (Ishmael and Isaac) the one by a bondmaid (Hagar) the other by a freewoman" (Sarah)

Verse 23, "But he who was of the bondwoman was born after the flesh: but he of the freewoman was by promise."

Ishmael was born after the lust of the flesh by Abraham. Abraham lusted after Hagar, the sexy black Egyptian young girl. And as a result, Ishmael was born. Now Isaac was born because God had promised Abraham that he would have a son within a year with his wife Sarah, who was the freewoman.

These two women, Sarah and Hagar, were being used by St. Paul as symbols of two covenants-that is, the old covenant, and the new covenant.

Paul continues to say in verse 24, "Which things are an allegory: metaphor for these (two women) are the two covenants, the one from Mount Sinai, which gendereth to bondage, which is **Agar/Hagar.**"

Verse 25, "For this Agar/Hagar is Mount Sinai in Arabia, and answereth to Jerusalem (below) which now is in bondage with her children"

St. Paul equates' **Agar' (Greek word) or 'Hagar' (Hebrew word) to Mount Sinai in Arabia,** because it was at Sinai where the Israelites were given their ten (10) commandments and their laws. Know this truth: **it wasn't the nations of the world who were given the Ten (10) commandments and the laws of the Israelites, BUT RATHER, THE ISRAELITES 'ONLY'**

St. Paul also equates Hagar as the ancient Jerusalem which was in bondage with her citizens under the Roman rule in the first century. I wrote all of this just to come to verse 26. St. Paul Continues: **"But Jerusalem which is above is free, which is the mother of us all".**

This Sarah is the mother of all Christians, because her husband Abraham is the father of all Christians who have faith in God and the Lord Jesus Christ. Indeed, Paul was telling those Jews **that there was / is a Jerusalem above and it was free and it depicted Sarah.** So Sarah symbolizes the Spiritual Jerusalem above. What about the other woman, Hagar, who she symbolizes? She symbolizes the former ancient Jerusalem on earth. So at this time St. Paul made this statement about Jerusalem being above, Jesus had already prepared New Jerusalem above for the Christians' Jews, or the ancient 144,000 spiritual Israelites.

And 'The New Earth' was already completed also for the '
all nations' of the righteous Christians to inhabit. This is 'The
New Earth' where all of those Christians who the apostle John
saw which were from every races, tribes and languages to inhabit,
or to live in. And this New Earth is the place you will go when
you leave this earth, provided of course, you make the passing
grade by believing in Jesus Christ, because he is the door to the
Kingdom of God.

This new Jerusalem above is the city which Abraham sought
for whose builder and maker is God. So both Abraham, Isaac,
Jacob, and David, and all of the heads of the former Israelites,
live up there worshipping God and the Lamb Jesus Christ,
who is also Melchizedek, the former king and priest of Salem/
Jerusalem. And this same Jesus is also the New Spiritual Adam.

CHAPTER 11

THE ASSYRIAN KING ON GOD'S HOLY MOUNTAIN IN EDEN

The Assyrian at this time were dominating the Jews in Jerusalem, and were upon 'The Holy Mountain of God, which was Mount Moriah / Mount Zion / Acra. But God's eyes were especially on Mount Moriah, because this Mount was his Holy spot on earth, then Mount Horeb. But the truth is...This Jerusalem was Eden in which he had planted his garden, eastward in front of his House (mount) facing the sunrise.

The prophet Isaiah writes in chapter 14:24-25,"The Lord of host sworn, saying, surely, as i have thought, so shall it come to pass as I purpose, so shall, it stand." Verse 25, "THAT I WILL BREAK THE ASSYRIANS…' IN MY LAND, AND UPON MY MOUNTAIN' TREAD HIM UNDER FOOT: then shall his yoke depart from off them (Jews) and his burden depart from off their shoulders".

This is crystal clear that the Assyrian king and his soldiers 'WERE IN THE LAND OF JERUSALEM', AND UPON GOD'S HOLY MOUNTAINS...IN THE LAND OF JERUSALEM, WHICH WAS GOD'S HOLY LAND.

It's also clear from the prophet that the Assyrians were a burden on the shoulders of the Jewish people. But God said he was going to remove 'the Assyrians...out of his land, and out

of his Mountains, especially Moriah where his Temple was
built.

When the nations in the ancient days would have invaded
Jerusalem, they always would have built a compound, or fortress
on Mount Acra. The reason is, because that mountain was
higher than Mount Moriah where God's Temple was built. And
they were able to 'look down on the Jewish Temple.' This Mount
Acra is located in Jerusalem...on the northside of Mount Zion,
between the Tyropoeon Valley and the Hinnom Valley.
After a while Mount Acra was lowered so that it would not be
higher than Mount Moriah.

THE KINGS OF ASSYRIA METAPHORICALLY AS SERPENTS

Here is what the prophet Isaiah prophesied to the ancient leaders
of Palestine, in chapter 14:29-32. "Rejoice not thou whole
Palestina, because the rod of him that smote thee is broken: **for
out of the serpent's root shall come forth 'A COCKATRICE',
and his fruit shall be, A FIERY FLYING SERPENT".**

Verse 30, "And the firstborn of the poor shall feed, and the
needy shall lie down in safety: And I will kill thy root with
famine, and he shall slay thy remnant."

Verse 31, "Howl, O gates: (leaders at the city gates) cry, o
City (the citizens) thou whole Palestina, art dissolved: for there
shall come from the north (Babylon) a smoke, and none shall be
alone in his appointed time"

Verse 32, "what shall one then answer the messengers of the
nations? That the Lord hath founded Zion, and the poor of the
people shall trust in it."

The leaders and the people were warned by the prophet,
not to rejoice because the Assyrian **'king Shalmanesser,'** was

broken, or died. The Assyrian king Shalmanesser also had his weight on the shoulders of the people of Palestine.

The prophet said to the Palestinians, don't rejoice yet, **because out of the serpent's root, shall come forth a Cockatrice. This Cockatrice was Shalmanesser's son, who was KING SENNA-CHE-RIB. And out of his fruit, or out of Senna-che-rib, came forth' A FLYING RED SERPENT, who was his son, ESAR-HA-DDON.**

SERPENT NUMBER ONE

Serpent number one, was Shalmanesser...Serpent number two, was his son...Senna-che-rib, 'a Cockatrice'...And serpent number three, was his son, **Esar-haddon...**"A RED FLYING SERPENT.

When the prophets speak about serpents, they were not addressing the devil, nor Lucifer personally, but rather the kings, or rulers **who portrayed the actions of the devil, or Lucifer.** God caused the serpent to mutate who was caught in the Garden of Eden, and told him he would crawl upon his belly. However. In the process of time the devil caused a serpent from his loins to mutate which brought forth a cockatrice. And that cockatrice mutated **and brought forth a red flying serpent.** The prophet referred to the three Assyrian kings as symbols of the serpents which were evil.

I personally saw a serpent flew, or pitched in the air to a distance of about twenty five (25) feet ahead, and it made a squeaking sound when it flew. Needless to say, I was stunned, because I had never seen a serpent flown, nor made any sound before. I never told my wife because she would have wanted us to move from our two (2) acres homestead.'

Consider this: The serpents who the prophet spoke about, were, 'father, son, and grandson. This is, king Shalmanesser, the first serpent-King Senna-Che-rib, the second serpent, or 'the cockatrice', and king Asar-ha-ddon, 'The flying serpent. These three serpents, or Assyrian's kings were: sly, deceptive, slick and crafty, as the serpent which was in the Garden who deceived Eve. The prophet spoke of these Assyrian kings metaphorically.

NOTES ON THE ASSYRIAN KINGS

On the 4th. Year of king Hezekiah, which was the 7th. Year reign of Hoshea, son of Elah king of Israel, that Shal-ma-nesser king of Assyria (serpent Number 1) came up against Samaria, and besieged it.

Hezekiah was the king of Judah, and Jerusalem was its capital. And Hoshea was the king of Israel, and Samaria was its capital. Judah represented two tribes of the twelve (12) tribes of Jacob, and Israel, represented ten (10) of the twelve tribes of Jacob at that time. This is so, because there was a split in the twelve tribes ' before' that time.

At the end of three years, the Assyrian king took Samaria, the capital of the northern kingdom of Israel. However, it was in Hezekiah's 7th. Year reign of the southern kingdom...and the 10th. Year of Hoshea, the king of Israel that Samaria was taken by Shal-ma-nesser, in 722bc. (Serpent # 1)

In the 14th year reign of king Hezekiah, (seven years later) that king Senna-Che-rib, the son of Shal-manesser who was serpent # 2, or the cockatrice, came up against Judah. As a result, he forced king Hezekiah to pay him 300 talents of silver, and 30, talents of gold.

Observe: 2 kings chapter 18:1, states, "And the king of Assyria do carry Israel (northern tribe) unto Assyria, and put them in...Halah and in harbor by the River Gozan, and in the cities of the Medes".

This invasion took place in the year bc,722, because they refused to keep God's commandments and to obey him fully'.

There are some people, even today, who are wondering whatever happened to the ten (10) tribes of Israel, and where did they go. And where are they today? The reality is, when they were taken into Assyria, the ten tribes **were placed in Halah, harbor by the River Gozan, and in the cities of the Medes.** This is where they were put. So they assimilated among the places where they were placed, and in time, disappeared.

THE FORMER GLORY OF THE ASSYRIANS

In Ezekiel chapter 31, we see where God gave him a message, and told him to speak to the Pharaoh king of Egypt. At this time, Pharaoh was flexing his muscle, as though he was the greatest nation that ever existed. God wanted Pharaoh to know that he wasn't even as great as the Assyrians in its beauty and greatness.

Chapter 31:3, says, "Behold the Assyrian' **was a Cedar in Lebanon with fair branches, and with shadowing shroud, and of an high stature; and his top was among the thick boughs"**

Here God describes the greatness of the Assyrian, **like a Cedar Tree in Lebanon,** and as to how beautiful his branches were. And as to how tall he was. God used metaphors to describe his greatness. God also used as metaphors the deep, and Rivers running around its planes.

God talks about how this Cedar Tree of Lebanon was so great, that the fowls of the heaven (air) made their nests in his boughs. And under his branches did the beasts of the field bring forth their young, and under his shadow **dwelt all great nations.**

Take a note of this: the end of verse 6th, proves that all of the various descriptions of 'The Cedar Tree, were in reference...

'TO NATIONS AND LEADERS" in the various nations. And the word, 'field' was in reference, 'TO THE WORLD'. God continues with the greatness of Assyria: Verse 8, he says, The Cedar of God could not hide him: The fir trees were not like his boughs, and the chestnut trees were not like his branches; NOR ANY TREE IN THE GARDEN OF GOD WAS LIKE UNTO HIM IN HIS BEAUTY."

The ancient people knew that Jerusalem WAS THE ORIGINAL EDEN IN WHICH GOD HAD PLANTED HIS GARDEN. This is why the nations of the past ages hated Jerusalem so much. We must remember that 'the Assyrian king was in Jerusalem in God's holy city and his holy mountains, until God chased him out.

Why would God through Ezekiel keep using, 'The Garden of God, if it wasn't in existence in the days of the Assyrian king? Think ! but how would you know where the Garden of God was? Simply by asking, ' FROM WHERE WAS THIS ASSYRIAN KING KICKED OUT? The answer is simply: 'FROM JERUSALEM'; So then, you see, that Jerusalem was Eden, and the Garden of God, was in Jerusalem. Do you see it?

Look at this: no one in the Garden of Eden was as beautiful, and as high in power as he was. But the important question is, WHEN WAS THIS KING IN EDEN?

So where-ever we find God kicking him out, we can safely say that that place was Eden. So we now know where the Garden of Eden was. It was in Jerusalem where we found him mistreating God's former holy people. (did you read between the lines?)

No nation's leaders could have arisen as high and powerful as this Assyrian king at that time even none 'in Eden' that is, none in Jerusalem, was as powerful as he was among the other trees, or other leaders – not only in Jerusalem, but in all the lands in

Israel. In fact, the powers in Jerusalem couldn't stand up to him in power and greatness.

Ponder this: this proves that Eden was indeed in reference to Jerusalem, because it was in Jerusalem **where we found the king of Assyria abusing God's people.**

The branches of this Assyrian king were those countries' leaders who had to pay tributary monies to him, and those countries which he controlled. Even the trees (leaders) 'in Eden' envied him. That is, even the leaders 'in Jerusalem' envied this Assyrian king. It was God who made this Assyrian king great, in the same way he made king Solomon great. This Assyrian king was indeed handsome and wise above all the kings, or trees. You may wonder why God made this Assyrian king so great, **even greater than the leaders in Eden, or Jerusalem?** Well, God is sovereign. He lifts up whoever he wants and when he desires. But we must remember that the Assyrians were also from the stock of Shem, just like the Israelites.

Because this Assyrian king had lifted-up his heart or mind to the heavens, God had to put a stop to him by bringing him down. He was getting too big for his britches. Man always falls down to the pit, when he storms the gate of heaven and tries to force his way inside, and demanding a seat, or position at the table.

In verse 11, God says, "I have therefore delivered him into the hand of the mighty one of the heathen; he shall surely deal with him, **I HAVE DRIVEN HIM OUT FOR HIS WICKEDNESS."**

So we see that God did drive out the Assyrian king **out of Eden, or out of Jerusalem, and out of his Holy Mountains-Moria/Zion and Acra.** Seriously consider the following reasoning: In order for God to drive-out the Assyrian king **'OUT OF EDEN', he had to have been in Eden.** But we have no history where we find the Assyrian king, ' in Eden-in the Garden of God and with the leaders of Eden. This should prove to you that this Eden and mountains of God, **had to have been in Jerusalem**, because this is the land where we find him abusing God's former people **and occupying his holy mountains. (I wonder if you see the reasoning?)**

When the prophet here speaks of Eden, he had to have been making reference to Jerusalem as Eden because the Assyrian king, **'was never in the original Eden,** but why not? Because he wasn't living in the days before the flood, in order to access it. But we find the Assyrian king in Jerusalem, so the prophet had to have been referring Eden as Jerusalem metaphorically. (yes?)

Now it was king Nebuchadnezzar who God had chosen to destroy the Assyrians. So when king Nebuchadnezzar was destroying the Assyrians, **'all of his branches fell off.** That is, all of his dominated countries under him were so happy he was defeated by Nebuchadnezzar, that they rejoiced greatly, because they were now free from tributary payments.

When verse 8 says, **'The Cedars (leaders) in the Garden of God could not hide him...proves that he was indeed...in the Garden of God. But again, we know the prophet was making reference to Jerusalem, when he says...'in the Garden of God'**

No trees in the Garden of God were like unto him in beauty. So we know that God could only have been referring **'to his holy city, and his holy mountains in Jerusalem.** The prophet knew that Eden, symbolically, was Jerusalem, the former holy city of God – **and that his garden was in his city of Jerusalem.** Therefore, Ezekiel knew that Jerusalem was the land of Eden, and he said so, but he used it as a metaphor. We know that God's holy mountain wasn't in Africa, Armenia neither in Europe, but rather in Jerusalem. **So Eden was truly the land of Jerusalem.**

Again, we can safely say that **Eden is the old city of Jerusalem, and the Garden of the Lord...was in Southeast Jerusalem, below Mount Moriah, or the Temple-Mount, in a low level field, facing the sunrise.** By this time, The Assyrian king was indeed, **'In the Garden of the Lord in Eden, that is, in Jerusalem.**

When Ezekiel speaks about' The Garden of God', which country do you believe he was speaking about? If you think hard, you would come up with Jerusalem which is in Palestine. God talked about the leaders **'in the Garden of God,' thousands of years...'after' the flood.** What all of this proves, is that the Garden of God **was recognizable, and its where-about known in the days of Ezekiel and the Assyrian king, because he was in it and chased out of it.**

By this time there were leaders and people living **in Eden, and the Garden of God.** But in Adam's days, there weren't any people or kings living in it. So this should open-up your eyes that the Garden of God, and Eden had to have been Jerusalem and Mount Moriah where God's Temple was built. (yes?)

Think about this: In the days of the prophets, there wasn't supposed to have been any leaders in the land of Eden and in the Garden of God...unless the prophet was making reference to the Garden in Eden, in Jerusalem, and Eden as Jerusalem, metaphorically.

If you're truly seeking the where-about of the Garden of Eden, **you only have to visit southeast Jerusalem-that is, the old City of Jerusalem 'BELOW' THE TEMPLE-MOUNT.** In ancient times, this area was a very lush green plain with trees, which was the Garden of Eden. But to find this location of the fountain of living water, **YOU ONLY HAVE TO GO UP TO THE TOP OF MOUNT MORIAH,... OR THE TEMPLE-MOUNT "AT THE CENTER OF IT TO THE SOUTH"**

Now if you were to stand in the center of the seven miles by three of miles,(7x3) at the south, in Jerusalem, up there. YOU WILL BE STANDING ON THE VERY SPOT WHERE THE JEWISH TEMPLE WAS BUILT...AND THE SPOT WHERE THE WELL, OR FOUNTAIN OF LIVING WATER WAS DUG OR WAS PLANTED, because the living water was coming out of the Temple.

TO WHOM IT MAY CONCERN

Whoever controls East Jerusalem and the Temple-Mount, should make these areas the most attractive tourist destination for the world to visit.

CHAPTER 12

THE KING OF TYRUS IN EDEN – THE GARDEN OF GOD

These verses will prove that Jerusalem was indeed Eden, and the king of Tyrus was in Eden,' the Garden of God. These verses will also prove that the Cherub' which covered, **WAS A MAN, AND HE WAS NOT LUCIFER AS SUPPOSED.**

You will also be convinced that the prophet was not addressing Lucifer but rather, the king of Tyrus. God didn't tell Ezekiel to address Lucifer, neither the devil, but rather,' **the Prince and king of Tyrus who was a human.**

JUDGMENT ON THE PRINCE OF TYRUS

Ezekiel chapter 28:1-19: "The word of the Lord came unto me again saying."

Verse 2, "son of man, say unto the Prince of Tyrus, thus saith the Lord God: because thine heart (mind) is lifted up, and thou hast said, **"I am a God, I sit in the seat of God in the midst of the SEAS (nations) YET THOU ART A MAN; AND NOT GOD, though thy set thine heart as the heart of God."**

Ezekiel says that God had told him **to prophesy to the Prince 0f Tyrus/Tyre.**

THE PRINCE OF TYRUS WAS THE HIGH PRIEST OF TYRUS

In all lodges or fraternities, you would find a high Priest. This high Priest in ancient times was called 'A Prince'. Even in Jewish ancient times, the high Priest was referred to as 'The Prince of the sanctuary'.

During the times of the Maccabeans' era, there was no Israelites' king. So the high Priest was the Prince, both of the spiritual things and the social things. In times past, God always worked with both king and Priest. But this Prince of Tyrus, was the high Priest, that is,...a spiritual Prince. This Prince believed that he had come to the position of a God. He believed this because he had so much influence over the various nations, which traded with his country and with him.

Here are some of the many nations which traded, honoured, and respected him; but whose priests he had influence over: Senior, Lebanon, Bashan, Ashurites, the Isles of Chittim, Egypt, the Isles of Elishah, Idon, Arvad, Gebal, Persia, Lud, Phut, Gammadims, Dedan, Syria, Judah, and the land of Israel, Arabia, Sheba, Raamah, Haran, (Turkey) Canneth and Eden."

Ezekiel 27:24,says, "These were thy merchants in all sorts of things, in blue clothes, and broidered work, and in chests of rich apparel, bound with cords, and made of cedar, among thy merchandise."

Verse 25, says, "The ships of Tarshish did sing of thee in thy market and thou wast replenished, and made very glorious in the midst of the Seas."

Because this king of Tyrus was so popular among 'the seas' (multitudes of people in the then known world) he believed that he was a God; and that he sat in the seat of God. That is, just as God sat in the midst of the congregation of the Israelites on the ark of the covenant among the Jewish people in his Temple.

So this man, or Prince of Tyrus believed that he now sits in God's place. **So he believed that...ALL THE GODS OF THOSE NATIONS WERE INFERIOR TO HIM, because he was superior to their Priests.** He also felt that he was superior to Israel's God, because he was superior to both Israel and Judah's Priests. **And even Judah sang his praises among the other nations in their lands.**

I wrote all of this in order to show you as to what caused Prince Tyrus to lose his mind, to believe that he was a god. He became proud and arrogant, because all of these nations were doing business with him, and making him and his country rich and beautiful. **He was a master sorcerer. His witchcraft was above all of the various nation's wisemen.** Just in case you may doubt that this spiritual king/priest was indeed the wisest one in his time, read the next paragraph.

God goes on in verse 3, of chapter 28, "**BEHOLD THOU ART WISER THAN DANIEL, THERE IS NO SECRET THAT THEY CAN HIDE FROM THEE.**" But who in the world could this be? **Observe: the prophet Daniel...WAS A SPIRITUAL MAN AND A PROPHET. So if this Prince of Tyrus...was wiser than Daniel...Then he had to have been a spiritual man, or a prophet/ Priest.**

So, this prince was indeed a spiritual prince, and 'not' a physical prince who was heir to the throne of Tyre. **You have to be a spiritual man to be wiser than Daniel.** This is why I say **he was a Prince of a spiritual fraternity.**

The scripture says, no one was able to hide any secret from this Prince of Tyrus. Because of the power of his witchcraft no one could have out-smarted him. The scripture here is not talking about hiding any physical objects, but rather, spiritual secrets. So, if God said this prince was wiser than Daniel, then this man must have been very smart indeed. You'll soon see that he was a man and '**not Lucifer**'

In verse 4, God goes on to say to the Prince of Tyrus, "**With thy wisdom and with thine understanding, thou has gotten thee riches, and hast gotten gold and silver into thy treasures.**"

Verse 5, "**By thy great wisdom** and thy traffick (trading) hast thou increased thy riches and thy heart (mind) is lifted up because of thy riches."

Verse 6, "Therefore, thus saith the Lord God, because thou hast set thine heart as the heart of God."

Verse 7, "Behold, therefore I will bring strangers upon thee, the terrible of the nations: and they shall draw their swords **against thy beauty of thy wisdom.**"

God brought king Nebuchadnezzar from the north, and defiled the Prince of Tyrus' brightness. **That is, his influences and popularity in addition to the beauty of his city of Tyrus. GOD ISN'T TALKING ABOUT LUCIFER THE FALLEN ANGEL.!**

Ponder this: If God said that this Prince '**was a man**', who are we to say that he was a fallen angel or Lucifer?

Verse 8, They shall bring thee down to the pit, and thou shalt die the deaths of them that are slain in the midst of the Seas" (nations of people)

This is not satan/Lucifer. This prince was going to be brought down to the pit, or the grave. **And he was going to die...like a man, or like those persons who were slain, or killed in battle**"

Verse 9, "Wilt thou yet say before him that SLAYETH THEE, I AM GOD? but thou shalt be...a man and no god, in the hand of him THAT SLAYETH THEE"

You may wonder why am I stressing the point that this Prince was a man and 'not' Lucifer-seeing that it's obvious that the Prince of Tyrus was a man. I'm stressing this point because thousands of religious preachers are pontificating that this person who God was talking to was Lucifer.

Are you now convinced that those persons who say that this Ezekiel chapter 28, speaks to Lucifer are in error? As you have read where God says, **'that this Prince of Tyrus…'was a man' and he was going to die also…like a man.** So don't allow anyone to deceive you that this Prince was Lucifer. It's time for truth to be told so that up-coming young Pastors, or spiritual leaders, wouldn't be teaching errors.

Verse 10, "thou shalt 'DIE' the death of the uncircumcised by the hand of strangers: for I have spoken it saith the Lord.

Again, it shows that this Prince was a human being who was going to die the kind of death as a human. This also proves that this prince of Tyrus was a man, because God said that he was going to die the death as an uncircumcised man.

JUDGMENT ON THE KING OF TYRUS

Verse 11," Moreover, the word of the Lord came unto me saying," Verse 12, "Son of man, take up a lamentation upon **'the king of Tyrus'**, and say unto him, thus saith the Lord God; thou sealeth up the sum, **full of wisdom, and perfect beauty."**

Indeed, the king of Tyrus was full of wisdom as the Prince, or the high priest of Tyrus. And that the city Tyrus was a beautiful golden city. In verse 13, God is now going to talk to **'the king of Tyrus…who was a man also. He says,"** THOU HAST BEEN IN EDEN THE GARDEN OF GOD: every precious stone (gem) was thy covering; the Sardus, Topaz, and the Diamond, the Beryl, the Onyx, and the Jasper, the Sapphire, the Emerald, and the Carbuncle, and Gold: the workmanship **of thy TABRETS**

AND OF THY PIPE WAS PREPARED IN THEE IN THE DAY THAT THOU WAS CREATED."

It's this 13th. Verse which the scholars believe that speaks to Lucifer the fallen angel. But you'll see that it refers to **the king of Tyrus who was a man and not Lucifer.**

It's obvious that when God said, the workmanship of his Tabrets and of his pipes were prepared in this king of Tyrus, in the days he was created...didn't mean that his tabrets, or Tamarines and pipes, were inside of him. **Those musical instruments were made for him and his kingdom. Pipes were made for playing music.**

You see, in the same way that the gem-stone was shaped and fashioned for the king of Tyrus in the beginning of his reign, **so were the Tabrets which were musical Tambourines and his musical pipes for dancing and enjoyment. Those Tabrets, or Tamberrines and pipes were INTRICATELY DESIGNED. They were very stylish.** These were designed when he was created. That is, **WHEN HE WAS ANOINTED, OR MADE, OR BECAME THE KING OF TAURUS.**

Note again for emphasis: God keeps telling all who want to listen **that the king of Tyrus, 'WAS A MAN'** He wasn't created as Adam was, but he was born of a woman. Not as Lucifer who was made out of gold. Note: In the day he was created means, **IN THE DAY HE BECAME KING, OR WAS CROWNED OR WAS ANOINTED AS KING.**

This king of Tyrus was decked-out with ten (10) precious gem-stones. And God also had Tabrets, or beautiful Tambourines, and musical pipes and other instruments of music, made for celebrations, or for the coronations of the king: But in the end, he disappointed God.

In addition to having these ten (10) precious gem-stones **in his kingly crown, he also had rhinestones embedded in his kingly robe.** He was trying to be like a glittering star, which shines at night. Those stones which were embedded in his robes glittered, especially when he would move around. These precious gem-stones, sparkled and glowed as he slid here and there. Indeed, he was covered all over with precious gem-stones.

Even a Peacock with its colorful and beautiful feathers opened-up, was not as beautiful as his kingly robe was. But his problem was, **he wanted to compare himself with God's beauty.** However, apparently he forgot that he was born from a woman, and not beamed-down from heaven. He forgot he came hollering and screaming when he came into this world.

As you can see, we are talking about a human man all along. So the rest of the verses from 14-19, are still speaking about **the same man, and not a fallen angel, or Lucifer.** I hope I've convinced you thus far that the king of Tyrus was a human man and not Lucifer as being preached.

PROOF: EDEN WAS JERUSALEM

Put on your thinking cap and make your own decision as to if ' Eden' is the same land as Old Jerusalem. Let's now reason together: **If the king of Tyrus had been 'In Eden' the Garden of God, as the scripture states in Ezekiel 28:13, Then I put it to you that the Garden of God was in Jerusalem.**

We must remember that I've proven that the king of Tyrus was a man. So if he was a man who **was in Eden, the Garden of God, then Jerusalem, had to have been the land of Eden.**

Now, let's continue to Ezekiel chapter 28:14. Here, God is still addressing the same king of Tyrus.

Verse 14, "Thou art the anointed cherub that covereth: and I have set thee so: thou was (past tense) upon the holy mountain of God: thou hast walked up and down in the midst of the stones of fire."

This king of Tyrus, was indeed a king that was anointed by God. He was 'like a cherub (angel) which glows like a meteorite bright star....and he was covered all over with precious gem-stones and gold, as stated before.

This Cherub was not Lucifer. The scripture keeps saying... THAT THIS SAME KING WAS A MAN. We can't lose sight of this reality. So the king of Tyrus...WAS LIKE A BRIGHT CHERUB.

It was God who had made the king of Tyrus beautiful. And it was God who had him anointed as king and covered him all over with the ten (10) precious gem-stone on his kingly crown, and on his robes. Here are a few questions which should give you some insights that Eden was the old City of Jerusalem. So southeast Jerusalem, is a very important site.

Where was the Holy Mountain of God? And what was the name of the Holy Mountain where God dwelt? Here's the answer: the Holy Mountain of God' was Mount Moriah'. And it was located within ancient Old Jerusalem on top of the Mountain of Moriah/ Zion, where Abraham attempted to sacrifice his son Isaac. This proves that the man: king of Tyrus, 'was on God's Mountain of Moriah, which was in Eden, The Garden of God, which was ancient Jerusalem.

Put another way: the king of Tyrus was in Eden the Garden of God, and on the Holy Mountain of God...but we know that the Holy Mountain of God Was in Jerusalem. Therefore, this proves that Eden...was the same land of Jerusalem. And the Garden had to have been in Jerusalem.

Know this truth: Eden was Jerusalem, and the Garden was planted at the southeastern part of Jerusalem below Mount Moriah as you already know. This is why king Solomon built the Jewish Temple at the East...in Jerusalem facing the sunrise– in the same way Moses says that the Garden was planted Eastward in Eden. coincidence? Oh no! This is also why God sent his friend Abraham to the land of Moriah, and told him that he will show him (Abraham) the Mountain to go up, to sacrifice his son Isaac. And this Mountain, or hill was the mount of Moriah where Abraham wrote the words, 'Jehovah-Jireh-' The Lord will provide'

BACK TO KING TYRUS

God goes on to say to king Tyrus in verse 15, "Thou was perfect in thy way from the day thou was created, till iniquity was found in thee." King Tyrus was perfect in his way from the day he was anointed as king, and kept the way of the Lord...until he became prideful, then God had to deal with him by getting rid of him. Like king Uzziah who was perfect in his way – that is, he did everything right to please God at the beginning of his kingship, **until he became arrogant and tried to burn incense in the Jewish Temple of God.** This sacrifice in the Temple was only for the office of the Priest. 'Not the king.'

However, this Jewish king Uzziah, felt that he could have done anything he wanted to do, because after all, he was the king. **But God struck him with the mark of leprosy instantly in his forehead.** So king Uzziah had to be a vagabond in the earth. King Uzziah had to move from house to house because of the plague of leprosy.

King Tyrus, just like king David who also was anointed and innocent, and perfect in his way and was chosen by God-did well in the beginning of his reign, But. he ended-up committing many sins, to the extent that he became unfit to build God's Temple. David also sinned by eating...the show-bread of the Temple which was only for the Priest. But he wasn't struck with leprosy like king Uzziah, because he and his soldiers were hungry. (Like Cain?)

David also sinned by causing the death of Uriah, the Hittite; then took his wife. And he sinned by numbering the Israelites. In short, David shed too much innocent blood. This is why he suffered so much as a king, **because God doesn't compromise with unrighteousness.... Unrighteousness is never on the table for discussion.**

Likewise, the king of Tyrus started out pleasing God, until he became so rich and powerful, that he believed that he had arrived, to the position...not only as a god, But as Israel's God himself. He had gone too far. He had crossed the line. He made the same error as Lucifer. The prophet Ezekiel didn't say that king Tyrus was Lucifer. However, he referred to him as being prideful and wicked as Lucifer. So the preachers should take another look at what the prophet said.

In verse 16, God goes on to address the king of Tyrus by saying: "By the multitude of thy merchandise, they have filled the midst of thee with violence, **and thou hast sinned: therefore, will I cast thee as profane...OUT OF THE MOUNTAIN OF GOD: and I will destroy thee, O COVERING CHERUB, from the midst of the stones of fire"**

It was by the abundance of king Tyrus' wealth, which caused him to sin against God. Apparently, he couldn't handle his wealth, and his influences which went along with it...even though he was a wise man. But his wisdom caused his destruction. This wisdom he had was how to extract the wealth from those nations mentioned before who traded with him.

As a result of his abundance of wealth, he got caught right up along with those nations' merchants, by craftiness and violence. **So God had to get rid of him, by casting him out of his Holy Mountain of Moriah, which was / is in Jerusalem/ Eden.** God removed him from among **'The stones of fire.** In other words, he was cut off from among the fraternities of the kings. The kings were, and still are, 'STONES OF FIRE. To be a true king, one must be anointed and given a crown of gold...BUT THE CROWN MUST HAVE STONES OF FIRES, that is, precious gem-stones which are really, THE POWERS OF THE CROWN OF THE KINGS.

Know this: there are spirits of the gem-stones, and in them. All gem-stones contain a spirit. So the king of Tyrus was covered with the ten(10) precious gem-stones. That is, he was covered by ten spirits of fires. Now you know as to why kings have precious gem-stones in their crown, which crowns are made of gold. The gold and gem-stones are spiritual.

Moses' brother Aaron, who was the Israelites' high Priest, had twelve (12) precious gem-stones embedded on a gold plate, hanging and resting on his chest. Do not think they were only for beauty. They were twelve (12) spirits in twelve different kinds of stones. Each stone had a spirit embedded in it. And each spirit was different from the other one. EACH SPIRIT REPRESENTED EACH OF THE TWELVE (12) TRIBES OF ISRAEL. That is, a gem-stone for Reuben, Simeon etc.

In the past in the USA, in the west, when some men would have discovered gold, they would even kill their friend to possess it. It's true that some became overjoyed because of its value, realizing that they are now rich...This is partly true, but really it's because the spirit of gold has an intangible effect on their spirit or psyche.

Again, in the west, in the USA, in the old days, if a gold prospector would have discovered a stash of a million dollars in paper money, he would have been excited and happy. But if the Old-timer found gold valued a million dollars, most likely, he would have laughed and cried all at the same time. Once he looked at it, he would have become hypnotized and got kind of crazy. But why didn't he laugh and cry when he would have found the million dollars in paper money? What is it with gold that would cause your heart to pulsate and skip a beat, more than the paper money?

In Genesis 2:11-12, Moses writes about the name of the first river and about gold. He writes "The name of the first is Pison: (river) that is it which compasseth the whole land 'of Havilah', **'where there is gold."**

Verse 12, "And the gold of that land is good: There is bdellium and the onyx (beryl) stone "Even though Moses meant that the gold and the precious gem-stones were beautiful and costly, however, **it is the spirits of these gem-stones and gold, which make them so good and beautiful.**

THE MOTHER OF THE PRECIOUS GEM-STONES

The city of New Jerusalem above is the mother of the precious gem-stones and gold. Here's how the apostle John sees it in the first century in his vision, **He writes in Revelation 21:18, And the building of the wall of it was of Jasper: and the city was pure gold, like unto clear glass."** Could you imagine a wall? 144 cubits / 216 ft. composed of pure Jasper? What a powerful spirit it must have possessed.

Verse 19, "And the foundation of the wall of the city were garnished with all manner of precious gem-stones."

John goes on to enumerate the twelve (12) precious gem-stones of which the foundation of the wall is garnished. So how could the king of Tyrus with his little ten (10) pieces of gem-stones, compare himself with God, who owns a city of pure gold, and a wall of 144 cubits / 216ft. Garnished with twelve (12) heavenly gem-stones, in addition to heavenly pearls?

Now, in verse 17, God continues to judge the king of Tyrus."
Thine heart/mind was lifted-up because of thy brightness" **I will
cast thee to the ground, I will lay thee before kings, that they
behold thee".**
Let me prove to you that God was not talking to Lucifer, the
devil, but rather, to king Tyrus.. 'a man.' God says in verse 17, 'I
will cast thee to the ground, I will lay thee before kings. Here is
your proof: During this time, God was speaking...Lucifer had
already fallen from heaven, thousands of years prior.

Do you see that God through The prophet Ezekiel was
referring to the king of Tyrus who was a man? It was also because
of the king's brightness, or popularity which caused him to sin.
**So God cast him to the ground, so that the various kings with
whom he traded, who made him rich, would behold, or see,
him DEAD, and his city/Tyrus/Tyre in ruin and in desolation.**

Some preachers say that Ezekiel was addressing Lucifer the
devil. But how could this be true, when God himself said, **"that
he was going to cast him to the ground so that the various
kings with whom he traded would see him dead?** So reader,
if God threw this angel Lucifer to the ground **to be seen by
human beings,** then the question is, How did he look when he
fell? Was he like a gem-stone, gold, iron, rock or what? Know
this: Lucifer was an evil spiritual being, and the kings of the
earth had never traded with him nor seen him. It was the human
man, king Tyrus with whom they traded.

God continues to address The king of Tyrus through Ezekiel.
Verse 18, "Thou hast defiled thy sanctuary by the multitude
of thine iniquities, by the iniquity **of thy traffic"** (tradings)
**Therefore I will bring forth...a fire from the midst of thee, it
shall devour thee, AND I WILL BRING THEE TO ASHES
UPON THE EARTH...IN THE SIGHT OF ALL THEM
THAT BEHOLD (see) THEE"**

Fact: history shows that the city of Tyrus/Tyre Was **destroyed with fire after king Nebuchadnezzar had attacked it...and it did become ashes, just as God said.**
So the people who saw the city of Tyre in ruin, lamented for it, just as when God brought king Cyrus to Babylon and destroyed it...then the people from home and abroad lamented over Babylon. So tell me, Do you still believe that it was Lucifer whom God had addressed, or the king of Tyrus?
Ponder this next paragraph: L Verse 19, "**All they that know thee among the people shall be astonished at thee: thou shall be a terror and never shalt thou be anymore**". If this person was the angel Lucifer, how is it that verse 19, says, '**All they 'that know thee'...among the people...shall be astonished at thee?** This would have to mean that the people had to **have seen Lucifer before with their eyes, in order to recognize him. But you see the people never saw Lucifer before personally. So all of this is to show you that it was not Lucifer whom God addressed, but rather the king of Tyrus.**
It's important for me to set the record straight before I leave this earth, because too many preachers are teaching that God; through Ezekiel was addressing Lucifer the fallen angel rather than the king of Tyre. Hopefully, this chapter would cause all to see the light and truth that it was the king of Tyrus whom the prophet addressed. It was this king who was wicked as Lucifer was wicked. And just like the Assyrian kings who were addressed as serpents.. Not that they were serpents, but their actions and behaviours were like the ways of the wicked and cunning serpent.

CHAPTER 13

THE TRUTH ABOUT THE FORBIDDEN FRUIT ADAM AND EVE ATE – FINALLY REVEALED

Your eyes will now be opened to the new truthful knowledge which has not been told fully to you, as it relates to Adam and Eve in the Garden of the Lord in Palestine. Moses gives us the narrative to the best of his knowledge and understanding, as to what happened in the Garden of the Lord/Eden in reference to Adam, Eve, and the Serpent.

Every time a preacher tells the story about Adam and Eve, he would always skirt around telling you directly what was the fruit they ate...and would never tell you what the tree of knowledge of Good and evil, and the tree of Life are.

Moses indicates that it was the devil who possessed the serpent's body in order to communicate to Eve. These events took place in the Garden of Eden...which Eden was Jerusalem. And they took place **'below' Mount Moriah, or 'below' the Temple-Mount... South East in Jerusalem, where the tree of life was planted.**

Now the serpent or the devil knew exactly where the 'Tree of Life was planted, but he wanted Eve to take off the wrong tree first, which was the tree of knowledge of good and evil. He knew that once she would've eaten of this tree first, then God would have chased her out of his Garden. He knew that God doesn't compromise with righteousness. He knew that God would not have allowed her to remain in his Garden in a sinful condition, and live forever.

The serpent just wanted to ruin God's plan by having righteous children. He wanted Adam and Eve to sin against God, just as he had sinned against him. Remember however, that this action of the serpent was the desire of the devil. Moses records in Genesis chapter 3:1: "Now the serpent was more subtle than any beast of the field which the Lord God had made. And he said unto the woman, yes, had God said, ye shall not eat of every tree of the Garden?

The devil looked for the most clever creature to possess in order to communicate with Eve. He looked for the creature which was wise and cunning, and compatible with his own nature. He found such a creature that was as close to human being as possible, **and one that was walking on its feet like a man.** But of course, not a natural man.

Know this: the original serpent which was walking in the Garden, was a good serpent, **'before the devil or Belial contaminated his body. This serpent was a male creature,** one that both Adam and Eve would've seen before and known, **How do I know this? Well, because it was Adam who gave him his name…'serpent'. Don't forget it was Adam who named all of the creatures in the beginning when everything which God made was good. So the serpent in the beginning was a good one.**

From the beginning it was the serpent who was next to man, or Adam in wisdom. The serpent was always a symbol of wisdom, authority, power and skill. This is also why God gave Moses… **A ROD OF A SERPENT AND OF POWER TO PERFORM MIRACLES.**

If you would remember from the scripture, that when Moses met God on Mount Horeb, in the burning bush. Now when he threw down his rod on the ground, as God told him to do, 'IT TURNED INTO A SERPENT'. After picking it back up, it returned to his stick, or shepherd's rod. Strangely enough, THIS WAS THE SAME ROD WITH WHICH HE DID HIS MIRACLES. So Moses' power was his rod of a snake.

Note this: The scepters which kings and priests used as their power, in reality, was the spirit of a serpent or snake. But it represented power. When kings in ancients days would've pointed his scepter, or serpent to an individual, it would've indicated, life, death, blessings, curses, or 'step forward.'

So the serpent in the Garden was a crafty and a wise one... of course not as wise, or crafty as Lucifer/the devil. But his form in the garden was somewhat different before he was cursed and began to crawl.

Let's not forget that Jesus told his apostles: To be wise as serpents, but harmless as a dove. But why would Jesus use a serpent or a snake, as being a symbol of wisdom, if it wasn't true? But the fact is, it is indeed a symbol of wisdom.

When king Hezekiah of Judah came to power, he did all that the Lord told him to do. He destroyed the brazen serpent which Moses had made in the wilderness.

2 kings 18:4 records: "He removed the high places, and brake the image, and cut down the groves, and brake in pieces the brazen serpent that Moses had made: for unto those days the children of Israel did burn incense to it: and called it 'NE-HUSH-TAN' '

In the process of time the Israelites used the serpent to perform sorceries. They worshipped the serpent Moses had Made in the wilderness to heal the people who were bitten by serpents; so Hezekiah destroyed it.

This shows that power can be used for good or evil. It all depends on the purpose you use it for. The serpent or the devil's whole intention was to ruin God's plans from the very beginning. He was jealous of Adam, because God had turned the planet-earth over to him, and had taken it away from himself. However, in the process of time, even after the flood of Noah, man still allowed Lucifer to control the powers of the earth-because they continued to be servants to him. This is why God had to scatter them from Babylon/Shinah.

The devil even reminded Jesus that he himself had the power and authority to give him Jesus, power over the nations – because the power was given to him...and he had the power to give to whosoever he so desire.

Before God had created Adam and Eve, **Lucifer was the bright and morning star of the earth, He was the light-bringer. The planet Venus or morning star symbolizes Lucifer. He was the first to bring light to the planet. He was the representative of the earth, AND PRINCE OF THE AIR, OR SPACE ABOVE IT. HOWEVER, JESUS IS NOW THE BRIGHT AND MORNING STAR IN GOD'S NEW EARTH ABOVE. WHICH IS GOD'S NEW CREATION ABOVE.**

This is why Jesus said that he who overcomes this world's evil, he will give him...'THE MORNING STAR'. Note: not the morning star of this earth, or Venus, but the one that is above. Jesus means that he will cause them to shine as the morning stars above in the spiritual realm in the spiritual New earth, **with New Jerusalem in the middle of it. Jesus did say: "My kingdom is not of this world"** However, even though his kingdom is not of this world, that is, **not set upon earth-he still holds the power over all the earth.** Jesus said to his apostle after he arose from the dead. **"ALL POWER IS NOW GIVEN UNTO ME BOTH IN HEAVEN AND EARTH" Matthew chapter 28: 18.**

Now what made Satan angry and mad at God was he turned the planet earth over to Adam. And worse than that,,,God gave Adam the power to name all of the creatures. But even worse, **God had even created Adam not only in his image like that of a man...but in his own likeness. That is, to look exactly like God's spitting likeness.** Yes, Lucifer was jealous of Adam because he was created like God, but he himself was not.

Lucifer **'was'** the controller of planet earth until he rebelled against God. In the beginning, God gave Lucifer **A SLICE OF PORKCHOP (earth)** but because of avarice or greed, he wasn't satisfied, **BUT HE WANTED 'THE WHOLE HOG':** that is, **THE WHOLE GALAXIES OR HEAVEN OF HEAVENS.** As a result of his greed, God kicked him out of the heavens, and deprived him of **being master of the earth. In the process of time, he is now taking-up residence in hell, and being dictated to by a hybrid female demon, whose name is SEMIRAMIS, NIMROD'S MOTHER, WHO WAS A FORMER HIGH PRIESTESS, WHO ONCE SERVED AND WORSHIPPED HIM. The devil is now the servant of his secretary in hell.**

This is the divine truth. The Lord God Almighty had allowed my spirit-man to see in my dream, many years ago as to how **a female human...yet part demon, defeated the devil-and as to the manner in which she destroyed him.** Even today as you read this book, **he is only a greyish golden – body, marred with dross in hell. So his former golden body can't shine anymore. 'THE LORD GOD BEAR ME WITNESS TO THE TRUTHFULNESS OF MY WORDS'.**

Here we have the serpent using **psychology on Eve,** by asking her if it were **'every tree'** that God commanded her not to eat from. Here is Eve's response in verse 2, "And the woman said unto the serpent, "We may eat of the fruit of the tree of

the garden"...She goes on in verse 3, **But of the fruit of the tree which is in the middle of the garden, God had said, ye shall not eat of it, neither shall ye touch it, lest ye die".**
Know this truth: Adam and Eve WERE THE TREE OF KNOWLEDGE OF GOOD AND EVIL THEMSELVES. Eve told the serpent that indeed, God told them that they could eat of every tree in the garden, **but this special fruit on this special tree (metaphorically) God said don't even touch it.: and don't eat of it, or you will die.** Adam and Eve were metaphorically referred to as trees, **BUT THE FRUIT OF THE TREE, AS THEIR SEX ORGANS.**

Now, the serpent responds to Eve in verse 4, "And the serpent said unto the woman," **ye shall not surely die."** The serpent had the nerve to tell Eve that God had told her a lie. Of course, this was very disrespectful, and insulting to God. But he being a merciful God, gave the serpent or the devil, **a long rope with a short catch'.** That is, many years to live freely, before he God, yanked the rope which was around his neck.

Before I continue to relate to you about the serpent's rudeness, as it relates to deceiving the woman Eve, Know this: **THE DEVIL / LUCIFER IS NO LONGER IN THE EARTH REALM. Even though his star Venus, or the morning star, still rises and sets. If truth be told again, He is in hell being dictated to by a female hybrid woman. She was the one who finally defeated him in hell, after Jesus Christ, or the seed of the woman had cast him down there.**

Because he had deceived a woman to ruin the earth...in the end, it was a female who had finally defeated him. One may wonder by asking: If the devil is in hell, why is there so much evil in the earth? First of all, **The morning star still rises and casts its influences on the earth while it goes from east to west: then circles around again to the east.**

Secondly: the original powers of darkness are still, not only here, but in the total universe. **It is part of what makes up the universe. If there is no darkness, there can be no universe. It was this kingdom which Lucifer had joined into, after God had expelled him from his heaven and stripped him from being the power of this physical earth.** Remember this: the powers of darkness were always in existence, **BEFORE GOD SAID, "LET THERE BE LIGHT" so the light came out of the darkness, in the same way you came out of the darkness from your mother's womb...and born into the light of day. But night or darkness was the first. And will be forever in the universe. But in God's case, he had created the light within the womb of the darkness.**

Know this too: Not only the darkness will never go away, it cannot go away. If it were to go away – the question is, to where will it go? So don't curse the darkness, just light the candle of God.

Thirdly: It's not God, nor the powers of darkness forcing you to do good or evil, the freedom of choice is in your hands. You have the power of choice to choose good or evil-light or darkness. However, there are consequences for your choices, because choices are decided upon...before action is activated. Even king David talked about how God's habitation is surrounded by darkness. Again, don't curse the darkness.

Okay: Now the serpent continues to accuse God by telling Eve that God had lied to her.

Verse 5," For God doth know that in the day ye eat thereof, then your eyes shall be opened, and ye shall be 'AS GODS', knowing good and evil."

The serpent says to Eve, "It's not true that you will die if you were to eat of the tree. In fact, God knows that on the day **you partake of this tree, your spiritual eyes would be opened**... not their physical eyes, because their physical eyes were always opened. But the serpent was referring to...Eve's mind's eyes...and her mind's eyes were indeed opened after she and Adam ate the forbidden fruit.

First of all, The serpent being crafty as he was, **told Eve the truth, and a lie at the same time.** When Eve took off the forbidden fruit of this special tree, she didn't drop-down dead, because when she partook of it with the serpent she didn't drop-down dead Even when she partook of it with her husband, Adam, they still didn't drop-down dead. **However, their spiritual covering dropped off.**

Question: Did Adam and Eve die when they ate off the forbidden fruit? I put it to you,'**that they did die'.** That is, they began to die from the day onward until they dropped-down dead and turned to dust.

Think about this: if you cut off a branch from a tree, or its source, the branch would automatically die the second you cut it off from the tree, despite the fact the branch may still look green and vibrant. (just like a zombie, living but yet dead). But as time goes on, you would notice that the branch begins to wither and eventually turn to dust, So Adam and Eve died in the same way in the day they ate from the forbidden fruit...from their own bodies. **So, like the branch – they were cut off from the spiritual life-force, or source from God.** Then as time went on-like the branch, they began **to wither or wrinkle,** and they eventually turned to dust as they were in the beginning when God had created them. **So they died on the day they ate from the forbidden fruit of their bodies. So God is vindicated.**

THEIR MIND'S EYES WERE INDEED OPENED AND THEY GAINED INSIGHT

Here is what happened when Adam and Eve ate the forbidden fruit of the tree of the knowledge of good and evil. The first massive civil war broke-out in their bodies. Now, when Adam released his sperms for the first time...but Eve for the second time...because her first time was with the serpent, **their neurons, or brain cells became confused, because they were ejected out of the regular rotation in their brains.** It was like getting 'the first hit' of cocaine. And they never experienced that same intense sexual thrill again. But they kept trying.

Know this: Their brain cells were knocked out of orbit, as a result a new abnormal circuitry path in their brains came into existence. So the universe in their brains were altered, so it's no longer aligned with the spiritual universe. This is because their brain cells got short-circuited and were disconnected from God's glory which covered them as a glow, that is, they blew a fuse in their brains and their light went out.

Not only did their brain cells get confused when they released their sperms and eggs for the first time, but all of their cells in their bodies began fighting one another. A declaration of civil war was automatically declared and began. Yes, total war broke-out throughout their bodies. The red cells, white cells, T cells, and all of the cells got confused and began to attack one another. As a result, the death process of their bodies began. And it continues even up to this day.

While some cells automatically died, some began to be created on their own. **But more cells were aging or dying than the new ones being formed. And there was a mutation of the cells.** However, Eve had already experienced her sexual encounter during the time she was deceived by the serpent. This is how she knew that the fruit, or the sex-act was sweet, and persuaded Adam to eat of it, that is, to perform the sex-act with her.

When Adam and Eve saw that they didn't die when they ate the fruit of the tree of knowledge of good and evil which were their bodies, they might have thought that the serpent, or the devil was right, because they didn't drop down dead.

The serpent, being as wise as he was, knew that once Adam and Eve, took of the sex-act, and would spill their sperm and eggs **(like 'Onan,' Judah's son)** he would have them hook, **then a massive civil war of good and evil would break-out in their bodies,** and they would have eventually died. Then God's plan would have been ruined. You see, Satan was jealous of God's physical son and daughter who were created in his own image and likeness. He hated Adam with a passion because when he sees him, he sees the likeness of God. But he didn't hate Eve yet, because she was created after the image and likeness of God's wife-his **Shekinah Glory who was Mother Nature of the earth, and Queen and Goddess of heaven.**

The serpent was indeed successful in ruining God's plans, by causing Eve, and by extension, **Adam to become zombies. That is, 'walking dead people'. As a result, the whole world became a world of zombies, or walking dead people.** So if one wants to become alive, **the only way out,** is to allow doctor Jesus Christ Eliakim, to inject one with the Holy Spirit of God, **which is the living water, or antidote, or vaccine.** Of course only if one wants to go where he is **in the New Earth above which is also in the Heavens.**

Now the serpent spoke a half-truth to Eve. Here is the truthful part he told her. **'That they will be 'AS GODS...TO KNOW GOOD AND EVIL'.** Yes, their minds' eyes **were truly opened when they had engaged in the sex act.** Why do I say 'Half-truth'? **Well, Right away, after the sex act, Adam's eyes were opened for the first time, and he realized that he was naked. That is, he noticed that the glow of light, or his covering had gradually disappeared.**

Again, Eve's eyes had already been opened from the time she engaged in the sex-act with the serpent before. **Her eyes** were opened 'before' Adam's mind's eyes, because she knew, or had the knowledge that the' FORBIDDEN FRUIT' was good for spiritual food, and her body or tree was to be desired 'BEFORE' she returned home to Adam. In fact, it was Eve who had returned home with this new found knowledge, and convinced Adam 'to eat it also with her.'

The mere fact that she admitted to God that it was 'the serpent' who had deceived, or beguiled her…PROVES THAT SHE WAS EXPOSED TO THE EATING OF THE FORBIDDEN FRUIT OF THE TREE, 'BEFORE SHE ATE IT WITH HER HUSBAND ADAM.

Do you see that Eve ate the fruit of the tree 'before Adam did'? But with who? Do you think that the devil would only told Eve about the use of the fruit, and not demonstrate, as to how to use it? The serpent told Eve that God knew that if she ate of the fruit, **that she shall be as Gods, knowing good and evil.** The serpent was one hundred (100%) percent right with this statement. He mixed truth and lies together and was successful. I will prove it to you soon. Bear in mind, at this time we only have Eve and the serpent in this scene. Here is what Moses writes in Genesis 3:16: "**And when the woman saw that the tree was god for food, and that it was pleasant to the eyes, and a tree to be desired to make one wise**" she took of the fruit thereof,…'AND DID EAT."

Observe the word, 'ALSO'. This shows that Eve did something, then gave Adam a piece of that something also. Note the word 'also' is an after action. So it was after she took off the fruit of the tree, that she gave her husband **also.** When the woman saw that the tree was good for food, and that it was pleasant to the eyes…that is, 'to lust over', she took off the fruit and did eat off it. Question, is Adam here at this time? The answer is 'NO' So bear in mind that in this scene, Adam wasn't there when she was being educated about this tree and its fruit which she took off and did eat. So it was only 'AFTER' she returned home to Adam that she ate from the fruit 'AGAIN', but this time,' WITH HIM'.

Observe: when Eve was engaged in the sex act with the serpent, ' there was a chemical imbalance took place in her brain. Her whole body had experienced a thrill that she never had experienced before and never had experienced that level of thrill again. So she wanted Adam to experience and to enjoy this newly found thrill. This is why Adam complained to God and said that it was the woman who made him eat off the fruit.

EVE GOT SWUNG OR DECEIVED

First, you must remember that you have a powerful fallen son of God who knew the workings of the Gods, speaking through a serpent's body, who knew the workings of heaven and the Gods. He was like the angel of the Lord who spoke to Balim through a donkey. Now this powerful being was using the highest degree of psychology to deceive and to trick this innocent young woman. And he was successful using his brand of sorceries.

Even though Eve was created with the body of a full woman, she didn't have the knowledge of a full grown woman, because her brain wasn't uploaded with experiences, activities and events. But instead, she was as a young child.

SCENE NUMBER TWO

The scene now shifts to Eve going back home, to encourage her husband Adam, to try-out the forbidden fruit. After persuading Adam, by causing him to partake of the forbidden fruit off the forbidden tree, they now eat the fruit together.

Don't forget, the scripture says,'" **she gave 'also' unto her husband.** Again, the word 'also' indicates that she took off the fruit first, then after experiencing the thrilling effect...**then she gave a piece of the fruit to her husband.** So the word 'also' should tell you **that Eve had to have taken, or eaten of this fruit...'before' she gave Adam a bite (yes?)**

Think about this: if Adam were there when the serpent was tricking or talking to his wife, and telling her about the forbidden tree and the use of its fruit...**then Eve wouldn't have to tell Adam about the fruit of the tree. But why not? Well, because Adam would have already heard what the serpent would have said.**So you see, Adam was not there with Eve and the serpent **when she saw that the fruit was desirable, and she did eat of it.** Now, 'did eat' means to activate her sex organ. So if you can agree that Eve had activated her sex organ, or her fruit, then it begs the question! Who did she had sex with?

Now there are no rational reasonable responses but to conclude that it had to have been with the serpent if Adam wasn't there...unless you believe that she was the first woman to sexually stimulate herself. This last option is unlikely because the serpent's plan was not only to get Eve to sin against God, But Adam also, so that the whole plan of God would be ruined, and so that he himself would be the father of the first hybrid human beings. And indeed he did become the father of the hybrid human **through Cain.** Now it wasn't until 130 years later, after the creation of Adam, that Seth became the second natural human being after Abel.

SCENE NUMBER TWO CONTINUES

It's not only me who believes that Adam wasn't there with Eve and the serpent, but St, Paul also believes this. He put the blame on Eve, But Adam was also guilty of sin, because God put him in charge of the physical Garden. So Adam was also punished for disobeying God by eating the forbidden fruit before God told them to go ahead. I'm saying that Adam was a criminal because he was found guilty for committing an ungodly sin-then was judged, and sent into exile **to do hard labor by the sweat of his face.** Adam was like a man who had committed a crime in a foreign country (Eden/Jerusalem). Then after being found guilty, he was deported back to his country, which was '**The City-Adam', near Zarethan, and Beth-shean, which was below Jez-reel, in the area of the Jordan Valley to the north in Israel.**

Here is what St. Paul told Bishop Timothy in 1, Timothy chapter 2:13-14. "For Adam was first formed, then Eve"verse 14, "**And Adam was not deceived but the woman being deceived... was in the transgression'"**

Again, Adam wasn't deceived by the serpent, so he couldn't have been the first one to eat from the forbidden tree. So Adam couldn't have been present while the serpent was deceiving Eve. So what I'm saying? Simply this, **that Eve ate the fruit, not only...in front of the serpent, but with him first.**

Here is what St. Paul says to the Christians in Corinth: "2,Corinthians 11:2-3," For I am jealous over you with Godly jealousy: for I have espoused you to one husband that I may present you **as a chase woman to Christ."** St. Paul wanted to espouse, or to present the Christians of Corinth, to one husband as a chase, or pure virgin to Jesus Christ. **Now watch St. Paul's contrast to Eve who was not a chase, or pure virgin TO ONE MAN, or to Adam.** It should be obvious that St. Paul was making reference to Eve as cheating on her husband.

St Paul knew that Eve wasn't a pure virgin to Adam. So who caused her to be an impure virgin to her husband? **Who caused her to lose her virginity? So if she was an impure virgin**

as Paul says, shouldn't this indicate that She lost her virginity with the serpent? And if this is true, doesn't this show that when she had this sexual affair with the serpent, that She got pregnant with Cain? (yes?)

Why would Paul talk about a pure virgin as being presented to Christ – if Eve was a pure virgin to Adam? Paul didn't want the Church at Corinth to be an impure virgin to Christ – as Eve was an impure virgin to her husband. IF EVE WAS A PURE VIRGIN TO ADAM, THEN ST, PAUL WOULD HAVE NO REASON TO MAKE A COMPARISON TO THE CHURCH ABOUT EVE'S IMPURITY.

Here is the definition of a virgin: "One who has never engaged in sexual intercourse...So why would St. Paul used the word, "Virgin", or a woman who had never engaged in sexual intercourse with the church which was classified as a woman-and the physical woman Eve-if it wasn't a sexual intercourse which Eve had engaged with the serpent? This is why Cain was her first born son...and the wicked one.

Think about this: The serpent just didn't tell Eve about this fruit, and the use of the tree...but he had demonstrated it with her as to how she should have used it with Adam 'also,' when she would've returned home. So there is no reasonable question, that Eve ate the fruit 'BEFORE' she returned home to Adam.

When Eve returned home to Adam, she was now a wise woman with insight. She now knows all about her newly found knowledge about having sex. She now understands more about the art and movements of this tree and its fruit-that is, about the use of her body and sex organ. Because after attending classes with the serpent, or the devil, she is now a smart student. But little did she know that she was playing 'the devil's roulette' with the devil himself. (poor child)

Eve's fault was, she listened to another voice instead of God's voice. Now with this newly found awareness of her body, and being told how great it was, she couldn't wait to get back to Adam **To pose before him and to do ' the cat-walk...naked.** She is now really naked with not even a fig leaf to cover her fruit. So what we have here is that Adam is now **'The student' and Eve is 'the tutor' in the art of having sex,** or the eating of the fruit from the tree of knowledge of good and evil-which was really, her own body. What Eve didn't realize was that when the serpent was demonstrating with her as to how to operate the forbidden fruit and the tree, **his seed or sperm was planted in her womb.** You'll see later where God would talk to Eve about, "her seed (child) and the serpent's seed or children.

You should know that if the sons of God were able to marry and had sex and children with the human women...as Moses says in Genesis chapter 6:1-2, then surely, Satan being a powerful fallen son of God, could have performed sex with Eve. Do you see that the fruit of the tree of the knowledge of good and evil, had to do with sex?

Verse 3, St. Paul goes on to admonish the church at Corinth: **"But I fear, lest by any mean, AS THE SERPENT BEGUILED EVE THROUGH HIS SUBTLETY (craftiness) so your minds should be corrupted from the simplicity that is in Christ."**

St. Paul was afraid that after he would have departed, or died, then another voice might have come and deceived them. Just like the serpent's voice who spoke to Eve. Paul was warning these Corinthian Christians, not to listen to no other voice, but to his, and of course, the apostles. He was warning them, **he knew that Eve had listened to another voice other than God's voice or command...that is...don't eat the fruit yet.** I quoted this so that you may see that Adam wasn't deceived. But his sin was that of disobedience to God's command. Therefore, it was Eve who was deceived, as Paul says, **then while she was being deceived by the serpent...then Adam couldn't have been present at that time.**

So if this is true what Paul says, then it proves that Eve had to have eaten the forbidden fruit with the serpent. And if this is true as I believe it is, **then she had to have gotten pregnant as a result. And produced her first son Cain, the first giant on the earth, then to be followed with the other sons of God who also came to earth and procreated, and caused the second sets of giants on the earth. Genesis 6: 1-2.** Here is what John says to the Christian' Saints about Cain. I John chapter 3:11-12, "For this is the message that ye heard from the beginning; that we should love one another."

Verse 12, **"Not as Cain who was of that wicked one (Satan) and slew his brother.** And wherefore (why?) slew him? Because his own works '**were evil' and his brother's righteous"**

Observe: Cain was the son of the evil one, because the evil one, or the devil was his father. Cain was the father of the first hybrid human giants.

Even though Moses says Adam knew his wife and she begat a son, he knew quite well Adam thought Cain was his son. But I feel certain after a while, Adam realized that when Eve ate the fruit with the serpent, or when she had sex with him, she got pregnant, or was conceived. **If you don't believe Cain wasn't Adam's son, just read the generation, or genealogy of Adam. (You will smell a rat.)**

In Genesis chapter 5:1-32, Moses left out Cain's name in Adam's generation, or genealogy, as being made in the image, or likeness of God. But Moses began with Adam's OWN SON SETH who was made in his own likeness. Moses separated Cain and his generation, or genealogy by themselves in Genesis chapter 4:17-24.

MOSES LEFT OUT CAIN IN ADAM'S GENEALOGY

Here is what Moses records in Genesis chapter 5: 1-4, as to who was of the generation, or genealogy of Adam.

Verse 1, **"This is the book of the generations of Adam, in the day that God created man, in the likeness of God made he him."**

Common sense should dictate that if we don't find Cain in this list of generations of Adam, then Cain could not have been in the likeness of Adam or God.(yes?) This is why Cain was different from the regular man like Adam. And the reason he was not like Adam is because **he was a giant and the hybrid son of Eve, and the serpent/the devil, the evil one.**

Verse 2, "Male and female created he them, and blesses them, and called their name 'Adam' in the day when they were created"

Observe verse 3, carefully, so that you may see **that Cain was not Adam's son. Cain's surname wasn't called Adam.**

Verse 3, "And Adam lived a hundred and thirty years, **and begat a son 'IN HIS OWN LIKENESS', AND CALLED HIS NAME SETH"**

Verse 4, "And the days of Adam **after** he had begotten Seth were eight hundred years. **And he begat sons and daughters."**

But the question is: why didn't Moses record the birth of Cain as Adam's firstborn son if he was convinced that Cain was Adam's son? Why did he record it from his son Seth who was in his own likeness?

Moses started the genealogy of Adam from his son Seth, **and by-passed Cian. Why?** All of this should indicate that the fruit which Eve ate was that of her sex organ. This I will prove as I go on.

We will see, according to Moses 4:1, that Cain was not created in the complete likeness of Adam nor God. Because in the book of the generation **of Adam**, wherein man was created, in the image and likeness of God, **Cain is not even mentioned in it.** Moses says that Adam lived 130 years, and begat a son... **in his own likeness.** What this also indicates is that Cain **was not in the complete image or likeness of Adam.** But this doesn't give Moses the right to **by-pass Cain as being of the generation, or genealogy of Adam just because Cain was not in Adam's likeness and image...unless Moses knew that Cain wasn't Adam's son. There is no other rational reason.** Cain was a hybrid human being. That is, part human from Eve's eggs, and part evil sperms from the serpent. You should know that the serpent was a real physical creature which the Lord God had made. It was his innocent body which the devil used to communicate with Eve. However, that serpent no longer exists in that form any longer.

HERE IS CAIN'S SEPARATE GENERATION/ GENEALOGY

In Genesis chapter 4:1. Moses records: "And Adam knew his wife: and she conceived, and bare Cain, and said, I have gotten a man from the Lord". It was Eve who said she had gotten a man from the Lord. It wasn't Adam who made this statement. And truly, Eve was the mother of Cain, but Adam wasn't the father of Cain. But Seth was his son who was in his likeness.

Again, when Adam knew, or had sex, or ate of the fruit with his wife, **the serpent had already planted his seed, or sperm into Eve's womb.** And it was his sperms and Eve's eggs which were combined which conceived Cain, the evil one.

In Genesis chapter 4:17-24, Moses now gives us the break-down, or generations, or genealogy of Cain and his seed. But why didn't Moses include Cain as Adam's son? Well, because Cain wasn't of the sperm, nor of Adam's genealogy. As a man, would you give a history of the genealogy of your family, or children, **and by-pass your elder son, just because he doesn't look like you, or in your likeness?** One can understand you doing this if you know he isn't your son, but your wife's son, or he is an adopted son.

So no matter how bad or sinful Cain might had been, Moses should have still numbered him 'after Adam's genealogy, even if Moses had said. 'AND ADAM BEGAT CAIN, HIS WICKED SON WHOM GOD HAD CURSED' But not to mention him, or include him as a man in the image and likeness of Adam, indicates that he wasn't fully human, but was a hybrid giant. Again, Moses didn't add Cain in Adam's generation, because he knew that Cain was the serpent's son, but not Adam's own.

BACK TO ADAM, EVE, AND THE SERPENT

After Adam and Eve had eaten of the forbidden fruit, or had engaged in the sex act, Moses continues to write in Genesis chapter 3:7, "And the eyes of them both were opened, and they sew fig leaves together and made themselves apron".

The fact that their Minds' eyes were opened, they became disobedient wicked gods with a small 'g. One may be inclined to say,' earth gods'-that is, because their aura was gone. **After having sex, Adam and Eve's minds were activated to the knowledge of good and evil. They then became aware that they were naked.** They even became knowledgeable, to the extent that they had to cover the very thing with which they sinned. So they got fig leaves and sew them together **and made 'aprons', and covered their sex organs...not their heads, nor feet, but their shame. But why this?**

Ponder this: if the sex organ wasn't the forbidden fruit which they ate, why did they cover this part of their bodies with fig leaves...as aprons? But what in the world were they hiding? When the serpent told Eve that if she ate the fruit, then she would become as gods, knowing good and evil...he was right-because we see that when Adam and Eve ate the forbidden fruit,...they did become as gods..to know good and evil. And their eyes were opened as Moses says. Note, this is exactly what the serpent told Eve would happen. I will prove it later from Genesis 3:7. (keep reading).

Note this: Many people always ask, why did God put 'the tree of the knowledge of good and evil in the Garden to test Adam and Eve? And after they failed the test, he still chased them out of his Garden? Please remember the following: Adam and Eve were symbolically, 'The tree of knowledge of good and evil in the Garden.

The serpent told Eve that God was keeping 'the knowledge of the gods from them' This knowledge was...TO KNOW GOOD AND EVIL.' They realized that they now have the power of choice, to do whatever they wanted to do, and they don't have to do what God says. But of course, they paid a heavy cost for it.

So when they engaged in sexual intercourse the potential of this knowledge which was locked up within their brains was activated. They became like gods, that is, to have the knowledge to distinguish between good and evil. So this knowledge was expressed by them using their brains to get fig leaves to hide their sexual organs. This was the first choice they made after gaining the knowledge of the gods.

Know this: sex was the action which activated the neurons in their brains causing their minds' eyes to be opened.

Ponder this question: Why did God put Cherubims, or angels with four faces **TO GUARD 'THE TREE OF LIFE'** so that Adam and Eve couldn't returned to the garden to eat of it and live forever...BUT HE DIDN'T PUT ANY ANGELS TO GUARD THE NEXT TREE?** Well, the next tree of 'the knowledge of good and evil, didn't need any angels to guard it.. **Because that tree of good and evil, was Adam and Eve's own bodies.**

So it wasn't a physical tree planted in the Garden with a fruit, which God put in the Garden to test them which caused them to sin. However, **It was the tree of life which was physically planted in the midst of the Garden which the angels had guarded after they were expelled out of it.** Soon you'll see Adam and Eve did become gods to know good and evil.

After Adam and Eve had eaten of the fruit of the tree, which was the sex organ...**THEY BECAME ASHAMED.** But what was 'the shame'? Know this: from the day they had engaged in sexual intercourse-**"The sex organ became a shame to be seen openly, or publicly.** This is why you should believe that the forbidden fruit was the sex organ-and the tree was Their physical body. And if you would notice. That the forbidden fruit, or sex organ, **IS SOMEWHAT NEAR THE MIDDLE OR CENTER OF THE BODY OR GARDEN: EVEN TO THIS DAY AS HUMANS.**

I'm not telling you to get a measuring tape and measure the distant from your sex organ, or from the top of your head to your sex organ which would be near the midst, of your body. However, it's the navel which is directly at the center of your garden or body. But the sex organ is still in the midst of the body. One may ask how could the sex organs **'be the sin or shame' seeing that it was God himself who had made them. Or had given them to both Adam and Eve?**

First, let's see what Moses writes in Genesis chapter 1:26, "And God said, let us make man in our image, after our likeness: and let '**Them** (Adam and Eve) have dominion over the fish of the sea, and over the fowl of the air, and over the cattle, and over the earth, and over every creeping thing that creepeth upon the earth."

So as you can see, God had created Adam and Eve to have children, **and to dominate the earth.** So in order to have humans to have dominion over the earth, **they had to have sex in order to bring forth these humans.** But God knew that their bodies, especially Eve's body, which was created years later after Adam, that it wasn't **yet ready to bear children without pain and agony.**

I'm sure whenever God was ready for Adam and Eve to engage in the sex act, and to have children, Eve would have brought forth children without pain and agony. Eve's body was still not matured enough internally **for children bearing, because this would have involved all of her body going through a significant change.**

Now I'm just asking you to think about the following: the mere fact that Eve had experienced **pain in the process of bringing forth Cain, through her sex organ, proves it must have been the sex organ with which she sinned.** Why do I say this? Well, God would not have created Eve to bear pain with her sex organ while bringing forth children. Eve experienced pain with her sex organ because she sinned with it.

THE BLESSINGS AND CURSES OF THE TWO TREES IN EDEN

Adam took off the fruit of the flesh of his body FIRST instead of taking from the fruit of the Spirit FIRST, which was 'the tree of life' which would have produced righteousness. As a result of taking the fruit of the flesh first, the following was the result.

Galatians chapter 5:19-21, Paul writes," Now the works of the flesh are manifest, which are these: "**adultery, fornication, witchcraft, hatred, variance, emulation, (jealousies) wrath, strife, sedition, heresies, envyings, murders, drunkenness, revelling" (carnality)** and such like: of which I tell you before, as I have also told you in time past, that they which do such things shall not inherit the kingdom of God (14 sins)

Know this truth: If Adam had waited for God to give him the go ahead, or the green light to engage in the sex act, then his children including all human beings would not be going through all of these evils in the world today. Do you see why we have all of these evils going on in the earth? Well, because of Adam and Eve picking the fruit of the flesh of their bodies '**BEFORE**' it was **full and ripe. Adam and Eve's fruits, especially Eve's fruit were still too green. They weren't even full yet. SO BEING RIPE IN ORDER TO PICK, WAS OUT OF THE QUESTION.**

God wanted them to have sex because this is why he had created their sex organs…'**BUT NOT AT THAT TIME YET'. this is why God told them to leave that thing alone:** That is, until he would have given them the okay. God was the manufacturer of Adam and Eve, so he knew when they would have been ready for sex to bring forth children. Even though Adam and Eve were created full-grown, they were like little children who picked a green fruit from a tree and ate it, and as a result, their stomach became painful. **Now had they taken from ' the tree of life' first, then their children including all of us would be enjoying the following:**

Galatian chapter 5: 22-24,.St. Paul now gives the working of the Spirit, compared to the working of the flesh. The work of the flesh is that of evil, but the work of the Spirit is good. Paul explains: "**But the fruit of the Spirit** (like the one in the Garden) **is love, joy, peace, long suffering, gentleness, goodness, faith, meekness, temperance, Against such there is no law. And they that are Christ's have crucified the flesh with the affection and lusts.**"

These are the nine (9) fruits of the Spirit. Paul ends by saying in verse 25, "**If we live in the Spirit, let us also walk in the Spirit.**" So what we have is a spiritual war going on between the Spirit of God, versus the spirit of the gods of darkness. Both of the spirits are trying to attach themselves to your mind, or to your spirit. So Adam and Eve brought on all of these pains, suffering and shame upon all of us. But thank God, there is a way out to escape. And that is to accept Jesus Christ Eliakim as Lord, and he will assign a holy spirit to be with you to help you bear all of what you may go through, **until you are brought to him by his angel...so that you may be assigned to your permanent home in the Spiritual new Earth above,**

FACTS; THE SEX ORGANS SYMBOLIZE SHAME

Here are a few scriptures to convince you **that the fruit which Adam and Eve ate together...' was the shame' of their sex organs.** If you are able to see and believe this, then you should believe that both Eve, the serpent, and Adam had performed the sex act in the Garden of Eden.

Here are the instructions which God gave to Moses as to how he and the Israelites should have built **his altar** in the remote past.

Genesis chapter 20:24-26. "**An altar of earth thou shalt make unto me,** and shalt sacrifice thereon thy burnt offerings, and thy peace offerings, thy sheep, and thine oxen in all places where I record my name I will come unto thee, and I will bless them "and if thou wilt make me 'an altar of stone', for if thou lift up thy tool upon it, thou hast polluted it."

Now read verse 26, slowly and carefully: "NEITHER SHALT THOU GO UP BY STEPS UNTO MINE ALTAR, ' THAT THY NAKEDNESS BE NOT DISCOVERED THEREON". When God said 'nakedness', he meant the former children of Israel's sex organs. God didn't want to discover or to see anyone's nakedness, or sex organs in the process of them walking up the steps of his altar. (this is crystal clear)

But wasn't it God himself who had made man's sex organs? One may ask: before Adam sinned, didn't he worship God without any clothes on? Yes, but you see, he was innocent and sinless, and two, he was clothed with a glory, or an aurora around him. But still, his sex organ was seen, because he and Eve had sex together, So his sex organ was indeed seen before he sinned.

After Adam had sinned, his glory vanished from around him. Then he realized that he was naked, because his covering, or glory had disappeared. This is why he was so ashamed, and afraid to meet God in the Garden, so he hid himself. However, the man or woman who accepts the second Adam does have an invisible covering, or glory around him just like the first Adam, even though one may not be able to see it.

In Jerimiah chapter 13:22, we see where God was speaking through him to speak to Judah: about them being taken captives into the northern country of Babylon.

Verse 22, "And if thou say in thine heart, wherefore come these things upon me? For the greatness of thine iniquity ARE THY SKIRTS DISCOVERED, and thy heels made bare" {bearfeet)

When the Israelites would have found themselves in such a dire situation, and being hauled into slavery in Babylon, they would have wondered, why were those things come upon them. The answer is, because of the greatness of their sins, and as a result, **THEIR SKIRTS WERE LIFTED UP OVER THEIR HEADS, CAUSING ...'THEIR SHAME, OR SEX ORGANS' TO BE SHOWN.** When a wind blows a woman's skirt over her head, what is the first thing she would do? Answer: she would try to pull down her skirt, **and would try to hide, or to cover her sexual part, especially if she isn't wearing any underwear.** So it's quite obvious that the sex organ was and still is **a symbol of shame. (do you see it?)**

Even a man would run for cover and hide, if for whatever reason, he finds himself without pants on, or underwear (shirt-tail) in a public place-or even in his dream. But how had this shame come about? Well, it started in the beginning in the Garden of Eden with Eve and Adam.

Here is a question: Why is one not ashamed if his hands, legs etc. are seen in a public view? Why is it shameful to allow one's sexual parts to be seen in a public setting? Why are you not ashamed if your elbow or navel being exposed in public view,..**but if your sex organ is exposed, you'll run for cover?** The answer is, because it's that same sex organ with which Adam and Eve had sinned in the beginning, **causing 'this shame'** to be traditionally filtered on down to all of us as a whole. **This shame of having one sex organ exposed in a public setting was passed on down through their' DNA' to us even today.**

And to prove that this was filtered 0n down to us – **is that you find it ingrained in all races. All of this proves that truly, the Homo sapiens, or all people on earth, derived from the first man Adam, and the first woman Eve.** As a result of their sinning in the garden, their spiritual covering disappeared – causing them to be naked, **and ashamed of their sex organs being exposed in a public setting.**

If you don't believe this, then give a good reason **why would you be ashamed to walk down town naked, even in the night?** Is it because it looks unattractive? Even if the law allows it you would still be ashamed to walk about naked. You would be ashamed because it's innate in you. **The shame is in your DNA.** so how do you think this shame of your sex organ got into your DNA? Well, it got there as a result of Adam and Eve being ashamed after they had sinned in God's Garden. And all of us had derived from them and if they were to call all of their children to them, then both, black, white, yellow, and brown would come running to them. Think about it.

Here now is what the prophet Jeremiah says to the ancient Israelites. Jeremiah chapter 13;23, "can an Ethiopian change his skin? (no) or the leopard with his spot? (no) then may ye (Israelites) also do good that are accustomed to do evil."

Verse 24, "Therefore, will I scatter them (ancient Israelites) as the stubble that passeth away by the wind of the wilderness"

God was heaven-bent in scattering the ancient Israelites because of their sins of forsaking him, and keeping sweet-hearts with other men. These other men were pagan gods. God was and is always a jealous God. This is also why human beings are jealous of their loved ones. When God loves you, he'll do good for you. But if you turned and forsake him by getting involved with other false pagan gods, or the world system, then it would have been better for that person, that he or she had not seen the light of day, nor even been born on this planet earth..

The following verses should make one shake in one's. boots. This is what God did to Judah, or to the ancient Jews. In verse 25, God continues to say to them: "This is thy lot, the portion of thy measures (judgment) **"from me' saith the Lord,,because thou hast forgotten me, and trusted in falsehood"**

So slavery into Babylon for seventy (70) years...was the portion of measure for Judah, from God. This should make one shake for fear, because if the creator has to reward one according to the proportion, or amount of one's sins then one would wonder where one will go to pay for one's sins? 'As for me, I'm not going to leave him nor forsake his son Jesus Christ Eliakim. This is especially for persons who once loved him, then switch back into the world system partaking of the works of the flesh. God goes on in verse 26, "THEREFORE WILL I DISCOVER THY SKIRT UPON THY FACE-THAT THY SHAME MAY APPEAR."

Are you now convinced that Adam and Eve's fruit, or sex organs were their shame as a result of involving in the sex act, before God was ready for them to use them?

Verse 26, is straight forward. God was going TO LIFT UP THE SKIRTS OF THE ANCIENT JEWS...OVER THEIR HEADS, so that their sexual parts may be seen. That is..'THEIR SHAME'. It is God who considers that the sex organs are shameful when they are exposed in public view.

Here is another case which proves that the sex organ was and still is one's shame. So if one is convinced that the sex organ is one's shame, then one should wonder how and when it had its beginning among human kind.

I want you to know that even after the flood of Noah, the sex organ was still considered 'a shame' if it was exposed publicly. So if it was ashamed to display one's sex organ 'before' the flood of Noah, then it had to have been ashamed to display it 'after' the flood. So do you see that this leads us back to Adam and Eve?

Moses writes in Genesis chapter 9:18: "And the sons of Noah, that went forth of the ark, were Shem, Ham, and Japheth, and Ham is the father of Canaan:"

Verse 19, "These are the three sons of Noah: AND OF THEM WAS THE WHOLE EARTH OVERSPREAD"

Verse 20, "And Noah began to be a husbandman, (farmer) and he planted a vineyard." So you see, in order for Noah to plant a vineyard after the flood, he had to have brought the vine – plants with him in the ark from the old world. This means that the people drank wine in the old world, or in the beginning before the flood.

Verse 21, "And he drank of the wine, and was drunken; **and he was 'UNCOVERED' (naked) within his tent"**

Verse 22, "And Ham, the father of Canaan, saw **the nakedness of his father,** and told his two brethren without"

Verse 23, "And shem and Japheth took a garment, and laid it upon both their shoulders, and went backward, **and covered the nakedness of their father; and their faces were backward, AND THEY SAW NOT THEIR FATHER'S NAKEDNESS"** (sex organ)

Verse 24, "And Noah awoke from his wine, and knew what his younger son had done unto him"

Verse 25, "And he said, cursed be Canaan; a servant of servant shall he be unto his brethren"

It's interesting to note that Noah didn't curse Ham who had exposed him to his brethren, **but he cursed Ham's fourth, or last son Canaan.** The reason Noah couldn't curse Ham is, because God had already blessed Shem, Ham and Japheth.

So whom God bless no one can curse. That is, one may use words to curse you, but it wouldn't work. They may work witchcraft on you, but it would never work.

IMPORTANT POINT TO REMEMBER

It wasn't Ham's first three sons whom Noah had cursed, but rather...HIS LAST SON CANAAN. And Canaan's tribe was the Canaanites. SO THE CUSHITES/ ETHIOPIAN,

THE EGYPTIANS AND THE PUTTIES...WERE FREE FROM THIS CURSE.

Remember this: Only Canaan's tribe was cursed – not Cush, his elder son, whose tribe was the Ethiopians people. Not Phut, the Phuties/lybians/ Nubians, 'not the rest of the Africans'... BUT IT WAS ONLY THE ANCIENT CANAANITES, HAM'S LAST SON WHO WAS CURSED. The Canaanites' tribe was the scape-goat who took the blame for their father's sin.

So what's the big deal if Noah's son or sons saw his private parts, or nakedness? Well, it was a big deal because it was already considered, **a shamed for one's sex organ to be exposed to others.** This is why Shem and Japheth got a garment and put it on their shoulders and walked backward, in order to prevent them from seeing their father's sex organ/nakedness/ shame.

Remember this also: The original name of the sex organ was not called, 'the sex organ'...**But it was called...'THE SHAME'.** And it got this name because God looked at it as Adam and Eve's shame. This was Adam and Eve's sex organs which were exposed openly to the beasts of the field. But before this, even though it was still seen, it was covered with an aura of light including the whole body.

Again the sex organ being exposed was always considered "a shamed" and it goes all the way back to Adam and Eve, whereby **they used their sex organs (fruits) to sin, 'BEFORE' they were given permission to use them.**

The sex organs today are still called, **'The private parts".** But what is so private about the sex organs? Why is it hidden under the clothes, and not to be publicly seen like the other parts of the body? Well, it evolved to be looked at as ' **the private parts because** Adam and Eve were ashamed for God to meet them naked without having on their spiritual garments. And later when their children were born, they made sure that no one would see **the very thing with which they sinned, and brought shame upon mankind.** So they made aprons out of fig leaves and covered them. So from that time to this day, we still hide or cover-up the sex organs, and rightly so.

FINAL PROOF FOR YOU JUROR

Here is another 100% iron-clad proof that Adam and Eve's sin was the engagement of the sex act. The following scripture by Jesus, will prove **that the fruit of the tree of 'knowledge of good and evil' was the sex organ.** Here is what Jesus told the apostle John to tell the Christians. Revelation chapter 16:15, "Behold, I come as a thief. Blessed is he that watcheth, and keep his garments **less he walk naked-AND THEY SEE HIS SHAME".**

Here is a question for you: Was the shame Jesus referred to when he told John to tell the Christians to keep their spiritual garments clean, otherwise when he would have returned, **'Their shame'** will be exposed; the sex organ? answer, Yes! So this shows that Eve did pick the forbidden fruit of her body and did share it with the serpent **'first'**, then she went home and shared it with her husband Adam.

I wrote all of the above scriptures so that you may see **that 'the shame' of Adam and Eve was indeed the shame of using their sex organs, or their fruits, before God was ready for them to use them.** This is why he warned them not to bother with it. All of this should make you understand that Eve's firstborn son Cain, was not Adam's son. Because she and the serpent had engaged in the sex act, before Adam did.

God indeed had intended for them to use their sex organs in order to have children. This is why he made them in the first place, But God also knew that Eve's body wasn't yet ready **to** bear children without pain, agony, and suffering. Now by Eve picking and eating this green fruit, it caused her to suffer for nine (9) months in misery. So from that day to this day, **uncontrolled sex is still the number one shame among human kinds.**

Know this: Great men are still tumbling down from lofty positions and high places-all because of stealing sex from the wrong woman. And picking fruits from the wrong tree, still exacerbates shame.

ADAM, EVE, AND THE SERPENT IN COURT

Scene number 3

Alas! The day of judgment has come for Adam, Eve, and the serpent to meet their maker for their disobedience to his command. All of this because of having sex without permission from the Lord.

When the Lord entered the Garden, or the court-room, he now called out for Adam. We now have two accused humans and one serpent in the Garden or in the court-room. **Here come Adam and Eve out of hiding, and dressed right up in a brand new outfit of green mini bikini aprons, and glued together with fresh fig leaves. No, 'not made in China', but made in the Garden in Eden/Jerusalem.** The serpent is also here in court, not as a crawling one, but standing on its feet like a man. At this time he wasn't yet cursed, so his head was elevated above the ground, and he is here to answer for his crime for deceiving mother Eve.

The Lord God is the judge, jury, and punisher. When Adam and Eve presented themselves, The Lord demanded Adam to explain himself, and to give an account for his obvious crime of being found naked, and for him committing a serious sin against this command. That is, for picking the forbidden fruit from the forbidden tree of knowledge of good and evil, and for given-in to the voice of his wife in committing evil.

Moses records in verse 9, "And the Lord God called unto Adam, and said unto him, "where art thou?"

Verse 10, "Adam responded: I heard thy voice in the Garden, and I was afraid, because I was naked and I hid myself."

First, let me show you that Adam was covered with the light of righteousness, but when he had committed, 'that sin'- his spiritual clothes fell-off, or disappeared. As a result, he was then cut-off from the divine light of God, AS A BRANCH IS CUT-OFF FROM A TREE.

Here is how you would know that Adam was wearing a spiritual robe. He replied to God by saying that he heard his voice in the Garden, so he hid himself because he was afraid. And he was indeed naked. This shows that Adam was wearing some kind of spiritual covering. You may ask, how could this be verified? **You see, if Adam said he was naked, it proves he wasn't naked all along so he had to have been wearing some kind of spiritual robe or coat.. You see, to have the knowledge to say, you are naked is to have the knowledge that you were wearing clothes before. (Yes?)**

Tell me what do you think of the following paragraphs.

Someone comes to the door of your house and knocks. When you finally open the door, you say to the person: **"I heard you knocking, but I couldn't come any quicker...BECAUSE I HAD MY CLOTHES ON'** This person may think that you may have lost your mind. And they should have a reason to be right.

Here is the question: why would Adam reply to God by saying, **"I heard your voice and I was afraid, and I hid myself, BECAUSE I WAS NAKED – IF HE WASN'T ACCUSTOMED OF WEARING CLOTHES?**

Note, if he was always naked, then he wouldn't have responded to God with those words. **So yes, Adam was spiritually clothed with a garment of a light around him, like an aurora.** Therefore, he who doesn't have the glow, or light of the Spirit of God around his spirit-man, **is indeed spiritually naked. Yes, Jesus says, that person is naked.**

This is why if I died without receiving Jesus Christ, I would end up in hell, naked, blind and in utter darkness. But if you accept Jesus Christ as Lord and savior, he promised to give you a beautiful robe made out of fine linen. Also he will give you **the brightness of the heavenly morning star. That is, the brightness of a star around your spirit-man.** So, what do you have to lose? Why take a risk? Even though I know what I speak is the divine truth. **What if when you die you find out that it's true...what would you do then? Just consider it.**

BACK TO ADAM

We now know by this time, **Adam's eyes were already opened. Because he wasn't supposed to know that he was physically naked.** This word 'naked'. Wasn't programmed into his brain. And for sure, God knew he never mentioned the word to him. So God who had created Adam's brain, wanted to know where he got this new word, 'naked' from? God wanted to know **how can Adam download a new word, that he God didn't upload into his brain, or his fleshly computer.**

Verse 11," And he (God) said, who told thee that thou was naked? Hast thou eaten of the tree whereof I commanded thee that thou shouldest not eat?"

Mind you, God had already known that Adam had eaten from the tree of knowledge of good and evil, but he wanted Adam to explain himself.

Verse 12, is Adam's defense: he accused his wife Eve for the crime. He responded to God's question by saying:. **"The woman whom thou gavest to be with me, she gave me of the tree, and I did eat." Do you see that Eve had to have tasted the forbidden fruit of the tree ' BEFORE' she gave a piece to Adam?** Do you see this leaves the door of understanding opened to believe that Eve had to have eaten the fruit with the serpent who was informing her about the tree and the fruit? This also indicates that when she first ate the fruit with the serpent, she got pregnant with Cain. This also lends itself to the understanding as to why Cain was wicked. This also explains as to how Cain became the first giant to walk the earth.

Here is Adam telling God, who is the judge, that it was the woman who gave him the fruit, so he didn't refuse but he did eat it also. Can you read between the lines that Eve had to have knowledge of the working of this tree, and the usage and function of this fruit **'BEFORE' SHE GAVE IT TO HER HUSBAND?** This was Adam's defense before God or the judge. Adam had no lawyer to plead to the judge on his behalf. So he had no other option, but to throw himself at the mercy of the court, or the judge.

THE SERPENT WAS IN LOVE WITH EVE

This is something you need to know. **The serpent was still hanging around with Eve and Adam – even after he had deceived her the first time – and at their dwelling.** The serpent also knew that Eve got pregnant with his child as a result of his seed he had planted, within her the first time they engaged in the sex act.

Might as well I tell you I believe that the serpent and Eve were still in love-even after he told her about the fruit, or her sex organ. God had to warn Eve about her desires. **At this time she didn't know that keeping sweet-hearts was wrong or desiring another being's fruit..There was no law against it yet.** But what in the world was the serpent doing living or hanging-out with Eve and Adam? It was because he still had a crush on Eve. Eve was under a spell of the devil until God stepped in.

Notice this: in this third scene, we have **'Adam, Eve, and the serpent'**. But in the second scene, we only have, **Eve and the serpent.** So as you can see, there was, **' a time lapse'** between the time the serpent was educating Eve about the fruit of the tree, and the time we are going to find him **'again' with Eve and Adam.** The serpent just wouldn't leave Eve alone. Was he watching her belly and counting the months in order to know when his seed, or child would be born? Now, if the sons of God, or fallen angels saw the beauty of the daughters of men that they were fair, or beautiful, **and even married to them...how much more Eve, the original woman, be even more beautiful?**

God now questions Eve about her involvement in this situation, **'and her relationship with the serpent, or the devil'.** Eve didn't know that when one is married, that one shouldn't have a desire, nor sexual relation with another man, beast, or serpent...other than her husband. But of course, God had not yet enacted any laws governing fidelity or morality, about marriage,

GOD NOW INTERROGATES EVE

Here is what Moses records in Genesis chapter 3:13, "And the Lord God said unto the woman, **'what is this that thou hast done?"** If you would ponder this question by God to Eve, you may conclude that one: God was angry. And two, It's the truth that Eve was the first one who ate the fruit. Again: this indicates that when Eve ate the fruit the first time, **that Adam wasn't** there. So the million dollar question is: ' **With whom did she eat the fruit, if it wasn't Adam?** Adam pointed his finger toward his wife Eve, and said to God, '**SHE MADE ME DO IT**'. Eve didn't deny what Adam said, but she in turn, pointed her finger toward the serpent – who was also present, and told God **that it was the serpent who deceived her and caused her to eat of the fruit from the forbidden tree.** Of course, he never even opened his mouth in his defense.

Here is Eve actual response to God in verse 13, "**And the woman said, ' the serpent beguiled me...and I did eat.**"

Eve didn't say to God, the serpent deceived '**US**' and "**WE**' did eat. She said he deceived '**ME**' and '**I**' did eat "Are you now convinced that Eve ate the fruit, or had sex with the serpent during the time the serpent was telling her, or deceiving her about the forbidden fruit of the tree?

Eve's defense to the Judge was that it was the serpent who beguiled or tricked her to partake of the sex act...'**And she did eat**' She didn't waste the judge's time, she admitted she ate the fruit from the forbidden tree, or partook of the sex act, **only because she was deceived.** When she said 'she did eat'...**There is no doubt it was the serpent with whom she ate the fruit, or had sex with. DO YOU SEE THAT ADAM WASN'T THERE WITH HER AT THAT TIME?** (yes?) **It was a later time when she ate the fruit with her husband Adam.**

Again, what this also indicates is that Eve's first son **Cain was truly the serpent's son. or seed. This Cain was the first hybrid human or giant upon the earth.** When Eve ate the fruit with Adam, or had sex with him, **it was the second time Eve would have eaten of the fruit, or having a sexual experience.** Think about this: when Eve went away from home, and left Adam at home...she had no knowledge of the benefits what she and Adam could have received by making use of their fruits, or sex organs. She was so blind that she didn't even know that her fruit and the tree were desirous.

Think about this: **but when she returned home, she was able to convince Adam to eat...the fruit, because they would be as gods knowing good and evil-and they would be wise as the gods.** Adam swallowed the whole bait, hook, line and sinker. He drank the Kool-Aid just as Eve drank it. I'm sure you can deduce from this narrative, that Eve had to have tasted this forbidden fruit, **'before' she returned home to Adam (this is the point!)**

This is really what Adam wanted to say to God: "I had no intention of eating this fruit until Eve...this same woman you brought to be my wife...from where you got her, I don't know, **It was her who convinced me and gave me a bite of the fruit, and I being so kind, I gave in to her request. Yes sir, I confess, I did eat it also.**

Again, all of this proves that Eve ate the fruit first,'**before she offered it to Adam. Adam was only trying to exonerate himself, or to clear himself as it relates to the eating of the forbidden fruit, or having sex.** But of course, it didn't work, because God still found him guilty as charged and sentenced him **to hard labor for life for his crime. And banished him to the Jordan Valley-area by the Jordan River...by Zarethan – below Jez-reel some sixty five (65) miles away from Eden/Jerusalem.**

GOD CAUGHT THE DEVIL RED-HANDED IN THE SERPENT'S BODY.

I want you to observe that the Lord God didn't ask the serpent, or the devil why he beguiled Eve, The reason is, because he knew how rude he was. And he knew that the devil, or the serpent would only have given him a condescending and disrespectful answer.

God knew the serpent had already told Eve that he was a liar. So God wasn't going to get in any debate, or argument with him at this time. So God just passed a judgment-sentence on him. God never questioned him because he didn't allow him to take the witness stand.

THE SERPENT'S SENTENCE

Moses writes the following in verse 14: "And the Lord God said unto the serpent, Because thou hast done this, **thou art cursed above all cattle, and above every beast of the field: "UPON THY BELLY SHALT THOU GO, AND DUST SHALT THOU EAT ALL THE DAYS OF THY LIFE." That was the serpent's curse 'before' he was cursed. One: 'crawl', and two, 'eat dust'. Which means he wasn't crawling before, and his head wasn't low to the ground sniffing dust. He was standing and walking upon his feet like a man.**

So, as you can see, the serpent was right there in the Garden at the time God passed judgment on Adam and Eve. Yes, the devil was caught red-handed in the serpent's body in this third scene. Ponder this: at the time the serpent had an audience with Eve, '**she was alone,** but in the process of time, we find him with both Adam and Eve in the Garden. Strangely enough, when God came into the Garden this time to pass judgment on all of them-**the serpent was there also.** So you should see that the serpent was indeed hanging-out with Adam and Eve.. But of course with his eyes on Eve and her belly.

Observe this: the serpent was going to be the devil's favorite creature on earth, even though God cursed him. But as for the devil himself who used his body, he was going to be free from this curse of crawling, which God had put on the physical serpent.

But his end would have eventually come by the hand of a hybrid human and demon woman.

So what we have here is the serpent, or devil who had deceived Eve, but in the end, it was a hybrid demon woman who had defeated him in hell after God had chased him and his demons down there. **I stake my soul on this reality before God, that is; I had seen the devil being destroyed in the land of hell by a hybrid demon woman in my dream. He is now only a golden statue with greyish dross covering his body hiding the shine of that golden body.**

Again, as for the physical serpent's curse in the Garden, this was the judgment-sentence God pronounced on him: "**upon thy belly shalt thou go: (two) and dust shalt thou eat all the days of thy life.**"

Know this: the serpent was walking upon his feet like a man at this time. And he wasn't crawling upon his belly eating dust. He became 'the scape-goat serpent because he took the blame for the devil's crime. So the devil used his body to communicate with Eve.

Think! Why would God curse the serpent by telling him,' **From now on you'll crawl upon your belly...if the serpent was crawling upon his belly all along?** It's like someone cursing you by telling you that, ' **from now on, you will see with your eyes, hear with your ears, smell with your nose, and walk upon your feet until the day you die-or from now on, you'll eat food with your mouth until you die, IF YOU WERE EXPERIENCING THESE THINGS BEFORE YOU WERE CURSED? So as you can reason, this wouldn't be a curse at all, but rather a blessing.**

So as you can comprehend, the serpent was indeed **walking on his feet with his head elevated above the ground, and he wasn't crawling nor eating dust in the beginning when he** communicated with Eve. Do you now believe that serpent was walking upright when he deceived Eve? I'll soon prove that Eve had sex with the serpent. So when you see a scene with a snake wrap-around a tree, and talking to Eve, you would know it's an error. KNOW THIS TRUTH: IT WAS AFTER THE SERPENT WAS CURSED THAT HE TURNED INTO THE KIND OF SNAKE YOU SEE THESE DAYS. But it was in the process of time. Just as it was in the process of time that Adam and Eve gradually grew old and turned to dust.

See if this makes sense to you. Why would God say to the serpent: "from now on you are going to crawl upon your belly...if the serpent was already crawling upon his belly before he was cursed? Therefore, this curse on the serpent, only proves that he was walking upright all along. Do you agree or disagree?

The serpent's body went through a gradual change, or mutation in the process of time. but he was walking upright just like a man at first. The fact that God brought him down to ground-level, shows that he was elevated in height, upon his feet. So from standing upon his feet, God brought him down to the ground and made him crawl, or dragged upon his belly; and put poison under his tongue, depriving him of his speech. So after that, he was no longer able to talk to Eve. So the devil was no longer able to use the serpent's tongue to speak.

The second part of the serpent's curse was that he was going to eat dust for the rest of his life. Observe: the serpent wasn't eating dust 'before' he was cursed. His mouth wasn't low to the ground. He was standing upon his feet like a man. However, he went through a process of a kind of' metamorphosis gradually. Again, just as Adam grew old, wrinkled and die,

189

GOD NOW BREAKS UP THE RELATIONSHIP BETWEEN EVE, AND THE SERPENT

God is now going to break-up this friendship between Eve and the serpent. Now after telling the serpent that he will crawl upon his belly, and will eat dust, for the rest of his life, God goes on to tell the serpent in Genesis chapter 3:15, the following: **"And I will put enmity (hatred) between thee and the woman, and between thy seed (Cain's children) and her seed (Seth's children) it shall bruise thy head, and thou shalt bruise his heel."** Question: Do you see that God is talking about two (2) sets of seeds or children? He is now making reference to Eve's children, and the serpent's children. So it's elementary for us to expect to see two kinds of seeds or two kinds of children. **And indeed they had to have looked some-what different.** Eve's children through her husband Adam, were normal in size, But the serpent's seed or children were abnormal in size. **And indeed they were giants in size.**

Look how God rebukes the serpent by telling him that he is going to break-up this relationship-by putting a spirit of enmity/ hatred/ division between them. So from that time onward, **the woman was going to hate the serpent, and the serpent was going to hate the woman...thus causing a division between them.** But it was God who had put this spirit of hate between them.

Have you ever wondered why God had to put enmity, or hatred between ...' **the serpent and Eve, if there wasn't a friendship going on between them? Note, in order to divide something... The something had to have been 'one thing' as a whole. so when you divide it, it then becomes more than one thing. So if God put a division between the serpent and Eve,** then, they had to have been one as a whole, or one in agreement, or one in accosiation. Think! Before this, Eve couldn't see how wicked the serpent was.

I have told you before that the serpent had a crush on Eve, that's why you found him hanging around the Garden all the time with Eve. God had noticed how close the serpent and Eve were, that's why he put an end between their relationship. **God wouldn't have made that statement to the serpent about division between him and Eve, if there wasn't a unity between them, or if they only had one encounter, or a one night stand, and never saw each other again.** But the fact of the matter is, they had more encounters, or meetings. God is still speaking to the serpent in verse 15, by saying that he was going to put enmity **between the serpent's seed (not beast) but children, and the woman's seed, or children.** God didn't mean for Eve's children to go and crush the head of the physical serpent which you see these days. Because of this mis-understanding of this statement God made, many people in time past and even these days, believe it was the kind of snake you see today. So whenever they would see a snake today, they would try to kill it by bruising its head.

Now think! Where was the serpent, or the devil going to get any seed, or children from? And we know God wasn't referring to the devil's angels, or any creatures or beasts. We know that the woman Eve was indeed going to have children...**but the serpent, who was going to be his seed or children?**

God knew the serpent and Eve had a sexual relationship. He also knew that Eve got pregnant as a result of that sexual intercourse with him. So God knew that the serpent, or the devil's seed, or children were going to come through Cain – Eve's firstborn son who was his first hybrid son. All of this should open-up your eyes to the reality that when the serpent had engaged in the sex act with Eve, she got pregnant, as stated before.

Now what we have upon the ancient world-stage in the very beginning, **is the serpent's seed, or children, who came through Cain, and the woman's seed/eggs, or children who came through Seth.** In a kind of a way as to how Jesus' father was God, and his mother was Mary, but he didn't have a physical father.. So He was a hybrid son of God. that is, part human and part divine, or spiritual. So this was the position of Cain's birth. His mother was Eve, but his father was the devil.

Isn't it interesting that God talked about **two kinds of seeds, or two kinds of children, EVEN BEFORE CAIN WAS BORN'? and do you know it did come to pass? It came from Seth's children who were the seed of the women.** And isn't it strange that Cain's children were the evil ones, whose spiritual father was the serpent/the devil? **All of this should prove to you that Cain had to have been the serpent's seed, or child...which would mean that indeed, the serpent had to have had sex with Eve during the time he deceived or beguiled her.**

THE SERPENT WAS A BEAST-LIKE MAN/ CREATURE

Allow me to quote Genesis 3:1,: Moses writes: "Now the serpent was more subtle than any beast of the field which the Lord God had made, and he said unto the woman, ' **Yea, hath God said, ye shall not eat of every tree of the Garden:?**

The serpent was subtle. That is, having a sharp, discernment, keen, skilful, sly, and crafty ability. This is who Moses says he was. Moses says he was more skilful, or smarter than all of the beasts of the field which God had made. He was so intelligent that he was able to speak the language which Adam and Eve spoke. He was also smarter than Adam, because he knew about the working of the Gods. But Adam didn't. He was here on earth 'before' Adam was created.

The serpent was observing Adam and Eve whom God had made in his own image and likeness. (He was jealous of Adam) He notice that they weren't having sex like the other creatures, So this is one of the reason he approached Eve about her body, and fruit. Who was this serpent? Was he man or beast? Even though the devil possessed his body, he by himself, was clever and wise. Yes, Moses says, he was wiser than all of the beasts of the field. **The serpent was a beast-like man, standing on its feet just like a man and even speaking human language.** So the devil spoke through his body to communicate to Eve. Just like how the angel spoke through a donkey to communicate to Balim.

Now it's obvious that God speaks about the serpent's seed or children, and Eve's seed, or children. Now if you would notice, it was God himself who said that there were going to be **two kinds of people, or children.** So it only makes sense to expect to see two kinds of people. **That is, they had to have looked somewhat different from each other.**

Now Eve's children from her husband Adam through her son Seth, **were to hate or to be against the seed, or children of the serpent, or Cain's children.** We know how Eve's children looked – they all looked like one hundred per cent (100%) human beings. But the serpent's seed, or children who came through Cain, not only looked like giants, **but were giants.** They were all hybrid people, because the serpent was not made in the complete image and likeness of God as Adam and Eve were. **But he still had a touch of the spiritual workings of the Gods.** This should indicate that the serpent who was talking with Eve, had to have been upright like a man, but not totally human.

So if the serpent's seed, or children looked somewhat like humans, and even to interact with Eve's children, then the serpent itself had to have looked somewhat like a man. However, everyone in the old world before the universal flood were drowned or destroyed in the flood of Noah – apart from eight (8) persons.

Here is the question: why was it Eve's seed or children who God said would bruise the serpent's head...**if it weren't Eve and the serpent who had this attraction to one another, until God put a stop to it? Why didn't God say, 'THE SEED OF ADAM, WHY THE SEED OF EVE?** Well, because the sexual affair was between the woman Eve and the serpent. Yes, the serpent was doing more than just talking to Eve. He was having sex with her in the process.

ADAM, EVE, AND THE SERPENT ARE STILL IN COURT

After God had ended pronouncing the sentence on the serpent, and telling him about **his future children (through Cain)** He then turned his attention to the woman Eve, and pronounced the sentence on her. Eve is now going to learn about her fate. I wonder if you see where God said that the serpent was going to have children? But what does this have to do with Eve eating or picking of the forbidden fruit? Unless, these were going to be the two kinds of people, and indeed they were.

Moses records in Genesis chapter 3:16: "And unto the woman he (God) said, "**I will greatly multiply thy sorrow AND THY CONCEPTION; and thy desire shall be TO THY HUSBAND, and he shall rule over thee**"

If your mind is sharp, which I believe it is, then you would see **that Eve was already conceived, that is, pregnant with the serpent's seed, or child during this time God is talking to her, and passing sentence on her.** This statement by God to Eve should convince you **that she was already pregnant.** What God wanted her to know is, she was going to bring forth, Cain in pain and sorrow.

After God told Eve he was going to multiply her sorrow ' **in child bearing'**, he added in the same breath,: '**and thy desire shall be TO THY HUSBAND, and he shall rule over thee. This indicates that she wasn't pregnant for her husband Adam, but rather for the serpent. (Yes)**

If you would notice that it was '**after'** God had addressed 'the serpent'-then he addressed Eve. **Not after he addressed Adam. (do you see it?)** God wanted Eve to know that **from now on, it must be your husband you should desire.**

I'm writing this in this simple manner so that all persons would finally know that the fruit which Eve and Adam and the serpent ate, or picked, was the act of a sexual action. Think about this: if the sin, or the eating of the fruit that Eve ate was not that of **sex, why would God talk to her ABOUT 'CONCEPTION, OR BRINGING FORTH CHILDREN, OR BABIES AT THIS TIME'? (do you see it?) If Eve's action didn't had to do with her sex organ, or vagina, God wouldn't have been talking to her about bringing forth children with pain and sorrow,**

Look At the time God made this statement to Eve **about being conceived or having children...and about her desire for her husband. Well, it was 'AFTER' telling the serpent about his seed, or FUTURE CHILDREN.(Do you smell a rat?)**

Ponder this: if Eve was pregnant **for Adam her husband, GOD WOULDN'T HAD TO TELL HER... HER DESIRE MUST BE FOR HER HUSBAND. Why do I say this? WELL, BECAUSE HER DESIRE WOULD HAVE ALREADY BEEN FOR HER HUSBAND.** Do you see God had to have been referring to someone else **who Eve had desire for...OTHER THAN HER HUSBAND ADAM?**

Question: What does picking or eating an orange, apple or fig, **had to do with conception or bringing for children, unless this fruit was that of sex?** Do you see that this whole affair was a sexual one? But you see, the mere fact that God told the serpent about 'HIS SEED, OR CHILDREN' AND EVE'S SEED OR CHILDREN AT THIS TIME shows that there was sex involved.

(yes or no?)

Think about this: in the same way Eve's children or seed... were human beings, so were the serpent's seed or children human; with the exception that they were giants in size, because Their father Cain was a hybrid giant who was a combination of Eve's eggs and the serpent's sperm. What this indicates is that the serpent himself had to have been a kind of up-right creature which looked somewhat like a human being, **but not fully in the image of God. Thank God he drowned them all.** Even though God destroyed all of the giants in the flood of Noah, we still find many giants in Palestine when Joshua and the Israelites crossed over into the promised land. But where did they come from? **Well, the answer is in my book... 'BLACK BIBLICAL HISTORY' on amazon.com**

Now watch this: God even told Eve, IN SORROW SHALT YOU BRING FORTH CHILDREN" are you kidding me? But why? Answer, BECAUSE OF THE FRUIT SHE ATE. Do you see that the fruit which Eve ate caused her to bring forth children in pain and sorrow? Can I now rest my case in trying to prove that the forbidden fruit was the sex organ, And that Adam, Eve, and the serpent were all involved in the sex act?

Seriously ponder this: **why would God talk about having children at this time to Eve-and the serpent if it wasn't the sex act they were involved in?**

Note this: not between Eve and Adam, but between Eve and the serpent. Again, God was discussing the bringing forth of children between Eve and the serpent. God went on to tell the serpent about his seed or children and Eve's children hating each other and about the bruising of the other's heel, and the bruising of the other's head.

God was talking about children to the serpent and Eve, because it was the serpent who first had a sexual encounter with her. So, if the fruit she ate wasn't that of sex with the serpent, **WHY WOULD GOD TALK TO HER ABOUT HAVING CHILDREN, BECAUSE OF THE FRUIT SHE ATE?** God wouldn't have had any reason to be discussing children with Eve, **if she had eaten a physical or natural apple, or fig etc.** But you see, this special tree of 'knowledge of good and evil', wasn't an ordinary tree like the other trees in the Garden.

Adam, Eve, and their children were supposed to have been trees of righteousness, but they all ended up, being trees of unrighteousness. But, as for Adam and Eve, they were symbolically as trees in the Garden.

Again, God now warns Eve about her desires. He says to her, **"And thy desire shall be to thy husband, and he shall rule over thee".**

God was conveying the message to Eve that after a marriage, there must be only one man, And in the case of Adam, one woman, or one wife. What God was doing here was laying-down, not only the rule for marriage, but the law.

During the time Eve was engaged in the sex act with the serpent, **she didn't mean to be unfaithful to her husband Adam.** She just didn't know any better, but from now on, God wanted her to know what it means; that is, one husband, and to the man, one wife-**no hanky-panky!**

PARAGRAPH OF PARAMOUNT IMPORTANCE

If God knew he was going to expel Adam and Eve, out of the Garden, why would he tell Eve-**that her desire must be for her husband-knowing quite well ' THAT THE TREE AND THE FRUIT OF WHICH SHE LUSTED OVER, AND ATE FROM, WOULD REMAIN IN THE GARDEN?** Let me put it another way: Let's assume that the tree of knowledge of good and evil **was a fixed tree in the Garden of Eden, as some people believe, why then would God warn Eve about her desire for the fruit, or the tree-IF HE KNEW THAT SHE WAS GOING TO LEAVE BOTH THE TREE AND THE FRUIT BEHIND IN THE GARDEN?**

This should prove that this tree of knowledge of good and evil, **WAS A MOVEABLE TREE-AND NOT A FIXED ONE PLANTED IN THE GARDEN. (please explain)** well, because Eve was the metaphorical tree, **and it was a tree which brought forth children, and the fruit was the sex organ in the middle, or center of the tree, or Garden as is ours also.**

Don't forget Eve was standing **right there 'in front of the serpent'** when God warned her about who she should desire, **and it must be Adam who should have rule over her.** But why would God warn Eve about who should have the right to rule over her-**if someone else wasn't already ruling over her, or influencing her before? And we do know that the culprit was the serpent.**

Look at this one: If God knew that Adam was the one who was already ruling over her or influencing her all along, **WHY WOULD HE STILL TELL EVE THAT IT MUST BE ADAM TO RULE OVER HER?** Well, because he wasn't ruling over her before. As far as Adam was concerned Eve was just a woman the Lord God brought to be with him. Even though Adam knew Eve was his wife he didn't know he had the right to rule over her. Adam too was kind of naive because his brain wasn't uploaded with wisdom or knowledge yet.

Now, Eve's mind might have gone back to the words which the serpent told her in verse 5, He said to her," **For God doth know that in the day ye eat thereof, then your eyes, (mind's eye) shall be opened, and ye shall be as gods knowing good and evil".**

Moses now speaks in verse 6, "**And when the woman (Eve) saw that the tree (her body) was good for food, and it was pleasant to the eyes (to admire) and a tree (body) to be desired to make one wise, she took...of the fruit (sex organ) thereof, and did eat, and gave also unto her husband...'WITH HER' AND HE DID EAT"**

The reality is, Eve ate the fruit of the tree when she noticed how desirable both the tree and the fruit were, That is, when she was told by the serpent how awesome they were. Then she became aware of the tree and fruit, that is, her body and her sex organ. And was able to see how desirable they were.

Eve didn't notice how desirable or sexy her tree or body, and her fruit were, **when she was in front of Adam; but rather, it was when she was in the present, or in front of the serpent, that after she was told by the serpent, that she realized how lustful and desirable they were.** Then after eating it 'with him', she went back home and 'Ate the fruit (sex act) with Adam 'also'.

You should know she **also** desired the body of the serpent, because she was bewitched by the devil. He had a spell over. You must remember that this devil, or serpent was a master deceiver...**a master psychologist.**

Remember this: it wasn't the serpent's body which was crawling on the ground which she desired, or lusted over- but rather, it was the serpent's body which was walking upon

his feet-'BEFORE IT WAS CURSED. Observe: the devil through the serpent's, **transformed himself into a handsome, beautiful, walking serpent in order to deceive Eve.** So Eve saw this beautiful transformed body of Lucifer/the devil, **and she loved what she saw.** She desired the serpent's body because the devil made her see a polished beautiful serpent.

Don't forget, the scripture says the devil was able to transform himself into an angel of light. So if he wanted to deceive Eve, do you think he would have transformed himself into an ugly being? **Eve was mesmerized.**

GOD IS STILL GIVING EVE FINAL INSTRUCTIONS

Back to God instructing Eve as to whose body and fruit she should desire, and it must be for her husband Adam. Here is the question: Why would God have instructed Eve that her desire must be to her husband-**IF GOD DIDN'T SEE THAT HER DESIRE WAS FOR SOMEONE ELSE BEFORE? Or if there was no one else in existence?**

Remember now, at this time, it was just Adam and Eve as full human beings. So when God told Eve her desire must be to her husband...**who else had God expected Eve to have a desire for, or to? Unless there was someone else she could have desired?** Yes, that someone else was the devil who was able to transform himself-not only as an angel of light, but as a man. After all, if the sons of God were able to transform themselves to look like humans, and even to marry human women, how much more Lucifer could have done the same?

Now the strangest thing is, Eve still didn't hate the serpent at this time, for what he did to her. The reason is, she didn't possess a spirit of hate as yet. So the serpent was still hanging-out with

them in the Garden. But it wasn't until God stepped in, **and put a spirit of division or hatred between her and the serpent, that she really saw how wicked he was...then she hated him. It's obvious something was going on between them.**
Here is a salient question again: WHY WOULD GOD HAD TO PUT 'A DIVISION', OR 'HATRED' BETWEEN EVE AND THE SERPENT...IF THERE WASN'T A UNITY OR RELATIONSHIP BETWEEN THEM? God put this spirit of division, or hatred between them **so that they would hate each other instead of ADMIRING EACH OTHER.**

Question: Can you see that there had to have been a unity between Eve and the serpent,? If the answer is no! Why then God had to activate this spirit of division and put it between them?

Now as a result of Eve being under this satanic influence, she wanted to engage in the sex act with the serpent. But she didn't know that she was under the devil's spell. So when God asked Eve why did she commit this sinful act, she said ' **she was beguiled by the serpent.** The word 'beguile' is **to cheat, to deceive, to delight, and to charm".** So we can classify this act by the serpent, or the devil as ' **THAT OF RAPE' You see, the serpent did deceive, cheat, delight, charm, and tricked Eve.** But to do what? Well, **to eat from the forbidden tree, and to eat the fruit of that tree.**

Note this: Adam isn't here at this time when Eve was being beguiled. This means she partook of the fruit without the presence of Adam. **Again, the serpent had her hypnotized and under his spell.** She never did come to her senses, until God made her aware of her sin. So God had to put a spirit of division between them-**and scolded her.**

As far as the serpent was concerned, it was easier than taking candy from a baby. But how do you know she enjoyed it? **Well,** because when she got back home, she encouraged her husband Adam to take a bite of it WITH HER. So they both ate the forbidden fruit together. Yes, the serpent was the first rapist on earth.

If Eve didn't enjoy the sex act with the serpent, she wouldn't have encouraged Adam to have sex with her. She knew it was sweet so she encouraged him to try it...and he did eat it with her.

BACK TO GOD SCOLDING EVE

God is now telling Eve...No more sweet-hearts...and no more eating your fruit with no other man, serpent of creature. But from now on, you must direct your desire to your husband's fruit and body or tree. Again, if there were no one else, why would God tell her this?

Don't forget, the serpent was her instructor, and he was educating her about her body and her fruit, or sex organ. But God wanted her to know that her husband was now in control. And it's his voice which shall prevail. God was still setting, not only the rules of marriage in order, but the laws.

ADAM'S SENTENCE

Here is Adam's sentence for listening to the voice of his wife, and not God's voice. Verse 17, " Unto Adam he said, because thou hast hearkened unto the voice of thy wife, and has eaten of the tree which I commanded thee saying, thou shalt not eat of it, Curse is the ground for thy sake; in sorrow shalt thou eat of it all the days of thy life"

Verse 18, "Thorns and thistles shall it bring forth to thee; and thou shalt eat the herb of the field"

Verse 19, "In the sweat of thy face shalt thou eat bread, till thou return unto the ground, for out of it wast thou taken: for dust thou art, and unto dust shalt thou return"

Moses records in verse 20, "And Adam called his wife's name, Eve (life) because she was the mother of all living"

Check-out this fresh revelation: In the beginning, Adam didn't call his wife's name, Eve. It was just, 'ISH-SHA', or WOMAN. After they begat children, then and only then, Adam gave her the name 'EVE'

Here is the proof hidden in plain sight of Moses' statement in verse 20., And Adam called his wife's name Eve, (life). Here is the clue: Moses goes on: because she was the mother of all living"

But why did Adam call his wife's name Eve? Answer: because she was the mother of all living'. What this statement proves is that after Adam's wife had gotten children-then and only then, Adam had decided to give her the name, 'EVE'. But why? Well, because she is now 'the mother of all living. That is, living children.

Adam couldn't give her the name, 'Eve' 'before' she had children. Why not? Because she wouldn't have been the mother of all living yet. This is why the name Eve, means, life. If she hadn't gotten any children, then Adam wouldn't have called her Eve. Just like a woman should not be called a wife, until she is married. So Eve couldn't have been called Eve until she had children. This revelation was just revealed to me while writing this chapter. Now back to Moses as he goes on in verse 21, "Unto Adam also and to his wife did the Lord God make coats of skins, and clothed them".

Before God had expelled Adam and Eve, he gave them a new set of wardrobe. A new change of clothing. He killed a few lambs and made coats for them to cover their whole bodies, including their sex organs. But before receiving a new set of lambs – skin out-fit, They only had their sex organs covered with some fig leaves glued together. **Again, and it was to cover their shame, or sex organ. Because that was the thing with which they sinned.**

Those skimpy, leafy-bikinis made out of fig leaves couldn't hold-up to well. Those glued fig leaves connected with some vine-G-strings couldn't stay firm. I believe they just kept slipping off. As a result of eating the fruit like the gods, they gained the knowledge of the gods...to know good and evil. They now know how to make covering to hide their sex organs. Even though God was disappointed in them, I believe he still had pity on them. And even as I write about their ordeal, tears are in my eyes. After all, they are our father and mother, and we came from them.

Now God makes nice lambs' skin clothing for them and sends them on their way.I'm sure God gave them a few extra suits of coats. So from now on they were on their own. **So Adam and Eve picked-up their Georgie-bundle and headed north-then ended-up some sixty five (65) miles in the Jordan Valley area which was later called, 'THE CITY ADAM', near Zarethan, Beth-shean, below Jez-reel. Joshua chapter 3:16.**

Yes, they were expelled out of the Garden which was in Eden, later called Jerusalem, which was facing the east, or sunrise. Some believe God had only killed one lamb which symbolizes Jesus Christ. But the reality is: God killed several lambs, because the skin from one lamb wouldn't have made coats for Adam and Eve. So there had to have been more than one lamb which the Lord God had killed.

ADAM AND EVE BECAME DIRT GODS

Do you remember I told you Adam and Eve became little gods, but evil ones? Two: Do you also remember Eve told the serpent God had told them not to eat of the fruit, because if they did, they would die? Well, the following is very interesting to follow.

Here is the serpent's response to Eve in Genesis chapter 3:4, "And the serpent said unto the woman,"**ye shall not surely die**".

Verse 5, "For God doth know that in the day ye eat thereof, then your eyes shall be opened (one)...AND YE SHALL BE AS GODS KNOWLEDGE GOOD AND EVIL". (two)

Again, the serpent told Eve that God had lied to them because he knew that on the day she would eat this fruit **SHE WOULD BE AS GODS KNOWING GOOD AND EVIL.** But the question is, did the serpent tell Eve the truth? Well, in-part, yes, but not the part where he accused God as lying to them. How can it be proven that the serpent told Eve a half truth, or part truth and part lie? Well reader, **if God himself told you that Adam and Eve...BECAME AS GODS, would you believe him?**

Okay! After God had passed sentence on the serpent, Adam, and Eve, he says in verse 22, of this same Genesis chapter 3: **"AND THE LORD SAID...BEHOLD (look) THE MAN (Adam) IS BECOME...'AS ONE OF US'...TO KNOW GOOD AND EVIL: and now lest he (Adam) put forth his hand, and take also OF THE TREE OF LIFE, AND LIVE FOREVER"** unquote.

So as you have heard God himself say to the other gods, **THAT THE MAN, OR ADAM HAD BECOME AS ONE OF THEM AS A GOD.** So if God himself made this statement, then Adam and Eve **had to have become 'AS GODS' of the earth.**

After Adam had taken of the tree of the knowledge of good and evil, the Gods had decided to expel him and his wife out of the Garden...**'BEFORE THEY PICK OR EAT THE**

FRUIT OF THE ...'TREE OF LIFE'...'ALSO' AND LIVE FOREVER.

Did you pick-up on God's confirmation that the serpent told Eve the truth, and that Adam and Eve had become gods? **I will quote the serpent's statement...then God's statement, then you make the comparison.**

THE SERPENT'S STATEMENT

This is the serpent's statement to Eve: "AND YE SHALL BE AS GODS KNOWING GOOD AND EVIL"
NOW GOD'S STATEMENT
Here is God's suggestion to the other gods in verse 22. "Moses writes, 'And the Lord God said: BEHOLD (look) THE MAN (Adam) IS BECOME...'AS ONE OF US' (Gods) TO KNOW GOOD AND EVIL"

Do you see that God had confirmed the serpent's statement which he made to Eve, **that they will become as gods to know good and evil?** The serpent said to Eve, "YOU WILL BE AS GODS KNOWING GOOD AND EVIL" Now here is God's confirmation to the other divine beings: **BEHOLD (look) THE MAN IS BECOME...'AS ONE OF US'...TO KNOW GOOD AND EVIL"..not will become, but 'IS' become.** But of course, God ran them out of his Garden, so they wouldn't eat from 'the tree of life' and live forever. So you see, we could have been living forever on this earth, but Adam and Eve blew it for us, But no love lost.

Do you see that ' **The same statement which the serpent or the devil made...'IS THE SAME' GOD MADE?** So if God confirmed the serpent's statement, what do you think this means? **Yes, it proves that Adam and Eve became gods...that is, to know good and evil.** But how? Well, because they ate the fruit from the forbidden tree. **That is, they ate the food of the Gods before the time.**

Think about this: **if Adam and Eve became Gods, to know good and evil, would you say that man had fallen, OR ROSE TO THE STATUS OF AN EARTHLY DIRT GOD?** Think about this also: When Adam and Eve's minds' eyes were opened-their understanding of good and evil were activated. So again, the question to you dear reader is this: **HAD ADAM AND EVE 'DESCENDED' IN KNOWLEDGE, OR HAD 'ASCENDED' IN KNOWLEDGE, AND UNDERSTANDING?** You see, it was God who stated that they had **'ascended' to the status of the Gods. I didn't say this, but God did, but you decide if man had fallen or was elevated.**

LET'S MAKE MAN IN OUR OWN IMAGE

Here is the fact: God had made Adam in his own image and likeness. But when he and Eve ate the fruit from the forbidden tree,, **or engaged in the sex act, THEY BECAME EVEN MORE, AS THE GODS...THAT IS, IN KNOWLEDGE AND UNDERSTANDING.** The devil spilled the beans, that is, he revealed the secrets of the Gods. So Adam and Eve had down-loaded the knowledge of the Gods by activating the sex act, and eating the forbidden fruit before permission was given. Even to this day, it's the number one cause for the toppling of man from power.

Moses records in Genesis chapter 1:27, "So God created man in his own image, in the image of God created he them." This means that Eve also became an earthly goddess. **That is, after the image and likeness of God's wife, 'The SHEKINAH WISDOM' of God, the queen of heaven, and the spiritual goddess of the earth known as MOTHER NATURE.**

Tell me, how would you know that 'ONE' of the 'US' WAS A FEMALE? Well, God said: "let us make them in 'OUR' not only image, but also in OUR LIKENESS, Note: the image was 'THE FORM, or kind of shape like the Gods.

That is, they were given the up-right image as God and as Goddesses – not the image of any beast, or birds.

Now, 'THE LIKENESS' In which the Gods had created the man and the woman, WAS THE LIKENESS, OR SIMILARITY LIKE THEMSELVES. SO ADAM LOOKED JUST LIKE THE LORD GOD, with a glow, or aurora around his body but of course, it vanished when he sinned. And by the way, Jesus Christ himself looked just like his father the Lord God also.

Now Eve however, LOOKED JUST LIKE THE WISDOM OF GOD: that is, God's wife. Therefore, ALL OF THE FEMALES ON EARTH TOOK ON THE IMAGE, AFTER GOD'S WIFE. Know this: it was only Eve who took on the exact likeness of God's wife, But all females' or women took on her image. However, I'm sure one of Eve's daughters or granddaughters had taken on her likeness.' This likeness of Eve is handed down. So some women even today look somewhat like Eve. I wouldn't be surprised if Jesus were to tell me...it's your wife ' URISMAE' I say this because she is the most pious and righteous woman I have ever known on earth. I also believe she is an angel disguised in human flesh. This is my opinion.

Even today, I believe that a man somewhere on earth looks like Adam. I don't know for sure, but I do believe that Noah, Abraham, Isaac, Joseph, Moses and king David resembled Adam, and by extension the Lord God himself. Because if you would notice, upon their birth, the scripture would say that they were outstanding or a proper child. But what made them look so beautiful or handsome even as a baby, I believe is because they blushed or looked somewhat like Adam, and Adam was in the **likeness of God himself.**

Now the reason the devil or Lucifer hated Adam so much, is because he looked exactly or had the likeness like God. And every time he would see him he would see the likeness of God; and this just put hell up in him..

Finally, if God said, let us make them **in ' our own image and likeness-then when you look to see what the Gods made 'in their own image and likeness' YOU SEE ADAM AND EVE-THAT IS...A MALE AND A FEMALE.** So wouldn't you conclude that one of the **'US', or Gods HAD TO HAVE BEEN A FEMALE, or A WOMAN?** Think about it. You see, Adam and Eve, **WERE THE REFLECTION OF THE GODS.** that is, **THE LORD GOD, AND HIS WIFE, 'MOTHER SHEKINAH WISDOM',** who is also the same as Mother nature, **(Sophia)**

THINK ABOUT NARRATIVE

Observe this also again: You walk into a room-you don't see anyone. You hear a voice emanating from another room, saying **LET US MAKE MAN IN OUR OWN IMAGE AND LIKENESS"** Now, tell me how would you know what they look like, even though you haven't seen them? Well, all you have to do is, to see who the Gods' made or created in their image and likeness. Then and only then you would know how the Gods' look.

Now if you were to see a man and a woman coming out of 'THE SAME ROOM' where you heard the voice emanating from...wouldn't you conclude that the voice, or person who said..."LET US MAKE THEM LIKE US ... that one of them, or Gods, HAD TO HAVE LOOKED LIKE A MAN, AND

ONE LIKE A WOMAN, OR A MALE AND A FEMALE, OR A GODDESS ALONG WITH GOD, BEHIND THE SCENE? And indeed she is God's wife. She is the divine Queen of heaven and the spiritual Goddess of the earth, or Mother nature. She is the Spirit that makes all things on earth germinate or come to life and grow. Now whenever a person or the pope kisses the ground or the earth, he kisses Mother Nature-God's wife. **See my book, "THE WIFE OF GOD" on Amazon.**

I am so pleased with Jesus Christ, my Lord. And so thankful to him for giving me this message to let the women of the earth know that they are made after the image of **Mother Shekinah Wisdom, God's wife. And all, both men and women should thank God for her, and respect her because she is their mother.** Mary was Jesus' earthly mother, but Shekinah Wisdom is **his spiritual mother. So it's her who should be praised instead of Mary.**

CHAPTER 14

MY FINAL CLOSING ARGUMENT

Ladies and gentlemen, before I begin to expand on my closing argument, allow me to give you an overview of the events, which occurred after Noah and family dis-embarked from the ark, from Mount Ararat. Now at the end of 1656 years, or ten (10) generations, from the creation of Adam to the flood of Noah, God had decided that his whole creation was not worth saving. So he destroyed all, leaving only Noah, his wife, and his sons: Shem, Ham, and Japheth, and their wives, and an assortment of creatures. God then put Noah and his family on a boat and pushed them to the east, to a mountain called Ararat. Satellite view is showing Mount Ararat,. To be a dormant complex volcano **in eastern Anatolia-region of Turkey close to the border to Armenia, about 60km. South of Armenia's capital, 'Yerevan, 5,137m. (16,854 ft.) the tallest peak in Turkey.**

Here is what Moses records in Genesis 9:18-19, "And the sons of Noah, that went forth of the ark, were Shem, and Ham, and Japheth: And Ham is the father of Canaan." Verse 19, "These are the three sons of Noah: **AND OF THEM WAS THE WHOLE EARTH OVERSPREADED.**"

The logical deduction of this is, that since it was only 'after' Noah and his family came out of the ark, **that the whole earth** was overspread...of course, apart from the land where they left from **proves 'the whole earth 'WAS NOT' over-spread 'before' the flood.**

Two: This also logically indicates that the various lands they would have discovered, **'after'** they would have descended the ark, and Mount Ararat, would have been, **'VIRGIN LANDS':** that is, lands or countries which had **'NEVER BEEN POPULATED BEFORE'' In this vein, THEY COULD NOT HAVE BEEN THE LANDS, OR AREAS WHERE THE GARDEN OF EDEN WAS LOCATED,** nor where the fountain of living water emanated.

Think about this: since Noah and the ark landed on Mount Ararat, in eastern Anatolia-region of Turkey, close to the border to Armenia; rules **''them out' as being the land of Eden, and where the Garden of Eden was planted.**

Check this out: If the ark landed there, obviously that's not the region, nor land where Noah and his family came from. And we know that Noah, and Adam lived in the same region in the beginning/ or Jordan Valley.

Genesis chapter 2:8. I now quote Moses. "And the Lord God planted a Garden **eastward in Eden:** and there he put the man whom he had formed." This land was indeed called, **'Eden' BEFORE the flood.** However, after the flood came upon the whole earth, the land Eden took on a change in name. So when the flood ended, Noah and family descended Mount Ararat. As they travelled away **'FROM THE EAST'** They found a plain, or Valley in the land of Shinar/ Babylon. And there the various tribes multiplied in great numbers.

Moses records in Genesis 10: 25, **And unto 'Eber'** was born two sons: the name of one was **'Peleg',** for in his days the earth was divided: His brother's name was **Joktan".**

212

IMPORTANT INFORMATION

Note: the number of years after Noah and his family had landed in the new world-to the birth of **Peleg was 701, years.** It was at this time the earth was divided. That is, the people were scattered all over the earth by God because of wickedness; and trying to reach into heaven by building a tower.

God now steps in, then confused their language so that they wouldn't understand one another's speech. At this time there was only one language **and it was spoken in the land of Shinar/ Babel/Babylon. This means that this is the same language spoken in the old world before the flood.** At this time, no other parts of the earth were populated by human beings.

Now it was 191, years from the birth of **Peleg,** or from the scattering of the people at Babel, **TO THE BIRTH OF ABRAM. But seventy five (75) years later at the time God called Abram, brings the numbers of years to 266 years.** So during these 266 years, the whole earth was already populated, including Europe, Africa, Asia and Palestine, or Canaan land.

Now the number of years after the flood of Noah, up to the birth of Abram, **was 892 years. But up to the time he met God, at the age of 75, years brought the total number of years to 967 years. This 'Peleg' was Abraham's great, great, great, grandfather.**

During this scattering, and confusion at Babel; **CANAAN WHO WAS HAM'S FOURTH SON, FOUND A LAND IN PALESTINE, OR MIDDLE EAST.** He was blessed to have found the very land where the original people lived for the first ten(10) generations, or 1656 years, **From Adam to Noah.** Canaan and his tribe, or family members took possession of this land and called it, **'CANAAN LAND' which was of course, later to be known, AS 'THE PROMISED LAND' BY THE**

HEBREWS. And it was later named, the land of Israel. And it was located, FROM DAN (Le-shem) IN THE NORTH, TO NEGEV IN THE SOUTH-even as far south as the Gulf of Eilat, at Israel's border.

Now before the Israelites conquered Canaan's land, and gave the lands names after his sons. Canaan and his descendants occupied these lands for hundreds of years before the Israelites conquered them and took them. Canaan's third son whose name is JEBUS took possession of a part of the mountainous land, and named it after his own name which is Jebus. So his clan was called, 'The Jebusites'. This Jebus' land was the original land called, ' **Eden' before the flood'**. It was Canaan who had discovered the original land where Adam and the first ten (10) generations of people lived-including the giants.

PROOF: JEBUS' LAND IS JERUSALEM

These two verses in 1, Chronicles 11:4-5, will prove that the land of Jerusalem was first called, 'Jebus' after the flood.

Verse 4, "And David and all Israel **went to Jerusalem, which is Jebus, where the Jebusites were, 'THE INHABITANTS OF THE LAND"**

Verse 5, "And the inhabitants of Jebus said to David, "Thou shalt not come hither,(here) nevertheless, David took the Castle of Zion, which is the city of David"

A fort is a fortified cluster of buildings...also a building similar to a castle. So

Know this: after David took **'the land of Jebus from the Jebusites, he called it, JERU-SALEM.** But before it was called Jerusalem, it was called, **'Jebus',** however, the Hebrews always called Jebus' land, **'SALEM'.** But after conquering Salem, David put a prefix to Salem, and called, it **JERUSALEM.**

ADVANCING MY CLAIM THAT JERUSALEM AND EDEN WERE THE SAME LAND.

Ladies and gentleman, allow me to further advance my claim in this final argument, by asking you a series of questions and making a series of statements.

One day when The Jewish prophet Ezekiel was in captivity in Babylon, he had the experience of being in a vision of the Lord. In his book, in the fortieth chapter, he claims that God brought him ' **to the land of Israel**' then set him upon a high mountain, with the city of Jerusalem being situated on the south side of it.

What is important for you to bear in mind, is that, ' **It was the land of Israel, and the city of Jerusalem he was brought to.** In this city, he even gives the dimension of Jerusalem '**as being seven miles long and six miles wide. 7x6miles.**

Ezekiel also says he was commanded by an angel to tell the Jews that when they would have been freed out of Babylon, or captivity, and would return to Jerusalem, **that they 'MUST' divide the city of Jerusalem, straight down the middle,** and they must use the half to the south which would be 7, miles long by 3, miles wide to be holy. And they must measure 875 ft. square, of this 7x3, exactly in the center.

He goes on: this 875 ft. Square will be the most holy place. This most holy place was the spot where they 'MUST' build his temple.

Ladies and gentlemen, this same land of Israel where Ezekiel was transported in his vision, IS THE SAME ISRAEL WHEREIN HE DESCRIBES THE GARDEN OF EDEN. So don't look in another country for the place of the Garden of Eden. Isn't this straight forward? So please Remember this.

I've come to the conclusion that in the process of time, after the flood, **that this same land of Eden which Moses refers to in**

215

Genesis 2:8, was called Jebus, by the Jebusites who first owned it 'AFTER' they travelled from Shinar, or Babylon, after the scattering of the various tribes.

LADIES AND GENTLEMEN, PONDER THE FOLLOWING:

Based on the information of the angel's instructions to the prophet Ezekiel, I've come to the conclusion that the Garden of Eden was planted some **one and a third miles (1, ⅓) or 9,333ft. From The Golden Gate/ Eastern Gate, of the wall which surrounded the Temple-Mount below, in a plain, Eastward in Jerusalem to where Ezekiel stopped touring with the angel... AND THE TREE OF LIFE WAS PLANTED SOME 4,666 FT. in the middle of the Garden with lush green fruit trees and plants.**

Even though the layout, or size of Jerusalem today may not fit the exact dimension of it as the angel told Ezekiel, nonetheless, the Temple-Mount is still in existence to prove that it's the point of reference to find the Garden of Eden.

One can't say that the angel was making reference to heavenly New Jerusalem, because the heavenly Jerusalem's dimension is, 1,500 by 1,500 by 1,500 miles square, as a cube, situated in the center of the New earth above. But the angel told Ezekiel that the earthly Jerusalem **'MUST' be measured-out to seven miles long and six miles wide.**

If you believe the scriptures, or the angel's words to the prophet Ezekiel, you would notice that **he started with the nation of Israel, but specifically, with the city of Jerusalem... and the Temple-Mount as being the starting point to go forward, or eastward to look for the Garden of Eden.**

If Mount Moriah, or the Temple-Mount in Jerusalem was the place where God dwelt among his ancient people, **Why** would he put his garden in another land? Even today we still put our gardens 'in front of our dwellings houses, because this was the way it was in the beginning, as it relates to his dwelling place, or house and his Garden. Think about it!

Ladies and gentlemen: the point isn't where the four rivers ended up, but rather, 'where it began to flow from'. And the scriptures say it began to flow from Mount Moriah in Jerusalem. And Moses says the Garden was in Eden.

Ezekiel gives us the description of the Garden of Eden, by telling us that the Garden 'WAS IN JERUSALEM. And the river flowed to the Garden of Eden '' BEFORE' it went and divided itself into four heads.

If you differ where the river of living water began to divide into four (4) heads, is not the main point. The point is, it began to be divided 'After' it passed the Garden of Eden.

It's a known fact that throughout the old testament, God had declared that he had sanctified, or set aside the land of Jerusalem 'as his holy land'. So among all of the nations, or lands on earth in the past, Jerusalem was always number one. Moses states that in the beginning of God's creation, he had planted his Garden 'in Eden' facing the sunrise, or the east. Therefore, if the land of Jerusalem was God's set-aside land, or sanctified holy land, where do you think he would have planted his holy Garden? I submit to you that it would have been in Old Jerusalem which was called 'EDEN' before the flood.

In your studies or research, have you discovered any other land among all the nations on earth, where God had called, his holy, sanctified, or special land...apart from Jerusalem, and Mount Moriah/Zion? If not, isn't it logical for you to extrapolate that Jerusalem had to have been God's holy land in the past, where he planted his Garden? So if Moses says, that the Lord's

Garden. 'was in Eden' and God says that his holy land 'Was in Jerusalem', shouldn't this indicate that his Garden MUST HAVE BEEN IN JERUSALEM? Think about it'

Ladies and gentlemen of the jury, please contemplate on the following: Here is what Jesus promises to all who overcome **the mirages of this life.**

Revelation chapter 2:7," He that hath an ear, let him hear what the spirit saith unto the churches: **TO HIM THAT OVERCOMETH, WILL I GIVE TO EAT OF THE TREE OF LIFE WHICH IS IN THE MIDST OF THE PARADISE OF GOD"**

As you have heard Jesus say, that the tree of life...**is now in New Jerusalem! And it's in the midst, or middle of the Paradise of God...This is in the Garden of God above...in the same way as it was in the first Eden, or Paradise on earth, in the beginning in Jerusalem below the Temple-Mount.**

Think on this: the paragraph above should prove to you **'That the tree of life must have been in Old Jerusalem below on earth, among the trees which Ezekiel saw below Mount Moriah/the Temple-Mount.** And the Garden of Eden which Moses says God had planted, 'east in Eden had to have been in Jerusalem in Palestine. So according to reason, can you deduce that the Paradise of God was below Mount Moriah/Zion?

GOD' BLESSINGS ARE CONDITIONAL

The following is very important for you to know, So that when you hear God promise a thing, and at times decline from doing that thing, at least you would know why. **Never forget, all of God's promises and blessings are conditional**. In the event you disbelieve me, let's see what God himself says about honoring or dishonoring his words or promises.

God says in the book of Jerimiah chapter 18:7, "**At what instant I shall speak concerning 'a nation' and concerning 'a kingdom', to pluck up and to pull down and to destroy it**"

Verse 8, "**If that nation against whom I have pronounced, turn from their evil, I will repent of the evil that I thought to do unto them**"

Verse 9, "**And at what instant I shall speak concerning 'a nation' and concerning 'A kingdom' to build and to plant it**"

Verse 10, "**If it do evil in my sight that it obey NOT MY VOICE THEN I WILL REPENT (change my mind) OF THE GOOD WHERE WITH I SAID I WOULD BENEFIT THEM**" (unquote)

I'm hoping you're learning something about the nature of God. So it's quite evident that God's words or promises **ARE CONDITIONAL, OR PREDICATED ON AN INDIVIDUAL, OR A NATION DOING EITHER GOOD OR EVIL. it's ALL UP TO US OR A NATION.** Therefore, all of the promises which God said he would have done **for ancient Israel,** or former nations, were based on them keeping his statues.

Example: take the city of Nineveh. God intended to destroy it because of their wickedness. So he sent Jonah to preach to them to repent. Now, because they repented, God repented, that is, he changed his mind and did not destroy them.

GOD CHANGED HIS MIND FROM RECREATING THE PHYSICAL NEW EARTH-DOWN HERE

Just bear with me for a short while in order to enlighten you as to why God changed his mind **FROM RECREATING THE NEW EARTH DOWN HERE, AFTER THE ISRAELITES CAME OUT OF CAPTIVITY FROM**

BABYLON. It was the prophet Isaiah who had prophesied that God would have driven the Israelites into Babylon. And it was also the prophet Isaiah who had said God would have created ' A NEW EARTH AFTER THE JEWS WOULD HAVE COME OUT OF BABYLON.

The first portion of the prophecy did come through, because the Jews did go into slavery into Babylon. But the part of the prophecy where God would have recreated **'a new earth' after the Jews would have come out of Babylon didn't come into fruition.** The reason this part of the prophecy didn't come to pass is because the people didn't please God after coming out of Babylon, but made God more angry by them worshipping other pagan gods. **Therefore, God changed his mind and didn't recreate 'The New Earth' down here anymore. Instead he built it above. So the New earth is above, just as New Jerusalem is above.**

Here now is the New earth which God promised to create, after the Jews would have come out of captivity from Babylon, but he never followed through with his plans, **but repented, or changed his mind.** So Isaiah prophecy was only partly fulfilled.

Here is the good news by the prophet Isaiah to the Israelites, **but never came to pass. Isaiah chapter 65:17-25, "For behold, I create new heavens 'AND A NEW EARTH':** and the former shall not be remembered, nor come into mind"

Verse 18, "But be ye glad and rejoice forever in that which I create: **for behold, I CREATE JERUSALEM A REJOICING, AND HER PEOPLE A JOY"**...This never happened on earth, but the 144,000 Israelites in New Jerusalem above are the ones who are rejoicing and living forever.

Verse 19, "And I will rejoice in Jerusalem, and joy in my people: and the voice of weeping **'SHALL BE NO MORE HEARD IN HER, NOR THE VOICE OF CRYING"**

It didn't come to pass, but this joy is now being experienced above in New Jerusalem.

Verse 20, "There shall be no more thence an infant of days, nor an old man that hath not filled his days: 'FOR THE CHILD...SHALL 'DIE' AN HUNDRED YEARS OLD; BUT THE...SINNER BEING AN HUNDRED YEARS OLD SHALL BE ACCURSED"

Verse 21, "And they shall build houses, and inhabited them: and they shall plant vineyard, and eat the fruit of them"

Verse 22, They shall not build, and another inhabit; They shall not plant, and another eat: **for as the days of a tree are the days of my people, and mine elect shall long enjoy the work of their hand"**

Verse23, "They shall not labour in vain, nor bring forth for trouble; for they are the seed of the blessed of the Lord, and their offspring with them"

Verse 24, "And it shall come to past, that before they call, I will answer; And while they are yet speaking, I will hear"

Verse 25, "**The wolf and the lamb shall feed together, and the lion shall eat straw like the bullock: and dust shall be the serpent's meat.** They shall not hurt nor destroy...**in all my mountain (Moriah) saith the Lord"**

God is speaking metaphorically in verse 25. The wolf, lamb, lion, and serpent, were in reference to the nations. Question: who do we find in God's mountain in Jerusalem hurting God's elect in the past? **It was the king of Tyrus, and the Assyrian king.** And what did the prophet say that God said he was going to do to the Assyrian king? Well, that he will take his yoke off the neck of the Israelites. And what else did the prophet say that God was going to do to the Assyrian king? Well, **THAT HE WILL DRIVE HIM OUT OF HIS HOLY MOUNTAIN.** And as we know already that the Assyrian kings were referred to 'as serpents'. Therefore, God referred to those nations metaphorically. Just as Russia is referred to as a bear-the united states as an eagle and originally, Ethiopia as the lion. So in the New Earth and New Jerusalem which God had planned to create **after the Jews would have come out of Babylon whereby those nations would have enjoyed peace and unity,,,whereby they would have beat their swords into pruning hook, and learn war no more...DID NOT COME INTO REALITY. THERE WAS A CHANGE D IN GOD'S PLAN BECAUSE MEN CONTINUED TO WORSHIP PAGAN FALSE GODS.**

Again, what you have just read was supposed to be the conditions **of the New Earth and New Jerusalem...after the Jews would have come out of captivity from Babylon, but God changed his plans.**

Some people may say this was in reference to the millennium reign. But you see, this could not have been referring to the millennium reign. At this time this wasn't even referring to the New Jerusalem and the New Earth above, It was afterward that God had decided to create New Jerusalem and the New earth above. This New Earth, and New Jerusalem **WAS PROPHESIED TO COME INT0 BEING...ON THIS EARTH BELOW, BUT NEVER HAPPENED.** Why Do I say this? You see, in New Jerusalem and the New Earth above, **There is no death up there...And no sinners up there.** The following is what Isaiah prophesied to occur in New Jerusalem, and in the New earth. **"FOR THE CHILD SHALL DIE"...AN HUNDRED YEARS OLD;...BUT THE SINNERS BEING AN HUNDRED YEARS OLD SHALL BE ACCURSED".**

You see, this New Jerusalem and New earth which Isaiah prophesied about, **never came about, and were quite different from the Spiritual New Earth and New Jerusalem above, as prophesied by John the revelator.**

So don't forget, God says he will change his mind from doing what he says he will do, if we don't keep his righteousness. Note: the Christian tribe is not being taught that they are going to go to the **New Earth above when they die.** But they are only being told that they are going to heaven. And yet they are of the opinion that they are going to New Jerusalem, instead of the New Earth. In fact, the Christians are not being told anything about the New Earth above. They believe that a future New earth **IS THIS SAME ONE DOWN HERE WHICH GOD WILL BURN DOWN AND THEN RENEW IT.** (how sad!)

So this revelation here will open-up your eyes, **that it is the New Earth above where you will live forever after death.** New Jerusalem above **is only for the 144,000 ancient pure Israelites' virgins. And no one else is going to live there.**

Of course, the Saints from the New Earth will visit there to partake from the tree of life, and to carry back home...leaves from that tree to use as medicine

PURE RIVER OF LIFE EMANATING FROM GOD'S THRONE

Contemplate on this: we see in the book of Revelation chapter 22:1, where the apostle John writes the following: and he shew me a pure river of water of life clear as crystal...**proceeding out of the throne of God and the lamb""**

So as you have read John says, **in New Jerusalem above..the pure river of water of life stems /flows/proceeds...OUT OF THE THRONE OF GOD AND THE LAMB.**

Here now is the question: which country on earth in the past would you reason **that the river of water of life, must have been flowing, or proceeding out of the throne, or dwelling place**

223

of God? Well, the answer should be, none other than ' **FROM MOUNT MORIAH / ZION IN JERUSALEM'.** If you concluded it should be ancient Jerusalem, then I say to you, **'THEN YOU WOULD HAVE FOUND EDEN', IN WHICH YOU WOULD FIND ALSO...' THE GARDEN OF THE LORD BELOW MOUNT MORIAH/ ZION, IN A PLAIN.** Know this also: Mount Moriah, or the Temple-Mount in Jerusalem...**was the dwelling place on earth in ancient times, where God himself says he dwelt. In time past.** Therefore, the former earthly Mount Moriah in Jerusalem, **Is now New Mount Moriah / Zion in New Jerusalem above.** And this is the pure and righteous Mount Moriah / Zion wherein dwells righteousness.

Now in this New Jerusalem above, Jesus Christ Eliakim...**is the second Adam, or the new spiritual Adam, and the 144,000 Israelites...is the Spiritual Eve.** This is the same Jesus Christ who was born on the 15th day, in the month of September/ Tishri, in the year bc.5. To the virgin Mary. (see proof in the next chapter)

Here is an eye-opening question for you. Who is the Spiritual Adam today? Answer, Jesus Christ Eliakim. Where does he live today? Or where is his throne today? Answer...**in New Jerusalem above.** So if we find him or the second Adam in the New City of Jerusalem above, **SHOULDN'T THIS INDICATE THAT THE FIRST ADAM MUST HAVE LIVED IN JERUSALEM ON EARTH, IN THE PARADISE OF GOD...'BEFORE' HE WAS EXPELLED?** Just contemplate on it.

The first Adam had to have lived in Jerusalem in Palestine, because he was the Adam of the flesh. **NO WONDER WE FIND THE SECOND ADAM OF THE SPIRIT...IN THE**

SPIRITUAL NEW JERUSALEM. Do you see the correlation between 'the first Adam' who lived in the earthly Jerusalem, and the 'second Adam' who now lives in 'New Jerusalem' above?

Ladies and gentlemen: the apostle John, the prophet Ezekiel, and Jesus **Positioned 'the tree of life' in the midst, or center of the Garden, or Paradise of God, Just as Moses positioned 'the tree of life'…in the midst or center of the Garden. coincident? Oh no!, because it was positioned in Jerusalem, on earth in the beginning, and is now positioned in New Jerusalem above.** Therefore, it should be obvious that 'the tree of life' which Moses writes about, and says it was in the middle of the Garden of Eden, **had to have been in Jerusalem. (Do you see it?)**

But what does the tree of life have to do with Jerusalem and with living waters proceeding from the Temple of God watering the Garden, or Paradise of God, as Ezekiel says, **if Jerusalem wasn't emblematically of the Garden of Eden?** Here is the question another way: **Why is Eden and Jerusalem synonymous? Or what relationship Eden has with Jerusalem, if they were not one and the same land? Also why is the Paradise of God and 'the tree of life' above, synonymous with the Paradise of God, Eden, and 'the tree of life' on earth…if 'the tree of life' and the Paradise of God weren't in Jerusalem on earth**

Ponder this fact: It was in Jerusalem Below the Temple-Mount where Ezekiel **saw all kinds of fruit trees on both sides of the banks of the river in his vision.** Juror, I submit to you this spot has to be **'The Garden of the Lord BELOW HIS HOLY MOUNTAIN, OR TEMPLE-MOUNT IN JERUSALEM. Right here, which was…one and a third mile in length, because this was how far Ezekiel could have followed the copperish angel, or 9,333 feet from the Golden Gate, or eastern gate of the 875ft. Square wall, which surrounded the Temple on Mount Moriah.** But the tree of life which was in the

middle of the garden, or in the middle of the 9,333 ft. HAD TO
HAVE BEEN 4,666 FT. FROM THE GOLDEN GATE/
EASTERN GATE.

In the process of the angel telling Ezekiel the direction the
river will take, he tells him in verse 11. "**But its Swamps and
Marshes will not become fresh; they will be left for salt**"

Ladies and gentlemen, read slowly, because herein lies
another proof that Jerusalem was indeed ancient Eden. The angel
goes on to explain to Ezekiel in verse 12, of chapter 47, "**ALL
KINDS OF FRUIT TREES WILL GROW ON BOTH
BANKS OF THE RIVER, AND THEIR LEAVES WILL
NOT DRY AND DIE. THE TREES WILL HAVE FRUITS
EVERY MONTH, BECAUSE THE WATER FOR THEM
COMES...FROM THE TEMPLE. The fruits from the trees
will be used for food, and their leaves for medicine**" (This is
the tree of life)

Question: to where did Ezekiel return after following the
copper looking angel? I mean, the one who was measuring the
distance from the Temple's Golden / Eastern Gate-to a mile and a
third, eastward-to the point where he couldn't cross over the river?

Here is the answer: It was the place where he left from.
'**Before**' he started to follow the angel. And where is this place?
Answer: ' **By the eastern golden gate which was a part of the
Temple-wall of 875ft. Square, which surrounded the temple
area in Jerusalem.**

Take observation of this: **When Ezekiel returned, he saw
many trees on both sides of the banks of the river...'WHICH
WERE NOT THERE WHEN HE LEFT TO FOLLOW
THE ANGEL WHO WAS MEASURING THE WATER.**
I do not need to say those trees had fruits on them.

The question must also be asked: Was this place where
Ezekiel saw many trees on both sides of the banks of the river, '

THE GARDEN OF EDEN'? Ladies and gentlemen, I submit to you that it was truly the Garden of Eden, or the Garden of the Lord which was just below God's house / mountain; on top of the Temple Mount. Remember, the Garden sloped downward and levelled-off at ground zero into a plain.

When the angel was speaking to Ezekiel, **they were not all the way down by the Swamps and Marshes, but they were by the Gate which leads to the Temple.** I say this because one might get the impression that it was the Marshes and Swamps where the Garden of Eden was planted. You see, the Garden of Eden couldn't have been that far south.'**In Israel/Judah, because both Moses and Ezekiel stated that the Garden was 'IN EDEN/JERUSALEM. But the Swamps and Marshes... ARE 'OUTSIDE JERUSALEM', all the way down passes EN GEDI. and also the dead Sea.** But verse 12, is in reference to verse 7.

THINK ABOUT THIS JUROR

You should bear in mind that in the process of explaining the living waters' route, Ezekiel stopped at Eilat/Aqaba. He only takes us up to the point at the south end of Israel's border. This indicates that the Garden of Eden had to have been watered... '**Before'** it reached to the end of Israel's border: or, '**Before'** we arrived at Eilat/Aqaba. So the Garden of the Lord had to have been planted in Israel's land.

However, the river of living water itself would have continued through Aqaba's Gulf, **then through to the Red Sea, to the southern end of it in order to get to Ethiopia.** So, if in your search, you have reached the point of Eilat's Gulf in Israel/Judah, you would have already passed the Garden of Eden. You would have to return, or back-track to the bottom of Mount Moriah, or below the Temple-Mount, Southeast, **in 'East Jerusalem / the old city.**

Verse 12 is the clue which should open-up your eyes to the fact that Jerusalem was Eden where the Garden of God was planted. Let this remain in your mind always: **It was in Jerusalem below the Temple-Mount where Ezekiel saw all kinds of fruit trees...GROWING ON BOTH SIDES OF THE BANK OF THE RIVER IN HIS VISION.** Ladies and gentlemen, I put it to you, that this has to be **'The place of the Garden of Eden... Right here!**

CONTEMPLATE ON THE FOLLOWING

One: in New Jerusalem above, THE LIVING WATER IS PRESENTLY FLOWING FROM THE THRONE OF GOD. Two: HIS THRONE IS...'WITHIN' HIS TEMPLE. AND THREE: THE LIVING WATER IS FLOWING TO HIS PARADISE, OR GARDEN AND IS CURRENTLY WATERING ALL OF THE TREES INCLUDING 'THE TREE OF LIFE'. And there is also a river like a street which leads from his throne...just like the river which flowed from Mount Moriah, or the Temple-Mount in the earthly Jerusalem to water the Garden of Eden.

So, if the above scenario **is in the Paradise of God – in New Jerusalem above,** then Ezekiel's vision had to have been **'the Paradise of God also on earth in the beginning with Adam and Eve in Old Jerusalem in Palestine. (yes)**

Now, by the time of St. Paul's ministry in the first century, **New Jerusalem was already completed with the 'tree of life' and the river of water within it above.** Think about this: In Ezekiel's vision, the Temple also had living water **flowing outward from the Temple's threshold, or from the main door** flowing toward the east. It also watered the fruit trees, **and the rest of the trees in the garden. Look at this: ' and the trees were also on both sides of the banks of the river, which was below the Temple-Mount,** So the Garden must have been planted in east Jerusalem.

In Ezekiel's vision, the Temple also had living water... flowing outward from the Temple's threshold, or from the main door flowing toward the east. It also watered all of the trees in the Garden. Look at this! AND THE TREES WERE ALSO ON BOTH SIDES OF THE BANKS OF THE RIVER, WHICH WAS BELOW THE TEMPLE-MOUNT. So the Garden must have been planted in; East Jerusalem/Old Jerusalem. (yes?)

Remember this: When Ezekiel returned from his walking tour with the copper angel, didn't he find trees on both sides of the banks of the River? So isn't it strange that Ezekiel saw these fruit trees and this special river, **In Jerusalem, rather than in any other countries? This could only mean that the Garden of Eden had to have been planted ...'in the land of Jerusalem.**

Ponder this also: **These trees also bear fruits once a month. And the leaves of the trees were also for medicine, or for the healing of the nations-just like John's vision in the book of Revelation 22:2. This my friend was indeed the Garden of Eden also which Ezekiel saw describing. But look where it is? Yes, on earth.**

John's vision was about New Jerusalem above with the Garden, or Paradise of God. But Ezekiel's vision was for the earth with the Garden of Eden, which of course, never came into being after the Jews were delivered out of captivity from Babylon. But he described the way it was in the beginning, and how God was going **to recreate it again** after the Jews would have come out of Babylon. But God being disappointed with the

Jews' behavior, changed his mind and did not recreate it on earth no more-**but instead, he recreated it above.**

Please read slowly: if the Garden was in any other country on earth...why would Ezekiel describe it as being at the east... "in Jerusalem"-and the living water flowing from the Temple's threshold, on top of the hill, downward' to water the Garden? Now watch this: Ezekiel also says the water will flow '**to the east country' (which is Jericho) which is also in the Jordan Valley.** Then it would have entered the Jordan River-then it would have entered 'the Dead Sea', and would have passed '**En-gedi'** all the way down to Negev, or Eilat at Israel's coastline. All of this information proves that Ezekiel was describing …' **The Garden of Eden, with the trees of life on earth, in the land of Israel-and not Africa.** So he wasn't describing John's vision of the Paradise of God, and the tree of life in New Jerusalem above. **Nor any Garden in the millennium reign.**

Now seeing that the first Garden of Eden had already come and gone by the time Ezekiel had his vision, then he couldn't have been referring to the heavenly Paradise, or Garden of Eden and the heavenly tree of life.

THE BILLION DOLLAR QUESTION

Here is the question for you to ponder. So please take time-out to really think about it before you go on.

Why did God replicate or duplicate what was in the Garden of Eden on earth, and made them new in New Jerusalem above...IF THE EARTHLY JERUSALEM WASN'T EDEN, AND THE GARDEN WASN'T IN EAST JERUSALEM/ OLD JERUSALEM?

If the original Garden was in Africa, Turkey, or Armenia, why would God duplicate it in Jerusalem above? Doesn't this lend itself to the understanding that the Garden of Eden must have originally been planted in Jerusalem? Think about it.

Marinate on this: if the pure River of living water proceeds, or flows from Mount Zion/Moriah **'in New Jerusalem' to water God's Garden, and tree of life today up there...where do you think it must have proceeded, or emanated from in the past in the earth?** The answer should be...'**From Mount Zion/Mount Moriah/ the Temple-Mount, in the earthly Jerusalem.**

In the book of Revelation chapter 2:7, we hear Jesus say that he will give you food to eat from '**The Tree of Life' which is in the midst of the Paradise of God.**

Where is the Paradise of God today? Answer, '**In New Jerusalem above. Therefore, it stands to reason that 'the tree of life' which is in New Jerusalem today, must have been originally' in Old Jerusalem/East Jerusalem'. (yes?)**

PENETRATING QUESTIONS

Here is the question to ponder so you may see that the land of Eden was truly Old Jerusalem/East Jerusalem. Now with all of those lands in Europe, Africa, and China, why would God promise his friend Abraham, 'Canaan land'? Why didn't he choose a portion of land out of one of the above? The reason is because it wasn't any of those mountains within them he had chosen to be his holy mountain to dwell in in the beginning. And by extension, **to plant his Garden below his house, or mountain.**

This is why God told Abraham to go to **the land of 'MORIAH' and to go up to one of the mountains which he will show him to sacrifice his son Isaac up there.** And we know that Abraham did go up to.**Mount Moriah'** to sacrifice his son. We know that it was up there on Mount Moriah where Abraham established and recorded the name, 'JEHO-VA-JIREH' WHICH MEANS...'THE LORD WILL PROVIDE' This is why the mount is called, 'MOUNT MORIAH'. It takes its name after the land of Moriah. This is the response Abraham gave to his son Isaac, when Isaac asked him, where was the sacrificial lamb to sacrifice to God. Then Abraham replied: "" The Lord will provide himself a lamb: What Isaac didn't know was, he was the sacrificial lamb.

Moses says the name 'Jehovah-Jireh, was still recorded up there on Mount Moriah, even to his own days while he was writing about the story of Abraham. So we see that even Moses knew about this special holy mountain of God in Jerusalem/ Salem. But we should keep in mind that this was some 470, years' after' God had promised this holy land to Abraham and his descendants.

But what is so special about this land and mountain in his holy land of Moriah, even 'BEFORE' the days of Abraham? Well, because it was up there where God dugged a hole... 'AND MADE A FOUNTAIN OF LIVING WATER'. And it was this living water which flowed down to the Garden of Eden, below his mountain. And two: it was this same Mount Moriah where God's first high Priest built his first Temple. His name is, ' Melchizedek' of Salem, and priest of the most high God.

King David revered the hills of Judea so much that he says in Psalm 121:1-2, "I will lift up mine eyes unto the hills from whence (where) cometh my help, My help cometh from the Lord which made heaven and earth". Strangely, king David didn't say he will lift up his eyes' up to heaven' from where his help came from, he says, 'the hills'. It's a fact in those ancient days, God did live among the hills, in and around Jerusalem,, and planted his Garden below one of those hills. This is the reason

232

David said he looked up there for help. He knew that God and his angels would always visit those Judean hills.

David writes in Psalm 133:3, "As the dew of Hermon, and as the dew that descended UPON THE MOUNTAIN OF ZION: FOR THERE THE LORD COMMANDED THE BLESSING, EVEN LIFE FOREVERMORE" The scriptures show that the Mountain of Zion, including Mount Moriah, was indeed where God himself dwelt in the past. So we see it was Mount Moriah where God had commanded the blessings, even life forever in the past. However, today the command of life forevermore, and the blessings, 'Come from Mount Zion/Mount Moriah, from above in New Jerusalem. So if Jerusalem was a part of the Old earth-then it is also a part of the Spiritual New Earth above. This then proves that Old Jerusalem below in Palestine, on earth, must have contained the Paradise of God, and the tree of life within it also. (yes?)

Ladies and gentlemen, I have presented you with a field of overwhelming evidence proving that the former land of Eden, was the same land as Old Jerusalem-and the Garden of Eden was planted...AT THE SOUTH EASTERN PORTION OF EAST JERUSALEM, BELOW MOUNT MORIAH / THE TEMPLE MOUNT. And the tree of life was planted some 4,666,ft. FROM THE EASTERN / GOLDEN GATE WHICH WAS ATTACHED TO THE 875FT.SQUARE WALL WHICH SURROUNDED THE FORMER JEWISH TEMPLE.

It was the prophet Ezekiel's understanding, according to the angel of the Lord, that the Garden of Eden, or the Garden of the Lord, was planted eastward in the land of Jerusalem, below the Temple-Mount. As a result of the angel's narrative to Ezekiel the prophet, I do agree, and submit to you that Eden was indeed the land of Jerusalem.

CHAPTER 15

100% IRON-CLAD PROOF OF THE BIRTH-DATE OF JESUS CHRIST – THE SECOND ADAM

I am delighted to be chosen by Jesus Christ himself to be the one to reveal to the world, the true date he was born-started his ministry, and the date of his crucifixion.

This 25th day of December, which the church had instituted, is already ingrained in our psyche, and as such, it's difficult not to commemorate it on this date. But if I'm to be truthful, it's a festival season I love to enjoy. But I know this date was only instituted because of the lack of knowledge of the true date.

Now seventy (70) days are not far from the true date of his birth. However, it's good, at least to know the true date he was born. So the mass which the church holds on the 25th day of December, is what the church calls, **Christ-mass which is Christmas.**

For posterity purposes, allow me to share with you the correct date, '**once and for all**'. Now even if you don't celebrate the following proper date of his birth, which I shall explain to you, at least you would be aware of it, and hopefully, pay him respect on this date, and say to him-'**Happy birthday Lord Jesus**'. And to remember to replace the name **Sunday, to 'Jesusday'. And**

Sunday morning to 'Jesusday morning' and Sunday after, to Jesusday afternoon, and Sunday evening, to Jesusday evening, and Sunday night to, Jesusday night.

It's my hope the world, especially the Christians-from now on begin **to celebrate and honor Jesus Christ-the second Adam on his correct birthday, which is, the 15th, of September, and continue to commemorate it on December 25th.**

Please share the following information to your relatives, friends and the world: **JESUS CHRIST WAS BORN...IN THE AUTUMN, ON THE 15TH DAY OF THE MONTH OF SEPTEMBER, BC.5. This is the seventh (7th) month on the Jewish calendar of the year called TISHREI. This is a fact. And I will humbly prove it.**

Jesus Christ died, or was crucified **ON THE 15TH DAY OF MARCH / NISSAN, IN THE YEAR 30AD, AT THE AGE OF 33 I/2 YEARS. This is the first month on the Jewish calendar. Jesus was born on the 15th, and he died, or was crucified on the 15th.** Again, this I will humbly prove as we go along.

HOW DID I FIND THE DATE OF JESUS' BIRTH?

Now because the world admits they don't really know when he was born, I have developed a burning desire to find out the truth for myself. I thought, who is better to ask but Jesus himself. And so, I prayed and asked him – then he inspired my spirit, by his holy spirit. Then as I studied the scriptures, my spirit-man's eyes were opened.

First, in my quest, I had to satisfy myself as to the true date of his crucifixion, and as how old he was at his death. **Then I had to calculate backward 33 i/2 years.. This date ended – on the 15th, day of September / Tishrei – in the year bc5. Then I** went forward from September / Tishrei, 15th, bc5, to March / Nissan 30ad, which took me exactly 33 ½ years.

This 15th, day of September, bc, 5, **is the true date of Jesus' birthday. This is the real Christmas day.** But we could still enjoy the festival commemoration on the 25th, day of December. But the 15th, day of September, is the date we all should celebrate Jesus ' physical coming in the flesh. I say in the flesh, because he first came to the earth as a spiritual man-God in the personage of Melchizedek, king and priest of the most high God, **in the land of Salem which is Jeru-salem.**

PROVING THE DATE OF JESUS' BIRTH AND DEATH

Follow me closely: Exodus chapter 12:1-3, Moses writes: "And the Lord spake unto Moses and Aaron in the land of Egypt, saying,: **Verse 2, "This month shall be unto you-THE BEGINNING OF MONTHS, IT SHALL BE,,,'THE FIRST MONTH OF THE YEAR TO YOU"**

Verse 3," Speak ye unto all the congregation of Israel, saying, **in the tenth (10) day of this month,** they shall take to them every man a lamb, according to the house of their fathers, a lamb for an house" Unquote.

After the flood of Noah, **GOD GAVE HIM A NEW BEGINNING-MONTH OF THE YEAR IN ORDER TO CALCULATE TIME.** This was because Noah was going to begin, **'A NEW DISPENSATION' OF TIME.** Now in the same God gave Noah a new beginning date of year to calculate time, He is now giving Moses, **A NEW BEGINNING OF MONTHS OF THE YEARS TO CALCULATE TIME.** Like Noah-Moses and the Israelites were going to begin a new beginning of a new dispensation of time. First, let's find out which month of the year was **the first month to the Israelites for them to calculate the months of the year.**

Let's go to exodus chapter 13:3-4, to get the answer. Verse 3, "And Moses said unto the people, '**remember this day**', **in which ye came out from Egypt, out of the house of bondage.** For by strength of hand the Lord brought you out from this place: there shall no leavened bread be eaten"

Verse 4, "**This day came ye out IN THE MONTH 'ABIB'**"

So now we know the month the Israelites came out of Egypt was ' **THE MONTH 'ABIB', AND IT WAS THE NEW MONTH OF THE YEAR TO THE ISRAELITES..**

Now God is saying again to Moses in Exodus chapter 34:18, "The feast of unleavened bread thou shall keep. Seven (7) days thou shalt eat unleavened bread, as I commanded thee, **IN THE TIME (15th) OF THE MONTH 'ABIB'**: for in the month 'ABIB' thou camest out from Egypt."

THE DATE OF THE MONTH ABIB

In verse 18, above, God didn't give us the date of the month 'Abib' when the Israelites should have begun to observe the seven (7) days feast of unleavened bread. But in the book of Numbers chapter 33:3, Moses gives us the date the Israelites departed out of Egypt.

Numbers 33:3, Moses writes, "And they departed from Rameses, **IN THE FIRST MONTH...' ON THE FIFTEEN (15) DAY OF THE FIRST MONTH, ON THE MORROW...' AFTER'** the passover the children of Israel went out with an high hand in the sight of all the Egyptian"

So now we are sure that it was truly **ON THE FIRST 'NEW MONTH' OF THE YEAR, 'ABIB when the Israelites** departed out of Egypt-Again, we can certify that it was ON THE FIRST MONTH ".ABIB

This is a fact: the month **Abib,** is the same month in the Jewish Torah as…'AVIV'. This 'Aviv' is also the same equivalent – month as the Jewish NISSAN, OR MARCH, OF THE GREGORIAN CALENDAR, which the Israelites accept. So we know that THE MONTH OF MARCH…IS THE FIRST MONTH OF THE YEAR TO THE ISRAELITES, and on their calendar-not January-but **March.** And I have informed you how it was given to Moses by God to initiate for the Israelites as the first month of the year.

Let's go to verse 6, of this same Exodus chapter 12. God goes on to say to Moses: "and ye shall keep it up (the lamb) **until the fourteen (14) day of THE SAME MONTH: ABIB / AVIV / NISSAN / MARCH)** and the whole assembly of the congregation of Israel shall **kill it (lamb) in the evening"** unquote.

So we know the Israelites were to select a lamb on the tenth (10th) day of **Abib / Aviv / Nissan / March,** and to keep it pen-up or tied up until the fourteen (14) day **of the same month of March / Nissan.** And they should kill it in the evening. Don't forget this 14th day of March.

I'M GIVING YOU AN OVERVIEW-BUT I'M LEADING UP TO JESUS' BIRTHDAY

Let's now look at the book of Leviticus chapter 22:4-6, where God continues to give instructions how and when his passover must be kept by the Israelites. The following verses are about the feasts of the Lord, even holy convocations, which they shall proclaim in their season.

Verse 5, "In the fourteen (14) day of the first month (Abib / March / Nissan) at eve is the Lord's passover"

It's important for you to observe the following: ON THE 15th, OR ON THE DAY...'AFTER'...the 14th, day of passover was going to be a new beginning for the Israelites. This was the day...' the Israelites left out of Egypt from slavery.

It was on this same date of the 15th Jesus Christ left the earth-realm, or died, and entered the realm of the dead, or hell for three (3) days.

LEVITICUS CHAPTER 23: 5-6

God says to Moses in verse 5, "In the fourteen (14) day of the first month Nissan/March at even is the Lord's passover"

Now. we are going to see what God is going to say as it relates to the feast of unleavened bread.

Verse 6, God goes on to say:: AND ON THE FIFTEEN (15) DAY OF THE SAME MONTH 'IS' THE FEAST OF UNLEAVENED BREAD UNTO THE LORD SEVEN (7) DAYS YE MUST EAT UNLEAVENED BREAD"

This 6th verse God says to Moses to begin the feast of the seven days unleavened bread, ' On the 15th day of the same month. This month is the month of ' Abib/Nissan/ March, the same month of the Lord's passover on. the 14th. So the Israelites were to eat unleavened bread FOR SEVEN (7) DAYS. This is from the 15th of Abib/Aviv/ March, to the 21st. Of the same month of march. Do you see why the 15th is the beginning day on the Israelites' calendar?

This 21st day is very important of which I shall explain later, because it is linked to this subject-matter.

Note again: Jesus Christ was born on the 15th day of September / Tishrei. Bc.5, and he died on the 15th, day of March/Nissan 30ad. These two dates also represent ...'A NEW BEGINNING'.

THREE BIBLICAL FACTS

You have seen that the first month of the Jewish year **is the month Nissan/March.**

You have read that the fourteenth (14th) day of the same month of Nissan/March, was the date the passover lamb was killed, and eaten in the evening. Then the seven days feast of unleavened bread began **from the 15th day to the 21st. Day; OR UNTIL THE DAY OF THE VERNAL EQUINOX.**

And you have also read that on the 15th day of Nissan/ March, **or the day following the Lord's passover – day of the 14th that Israelites left Egypt. But the seven (7) days feast of unleavened bread festival....BEGAN FROM THE 15th TO THE 21st. (seven days)**

Note this: and it was on the 15th day that the real lamb of God was killed, or crucified. **Not on the 14th day like the symbolic earthly lamb, but rather...ON THE 15th DAY, AS THE SPIRITUAL LAMB OF GOD.**

Therefore, if you can see these biblical facts and believe them, then you should believe that Jesus Christ, the lamb of God, truly died on the 15th day of March. (no other month, nor date)

COMPELLING EVIDENCE FOR YOU

Didn't Jesus die, or was crucified the day, **'After' Thursday, the passover day?** If you say yes; then the next question is,**'what was the date-'after' the 14th of the killing of the passover lamb?** The answer is: **the 15th...**the day when not only the seven (7) days of unleavened bread feast began, but naturally, when Jesus Christ died, or was crucified. Can this be denied?

Ponder this: Jesus didn't die on the 14th day of March/ Nissan...because on this evening, according to the book of Luke 22:14-16, we find him eating the passover lamb on **this**

14th of March/Nissan, with his apostles …'ON THURSDAY EVENING…then he went and prayed to his father God, in the garden of Gethsemane on this same Thursday evening on the 14th of March / Nissan, and was crucified on the following day on Friday, at 3:oopm. I know you know this, But keep reading.

CONTINUOUS PROOF FOR YOU

Jesus Christ was born on the 15th day of September/ Tishri, bc,5 – some seven (7) days 'Before' – THE AUTUMNAL EQUINOX WHICH FELL ON THE 21st. OF THE JEWISH MONTH TISHRI / SEPTEMBER…and there was a high festival observance during that time.

Now compare that with Jesus' death. Again he was crucified on the 15th day of March, 30ad-some seven (7) 'Before' the vernal equinox, which fell on the 21st. Of the Jewish month Nissan / March. And incidentally, there was also a festival feast of unleavened bread during that time. Coincidence? Oh No ! there are no coincidental events with God. He does all things according to his plans, sequences, numbers and dates.

Again, Jesus was born seven days before the /autumnal equinox-and he died, or was crucified, seven days Before the vernal equinox-and he arose on Sunday morning / the first day of the week / Jesusday morning **on the 17th day of March / Nissan.**

If you were to read between the lines, you would discern that this seven (7) days 'Before' the autumnal equinox of his death or crucifixion, is no mere coincidence, but rather planned by his father God Almighty.

Whenever God would do a new thing on the earth, he usually does it, some seven days 'Before the autumnal, equinox. Or vernal equinox.

The literal lamb was killed on the 14th of March/Nissan, in the evening which was eight (8) days before the vernal equinox-but the lamb of God, the man-God, Jesus Christ, was killed, or crucified on the 15th day of March/Nissan in the evening also, at three pm (3pm)...seven days...Before the vernal equinox.

Now seeing that John the Baptist was born six (6) months 'Before" Jesus Christ, Therefore, it stands to reason that he was born in the month of Nissan / March – and I believe that it was on the 15th, day 'before the vernal equinox which fell on the 21st. In March.

Again here is what God told Moses in the book of exodus chapter 12:18. "In the first month (March / Nissan on the fourteen (14) day of the month at even, ye shall eat unleavened bread, until the one and 21st. Day of the month at even"

Observe this: God had Jesus Christ to be born on the fifteen (15) day of September, or the Jewish month, Tishrei BC.5, – BECAUSE ON THE SEVENTH (7th) day later was going to be the Autumnal Equinox.

Here is one definition of Equinox: "Now equinox: either of the two (2) times a year, when the sun crosses the celestial equinox, and day and night are – approximately the same length.

Now, it's important for me to prove to you the exact date Jesus was crucified which was the 15th, day of March / Nissan 30ad, in order to come to the true date Jesus Christ was born, which was on the 15th, day of September, bc 5.

One may argue that passover may occur on various dates based on the cycle of the moon. It may sometimes occur 'in April', which may be true, but you see, God had commanded Moses and the Israelites to observe his passover, on the 14th day of the first month. And this first month was / is, Abib /

Aviv / Nissan / March. **All of these are the same month.** And we know that every year has the month Aviv or March in it. So it shouldn't matter which month of the year the moon appears on, but the Jewish passover should always be in the first month of the Jewish calendar, Nissan / March 14th. But the Christians should observe **this same month of March-but instead of the 14th of March, like the Jews, we should observe 'THE 15th, DAY OF MARCH, BECAUSE THIS WAS THE DAY OUR LORD JESUS CHRIST, THE SPIRITUAL LAMB OF GOD WAS CRUCIFIED, OR DIED, ON GOOD FRIDAY: MOON OR NO MOON.**

PROOF: JESUS BEGAN HIS MINISTRY IN THE YEAR 26 AD.

Now to further prove that Jesus truly was born in the year BC,5, is to see if it will line-up with the year he started his ministry in 26ad-And to see if it also lines up with his crucifixion, or death in 30 ad. And to see if it all lines-up,or corresponds with his 33, ½ year on earth.

Now, if all of these events line-up compute, or fall in place from BC.5, to 30AD, **corresponding with him being 33,½ years old at death, THEN THIS SHOULD PROVE TO YOU THAT JESUS cHRIST TRULY WAS BORN ON THE 15th DAY OF SEPTEMBER / TISHRI BC, 5.**

Now, Tishri is the seventh month of the year on the Jewish calendar. But September, is the Roman name. We should know the ancient Jewish months are from the 15, to the 15, of each month This is seven (7) days before the equinox.

So from the 15th of September, BC 5, to the 15th of September BC.4 = **one year.** From the 15th, of September, BC4, to the 15th of September BC 3, = **one year.** From the 15th of September

BC,3, to the 15th of September 2, = **one year.** From the 15th of September BC. 2, to the 15th of September, 1, BC, = **one year...** Therefore, from the 15th of September, BC 5, at which time Jesus Christ was born, to the 15th,of September BC 1 = **4 YEARS.** So we have four (4) years in BC, Let's begin now to calculate the years of AD, up to 26,AD, at which time Jesus Christ started his ministry at the age of 30, years.

Now from the 15th of September BC, 1, to the 15th of September 1,AD = **1, year.** And from the 15th of September, 1 AD, to the 15th of September 2,AD = **1 year.** Now as you continue to calculate in this way from the 15th of September, to the 15th of September, of each year, '**Stop' when you reach the 15th day of September, 26ad. It was this year Jesus had begun his ministry.** Now notice how all dates begin and end on the 15th.

So from the year September, 15th, 26 AD, to the 15th of September, **27, AD, = 1, year.** And from September, 15th,27, AD. to the 15th of September,28, AD.= **1,year.** And from the 15th of September,28,AD. To the 15th of September, 29,AD. = **1, year.** So we have **3 years. But this additional 3 years from 26, AD. To 29, AD, ONLY ADD UP TO JESUS BEING 33, YEARS OLD CALCULATING FROM BC 5.**

But if Jesus preached for 3,½ years, and died at age 33,½ – then we still have six (6) more months to calculate to add up him dying at age 33,½, years, and ending his ministry in the year 30 AD. You see all of the dates must add-up or compute in order for him to die at age 33,½ years old. You can only come to this date of 30,AD **if you start calculating his birth-date from BC 5. And ending in 30AD.** So now, let's calculate the six, (6) months we have left in order to complete Jesus'33,½ years on earth. **So from the 15th of September, 29,AD, to the 15th**

of October, 29AD, = 1, Month' from the 15th of October, 29AD to the 15th, of November, 29AD, = 1, Month. From

the 15th of November, 29AD to the 15th. December, 29 AD = 1, month. From the 15th December, 29,AD to the 15th of January, 30, AD.= 1, month. From the 15th of January, 30, AD, to the 15th, February, 30, AD = 1, month. From the 15, of February, 30 AD to the 15th of March, 30 AD, = 1, month.

Note: this gives us a total of six (6) months. This is the six months which add up to Jesus being 33,½ years at his crucifixion, or death. And these six (6) months also bring us to the year, 30,AD. Do you think all of this is just a coincidence? Oh No! It was all divinely planned by God, to have his son Jesus, '**His lamb', to be born on the 15th of September, BC 5. And to start his ministry on 15th of September, 26, AD. And to die on the 15th, of March/Nissan, at evening, just as the passover lamb was killed during the evening.**

YOUR HOMEWORK

Now to satisfy yourself that Jesus Christ was truly born on the 15th day of September / Tishrei, then just calculate backward from the 15th, day of March, 30 AD. to the 15th day, of September, BC. 5, **AND SEE IF YOU WOULDN'T END UP WITH 33,½ YEARS.** All of this would prove that Jesus truly was born on the 15th day of September, BC5, and died on the 15th day of March/Nissan 30 AD… And he is 33,½ years old. DO YOU THINK ALL OF THESE DATES JUST HAPPEN TO COMPUTE?

ANOTHER PROOF OF THE BEGINNING OF JESUS MINISTRY

Here is another proof that Jesus Christ started his ministry on the 15th day of September/Tishri, 26 AD..

First let me quote Daniel chapter 9: 25, in order to show you that the count-down to Jesus Christ, the messiah, began from the time the commandment, or decree went forth from king Artaxerxes in the year BC 457. The angel goes on to say to Daniel in chapter 9: 25 The following:

"Know therefore and understand, that from the going forth of the commandment to restore and to build Jerusalem, **unto the Messiah the Prince, shall be seven (7) weeks, and three score and two weeks: the street shall be built again, and the wall, even in troublous time "**

When I would prove when the command, or decree would have gone forth, then you only have to calculate 483 years from that time, or that decree, **'to the Baptism of the Messiah at Jordan River.**

Know this: these weeks were prophetic weeks. That is, ' **a day for a year'. So seven (7) weeks were literally, 49, years, and the 62, weeks were literally, 434 years. So the 69, prophetic weeks were literally 483 years.**

PROVING THAT BC. 457, WAS THE COUNTDOWN STARTING DATE

For historical facts, when the commandment,or decree was signed by King Artaxerxes 1, Longimanus, so that you may have a point of reference to begin your calculation.

One: in the year BC539, the armies of king Cyrus entered Babylon/Iraq and took its power by conquering it. He reigned until BC 529. (10 years)

Two: Cambyses, who was Cyrus' son, took over from him and he reigned from BC 529, to BC 522, (7 years) Cambyses conquered Egypt which remained under Persian's domination until BC400 (129Years).

Three: Darius 1, took over from Cambyses, and he reigned from BC 522,to BC, 486 (36 years)

Four: Xerxes 1, who was the same king as 'Ahasuerus' in the old testament, took over, then he reigned from BC486, to BC 465, (21 years)

Five: Now Artaxerxes 1, Longimanus, took over from his father Xerxes 1, as king elect in BC 465, but his first year reign as king after being crowned was in BC. 464. So he reigned until BC 423 (41 years)

Now this is the same Persian king who made the command or decree that the Jews who were living in his kingdom as captives, could be freed and go back to Jerusalem. This happened so that Daniel's prophecy may have been fulfilled (Daniel chapter 9:25)

In order to find out when we should begin to calculate the time from the going forth of the commandment, we have to go to the book of Ezra chapter 7: 12-13.

Now when Ezra started his journey to Jerusalem from Babylon, on the first day of the first month, **in the 7th year reign of Artaxerxes-that the 7th year time was reckoned, or started from the year 457.**

I went through this process in order to establish the first year reign of Artaxerxes, **as being BC464.** Now let's calculate seven (7) from this year, BC 464, and see which year we end up in.

Counting down from BC 464, to BC 457 = seven (7) years. **So it's clear that 457...was the year the decree, or commandment went forth from the Persian king Artaxerxes.** So let's go forward 69, prophetic weeks, or 483 years from BC 457, to see which year we arrive in. Okay, Now that we end up in the year 26AD, then it's plain to see that it was in 26 AD, where the 69th prophetic week, or 483 years lands us **and not in 27AD,28AD, 29 AD, nor 30 AD.**

This 483 year was up to the time the Messiah was anointed, or was baptized by John the Baptist in the River Jordan. Jesus

then preached from 26 AD, to 30 AD, at which time he was cut off or died.

HERE IS KING ARTAXERXES' DECREE OR COMMAND

Here is the decree or command the angel told Daniel about- which when this decree is given, then he could begin the countdown **to the anointing of the Messiah.**

Ezra chapter 7:11-13. Verse 11, "Now this is the copy of the letter that king Artaxerxes gave unto Ezra the priest, the scribe, even a scribe of the words of the commandment of the Lord, and of his statutes to Israel"

Verse 12, "Artaxerxes, king of kings unto Ezra the priest a scribe of the law of God of heaven, perfect peace and at such a time"

Verse 13, **"I make a decree that all they of the people of Israel, and of his priests and levites, in my realm, which are minded of their own freewill to go up to Jerusalem, go with thee"**

Know this: this 13th verse of Ezra chapter 7...IS THE COMMANDMENT WHICH WAS TO GO FORTH IN ORDER...TO START 483 YEARS TO THE COUNTDOWN TO THE MESSIAH, THE ANOINTED ONE.

Now that you see the decree, or commandment did go forth as the angel told Daniel in his book, which is Daniel chapter 9:25, Let's go to the seventh verse of this same Ezra chapter 7, for further proof.

Ezra chapter 7, verse 7, states the following: "And there went up some of the children of Israel, and of the priests, and the Levites, and the singers, and the Porters, and the Nethinims, unto Jerusalem, in the seventh (7th) year of Artaxerxes the king"

Again since king Artaxerxes started his reign in BC.464, you only have to count seven (7) years from BC, 464. So seven (7) years from BC, 464 brings us to BC. 457, Now, calculate from BC 457 when the commandment, or decree went forth, to 483 years, or which is 69, prophetic weeks, or 173,880 days... YOU WOULD END UP IN 26, AD. SO, 26AD...WAS THE TIME JESUS CHRIST HAD TRULY STARTED HIS MINISTRY.

Here is a simple sum. If you just minus 457, from 483, you would come up to 26AD. Coincidence? O No! Of course, his ministry lasted for three and a half years, which ended in 30 AD, or when the Messiah was cut off, or was crucified.

I will now give you **my final proof** that the Messiah, or Jesus. or the second Adam, did begin his ministry in the year 26AD, and not 27, 28, 29, nor 30ad.

HERE IS MY FINAL PROOF JESUS STARTED HIS MINISTRY IN 26AD

Let me prove from another angle, that it was indeed 26AD, when Jesus Christ, the Messiah started his ministry. Now we know from the scriptures that a generation is equaled ' **FORTY (40) YEARS.** Therefore, if we want to be sure our Lord Jesus did begin his ministry in 26AD, let's go to the book of Matthew chapter 1:17.

Verse 17, states "**So all the generations...from Abraham to David are fourteen (14) generations; and from David until the carrying away into Babylon are fourteen (14) generations; and from the carrying away into Babylon unto Christ are fourteen (14) generations**" unquote.

This 17th verse gives us a starting point of reference, **which is from BC 586**-that is-the time the Jews were carried away

to Babylon, or Iraq, **TO THE ANOINTING OF JESUS CHRIST, AT THE RIVER JORDAN.**
Remember, each generation is equal to forty (40) years. So if we calculate 14, generations from Abraham to king David, **WE WOULD HAVE 560 YEARS. Which is, 40, years for each generation, times 14, equal 560 years.**
Two: if we calculate 14 generations from king David, to the carrying away of the children of Israel into Babylon in BC 586, **we would have another 560 years. Keep following me, you'll soon see the point.**
Three: take special notice of this: Now, calculate another 14, generations, times 40, years, per a generation, from the time the Jews were carried away into Babylon in BC.586 – to the time of Jesus' baptism at Jordan River, equal 560 years. **So in all, we have 42, generations, times 40, years per a generation EQUAL 1680 YEARS. So we have 1680 years from Abraham, TO THE** ANOINTING AND BAPTIZING OF JESUS CHRIST. (re-read Matthew 1:17)

TAKE SPECIAL NOTE

Now if you minus 14, generations, or 560 years from the year BC. 586, at which time the Jews were taken into Babylon to Jesus Christ, the Messiah. **IT WILL BRING YOU TO 26AD.**
My revelation, or inspiration of minusing 40, generations, or 560 years **FROM BC 586, TO 26AD, SHOULD PROVE TO YOU WITHOUT QUESTION THAT JESUS HAD STARTED HIS MINISTRY IN THE YEAR 26AD.**
Note, BC,586, was the year the Jews were carried away into captivity.-560 years or 14 generations brings you to 26 AD. All of this should be your proof (yes?)

In ancient times, especially in Jewish life, and history, a month was considered 30 days. And a year was considered 360, days. So do this: **multiply 360 days by 483, it would equal 173,880 days up to Jesus' anointing by the holy Ghost at his baptism..** 'AND 'NOT' ON HIS ENTERING JERUSALEM ON PALM SUNDAY: but rather at the beginning of his ministry at Jordan River, when God himself spoke and confirmed him as his beloved son.

Finally, just put down BC 586, and minus 560 years, and you would have your answer. So don't allow anyone to tell you that Jesus Christ started his ministry in 27ad,28ad, 29ad, nor 30 ad.. I do hope I've satisfied your quest about the true date Jesus Christ,the second Adam was born...And the date he started his teaching ministry...and the date he died.

Now if you're convinced of my inspired date of Jesus' birth, then **don't forget to wish him...'HAPPY BIRTHDAY' ON THE 15TH OF SEPTEMBER EVERY YEAR. PLEASE SHARE'**

Contact: **www.sbprabooks.com/IsiahLawrenceNottage. Or isiah lawrence nottage.com.**

The shepherd.
blessings.

Review Requested:

We'd like to know if you enjoyed the book.
Please consider leaving a review on the platform from which
you purchased the book.